THE GREAT COMPOSERS
THEIR LIVES AND TIMES

Index

MARSHALL CAVENDISH
NEW YORK · LONDON · SYDNEY

Staff Credits

Editors
David Buxton BA (Honours)
Sue Lyon BA (Honours)

Art Editors
Debbie Jecock BA (Honours)
Ray Leaning BA (Honours),
PGCE (Art & Design)

Deputy Editor
Barbara Segall BA

Sub-editors
Geraldine Jones
Judy Oliver BA (Honours)
Nigel Rodgers BA (Honours), MA
Penny Smith
Will Steeds BA (Honours), MA

Designers
Steve Chilcott BA (Honours)
Shirin Patel BA (Honours)
Chris Rathbone

Picture Researchers
Georgina Barker
Julia Calloway BA (Honours)
Vanessa Cawley

Production Controllers
Sue Fuller
Steve Roberts

Secretary
Lynn Smail

Publisher
Terry Waters Grad IOP

Editorial Director
Maggi McCormick

Production Executive
Robert Paulley BSc

Managing Editor
Alan Ross BA (Honours)

Consultants
Dr Antony Hopkins
Commander of the Order
of the British Empire,
Fellow of the
Royal College of Music

Nick Mapstone BA (Honours), MA

Keith Shadwick BA (Honours)

Reference Edition Published 1987

Published by Marshall Cavendish Corporation
147 West Merrick Road
Freeport, Long Island
N.Y. 11520

Typeset by Walkergate Press Ltd, Hull, England
Printed and Bound in Singapore by
Koon Wah Printing Pte Ltd.

© Marshall Cavendish Limited MCMLXXXIV,
MCMLXXXVII

Library of Congress Cataloging-in-Publication Data

The Great composers, their lives and times.

Includes index.
1. Composers—Biography.   2. Music appreciation.
I. Marshall Cavendish Corporation.
ML390.G82   1987   780'.92'2 [B]   86-31294
ISBN 0-86307-776-5

ISBN 0-86307-776-5 (set)
    0-86307-787-0 (vol)

Contents

How to Use this Index

The following pages are a complete index to volumes 1 to 10 of *Great Composers: Their Lives and Times*. The index consists of three sections: a General Index, an Index of Composers and an Index of Music.

The General Index

This index includes all topics – historical events, technical terms, countries, people and, of course, music and composers – that appear in the ten volumes. Where possible, people are indexed under surnames; where this is inappropriate (for example, Frederick the Great, King of Prussia), the person is listed under his or her most familiar name. Works of art (paintings, books and plays) are also indexed in this section with the artist's name following in parenthesis. There are general entries on types of music – symphonies, concertos, operas, for example – but for detailed entries on composers and on specific pieces of music, turn immediately to the Index of Composers or the Index of Music respectively.

The Index of Composers

In this section all composers appearing in the ten volumes of *Great Composers: Their Lives and Times* are listed with detailed subentries. Composers are indexed under their best-known names – usually their main surname as in Mozart, Wolfgang Amadeus or Beethoven, Ludwig van – with their dates of birth and death following in parenthesis. The subentries beneath each composer's name detail his or her life and works, but specific pieces of music are listed in the Index of Music.

The Index of Music

All pieces of music referred to in this series are included in this index, not under their individual titles, but under their types – arias, concertos, oratorios, etc. Under these headings, composers are listed alphabetically by surname and their relevant works follow.

Using the index

The number immediately following an entry is the number of the relevant volume. This is followed by a colon and then the page numbers on which the entry appears. If an entry can also be found in other volumes, these volume and page numbers are printed in numerical order and are separated by a semi-colon. Page numbers which refer to illustrations are printed in italics in all three indexes, as are titles of books, paintings, movies. Names of works of music – for example, Chopin's Etude in G flat major op. 26 no. 9 – are not printed in italics unless they are titles of operas, songs, ballets or are general titles of groups of works – for example, Vivaldi's four violin concertos, *The Four Seasons*. The composers who feature in the ten volumes of this series are printed in bold type, both in the General Index and the Index of Composers.

THE
GREAT COMPOSERS
THEIR LIVES AND TIMES

Contents

How to Use this Index

The following pages are a complete index to volumes 1 to 10 of *Great Composers: Their Lives and Times.* The index consists of three sections: a General Index, an Index of Composers and an Index of Music.

The General Index

This index includes all topics – historical events, technical terms, countries, people and, of course, music and composers – that appear in the ten volumes. Where possible, people are indexed under surnames; where this is inappropriate (for example, Frederick the Great, King of Prussia), the person is listed under his or her most familiar name. Works of art (paintings, books and plays) are also indexed in this section with the artist's name following in parenthesis. There are general entries on types of music – symphonies, concertos, operas, for example – but for detailed entries on composers and on specific pieces of music, turn immediately to the Index of Composers or the Index of Music respectively.

The Index of Composers

In this section all composers appearing in the ten volumes of *Great Composers: Their Lives and Times* are listed with detailed subentries. Composers are indexed under their best-known names – usually their main surname as in Mozart, Wolfgang Amadeus or Beethoven, Ludwig van – with their dates of birth and death following in parenthesis. The subentries beneath each composer's name detail his or her life and works, but specific pieces of music are listed in the Index of Music.

The Index of Music

All pieces of music referred to in this series are included in this index, not under their individual titles, but under their types – arias, concertos, oratorios, etc. Under these headings, composers are listed alphabetically by surname and their relevant works follow.

Using the index

The number immediately following an entry is the number of the relevant volume. This is followed by a colon and then the page numbers on which the entry appears. If an entry can also be found in other volumes, these volume and page numbers are printed in numerical order and are separated by a semi-colon. Page numbers which refer to illustrations are printed in italics in all three indexes, as are titles of books, paintings, movies. Names of works of music – for example, Chopin's Etude in G flat major op. 26 no. 9 – are not printed in italics unless they are titles of operas, songs, ballets or are general titles of groups of works – for example, Vivaldi's four violin concertos, *The Four Seasons.* The composers who feature in the ten volumes of this series are printed in bold type, both in the General Index and the Index of Composers.

General Index

A

a cappella 9:100
Abbado, Claudio 8:51, *51*
Abbado, Michelangelo, on Paganini 6:106
abbati, and opera criticism 10:11
Abel, Carl Friedrich, and J. C. Bach 5:*18,* 19
Abendmusiken, Lübeck 5:9, *9*
Académie Royale de Danse (French) 1:97;
    3:97
    see also Paris Opéra
Académie Royale de Musique (French)
    1:97
    enforcement of monopoly 10:24
    first controller 10:18
    foundation of 10:18
    permanent home 10:18
    and Théâtres de la Foire 10:24
Académie des Sciences (French) 4:106-107
Academy of St Martin-in-the-Fields 4:91
Accademia Filarmonica, Bologna 1:*22,* 23
    Corelli and 4:12
    Mozart accepted for membership 1:23
accelerando 9:100
accidental 9:100
accompagnato 9:100
'Accompagnist' to Crown Prince of Prussia
    5:*17*
acoustics 9:100
actor-managers 8:107
ad libitum 9:100
adagietto 9:100
adagio 9:100
Adagio for Strings and Organ in G minor
    (Albinoni/Giazotto) 4:16
added numbers 10:85
Addison, James 4:99
Adelsverein 7:65
aelomelodicon 6:63
aelopantaleon 6:63
affettuosso 9:100
Affligio, Giuseppe d' and *La finita semplice*
    1:22
agitato 9:100
Agnus Dei 9:100
agogic 9:100
Agoult, Countess Marie d'
    Liszt and 6:66, 90, *91-2,* 92
    Nelida 6:91-2
Ahle, Georg, attack on Bach's style 5:25
air 9:100
Aix-La-Chapelle
    Handel in 4:64
    music for peace of 4:66, 84-6
    Treaty of (1668) 1:93
Albani, Cardinal 1:84
Albert, Prince Consort of Queen Victoria
    8:71ff
    acceptance in England 8:75-6
    death of 8:78
    and 'fatherliness' 8:73
    and The Great Exhibition (1851) 8:23, 75
    and household management 8:73
    and Mendelssohn 8:39
    love of music 8:76
    see also Victoria, Queen of England
Alberti bass 9:100
ALBINONI, Tomaso Giovanni *see Index*
    of Composers

ALBRECHTSBERGER, Johann *see Index of*
    Composers
Alcott, Louisa May, and tourism 7:78-9
Alcubierre, Roque de 1:83
aleatory 9:100
Alexander I, Tsar of Russia
    and Chopin 6:63
Alexander II, Tsar of Russia 3:*78*
    and abolition of serfdom 3:78-80, 82-3
    assassination attempts 3:*82-3,* 84
    coronation of 3:*78*
Alexander III, Tsar of Russia
    coronation of 3:26-7, *84*
Alexander Nevsky monastery 3:13
Alexius Comnenus, Emperor of
    Constantinople, and Venice 4:49
Alfano, Franco, finishes Puccini's *Turandot*
    10:50
Algarotti, Count Francesco 5:60
    Neutonianismo per le dame 5:60
Alkan 6:104
allegretto 9:100
ALLEGRI, Gregorio *see Index of Composers*
allegro 9:100
allemande 9:100
    use in suites 5:46, 49
Allgemeiner Deutscher Musik Verein
    and 'New Music' 7:29
    president of 7:29
Allgemeine Musikalische Zeitung 2:50;
    8:101
Almac's Club 4:98
Alt-Bachisches Archiv 5:14
Altdorf University, Pachelbel at 4:8
'alternative religion' 9:8
alto 9:100
Alva, Luigi 10:76
Amadei, Filippo 4:71
Amati family 4:47; 9:9
Amalia, Princess, of Prussia and J. S. Bach
    8:55
Amenda, Karl
    on Beethoven's violin playing 2:59
    letter from Beethoven 2:10
America
    exhibits at The Great Exhibition (1851)
        8:29
    1890's high society 3:104ff
    'finding a duke' 3:109-110
    German emigrants to 7:57ff; 8:109
        destinations of 7:62
        reasons for emigrating 7:60
        social life in 7:65-6
    legislation on shipping 7:62
    piano manufacture in 7:41
    start of cotton-growing in 6:43
    'white elephants' 3:106-107
    Tchaikovsky in 3:13, 16ff
        diaries for 3:17
        homesickness in 3:19, 21
    see also United States
'American Girl Abroad, the' (illustration)
    3:*109*
America's Cup 3:110
Ampère 4:110
amputation 2:105
Amsterdam
    'bourse' 5:*68,* 72; 9:*9*
    centre of European finance 5:*68*
    Vivaldi in 4:40
andante 9:100

anaesthesia, development of 2:104-105,
    107
Anfossi, Pasquale
    Le gelosie fortunate 1:70
Angiolini, Gasparo 3:100
Anglo-Dutch War, Third (1672-4) 4:25
Anglomania 6:47
'angry young men', first 9:15
Anhalt-Bernburg, Princess Friderica of 5:11
Anhalt-Cöthen, Prince Leopold of
    and J. S. Bach 5:10
    remarriage 5:11
Anna Amalia of Prussia, Princess 1:19
    and W. F. Bach 5:17
Anne, Queen of England
    and Handel 4:61
    birthday ode for 4:62
Anna Ivanova, Empress of Russia
    and musical entertainment 10:41
'Annina della Pietà' 4:38
Ansbach
    Handel in 4:63
Ansermet, Ernest 3:48
answer *see* FUGUE
antefatto 10:85
ANTHEM 9:100
    full 9:106
    see also Index of Music
'anti-cholera' outfit 2:*105*
anticipation 9:100
antiphon 9:100
Aotouru 1:118
appassionata 9:100
appoggiatura 9:100
apron, Masonic 1:*34*
Apukhtin, Alexey, Tchaikovsky and 3:26
arabesque 9:100
Aragall, Giacomo 10:76
ARAIA, Francesco *see Index of Composers*
Arcadian Academy 4:12
archaeology, growth of 1:82ff
architecture
    effect of Baroque era on 9:8-9
    influence of ancient 9:13
Arco, Count 1:29
    Mozart argues with 1:41
ARIA 9:100; 10:72
    different emotions in 18th-century 10:13
    'pecking order' in 18th-century operas
        10:13
    use in Romantic opera 10:39
    see also Index of Music
ariettes 10:24
aristocracy (Russian), Europeanizing of
    3:82
Arlecchino in Commedia dell'Arte 10:20,
    21
ARNE, Thomas *see Index of Composers*
Arnim, Bettina von, and Liszt 6:91
ARNOLD Malcolm *see Index of Composers*
Arnold, Thomas, and education 8:81
Arnstadt
    C. Bach in 5:15
    J. S. Bach in 5:9, 25, 39
arpeggio 9:100
arrangement 9:100
Arrau, Claudio 2:57; 3:73, *73*
Arsenal, Venice 4:50, *50-51*
arsenalotti 4:51
art-songs 6:28
    Hungarian 7:35

Artaria (music publishers):
    Beethoven and Haydn and 5:90
    Mozart and 1:12
'Arthur's Seat', Edinburgh 8:44, *44*
'artists as hero' 2:39
artists
    during Baroque era 9:8
    'duty' during Romantic era 9:15
    image of the Romantic 2:76-7
Artois, Comte d' 5:106
Artôt, Désirée 3:*68*
    Tchaikovsky and 3:8, 29
arts
    militant trend in *see* Romantic era;
       Romanticism
    'modernist' revolt in 9:32
assignat 2:85
Assier, Alexandre *see* Tchaikovsky,
    Alexandre
Astor, John Jacob 3:105, *105*
Astor, Mrs William Backhouse 3:109
asylum, Endenich 8:*93*
    Schumann in 8:93
Athletics Club, New York 3:18
Atlantic, length of voyage across 7:62
atonality 9:100
attacca 9:100
Attwood, Thomas
    on Mozart 1:14
    Mendelssohn and 8:45
Attwood, steamship 8:42
AUBER, Daniel *see Index of Composers*
Aubrey de Mont Didier's Dog 8:107
audiences
    changes in class of 2:34
    reaction to Beethoven's works 2:34
auditoria 18th-century 10:10, *12-13*
Auenbrugger, Leopold 2:104
Augarten, Vienna 1:*40-41*
'augmentation' 5:33; 9:100
Augsburg, Mozart in 1:11
Augustus II 1:83
Austria
    anti-Semitism in 7:104, 105
    Biedermeier style in 6:52ff
    catch-phrase after French invasion 6:56
    censorship in 6:56
    complexity of civil service 7:104
    and Congress of Vienna (1814-15)
       7:68
    curb on revolutionaries 9:24
    death of liberalism in 7:105-106
    early 19th-century painting in 6:*53*,
       53-4, *54*
    effect of *Zollverein* in 7:70
    and French Revolution 5:107
    German allegiance to 7:68
    Habsburgs restored to 9:23
    impact of Italian opera in 10:15, 28
    insurrection in 9:25
    literacy in the 19th century 8:79
    nationalism in 7:72
    opera houses *see* individual names
    the plague in 5:76
    as police state 6:56-8
    politics in 7:105-106
    rebuilding the Empire 2:95-6
    revision of universities 6:56
    stock market crash 7:104
    Vivaldi in 4:40
    and World War I 9:27

    wars 7:104
       and Schleswig-Holstein 7:73
       loss of Venice 7:73
    see also Hapsburg, House of
Austria-Hungary, wars with Prussia 5:60-63
Austrian Netherlands, Mozart in 1:19
Austrian Succession, War of the 4:84
Auswanderung (emigration) 7:58, *61;*
    8:109
    to America 7:57ff; 8:109
       destinations 7:62, 64
       effects of war on 7:64
    last great 7:64-5
Avignon, Rameau in 4:11
Avoglio, Signora 4:76
ayre 9:100

B

Bach, Ambrosius 5:*8*
    employment 5:8
Bach, Anna Magdalena 5:11, 26
    Clavier-Büchlein of 5:*11*
    Carl Philipp Emanuel
BACH *see Index of Composers*
Bach, Christoph 5:8, 15
Bach, Gottfried Heinrich 5:*13*, 16
Bach, Johann Ambrosius 5:15
    musical training 5:15
Bach, Johann Bernhard 5:15
BACH, Johann Christian *see Index of*
    Composers
BACH, Johann Christoph *see Index of*
    Composers
BACH, Johann Christoph Friedrich *see*
    Index of Composers
Bach, Johann Gottfried Bernhard 5:16
Bach, Johann Jacob 5:15
Bach, Johann Ludwig 5:15
BACH, Johann Sebastian *see Index of*
    Composers
Bach, Johannes 5:13
Bach, Maria Barbara 5:9, 25
    death of 5:10, 26
BACH, Wilhelm Friedemann *see Index of*
    Composers
Bach, Wilhelm Friedrich Ernst 5:13
Bach family, musicians in 5:13-14
Bach memorial, Leipzig 5:*10*
Bach Society, foundation of 8:55
'Bach Werke Verzeichnis' (Bach
    cataloguing system) 1:67
    publication of 8:55
Bachgesellschaft, completion of 7:68
Bacon, Francis 4:103-104
Bad Godesburg, Haydn in 5:92
Bad Ischel, and tourism 7:83
Bad Teplitz, Beethoven at 2:*18-19*, 19
Baden-Baden
    'cures' at 1:14, 30, *31*
    and tourism 7:82-3
badinerie/badinage 9:100
Baedeker, Karl 7:78
bagatelle 9:100
bagpipes 10:87
    Mendelssohn's opinion of 8:37
Bahr, Hermann, on Ringstrasse era 7:107
Baillot 2:62
    Chopin and 6:787
BALAKIREV, Mily *see Index of Composers*

balalaika 9:100
Balanchine, George 3:44
Balfe, Michael, and an English opera house
    10: 46-7
Balkans, nationalism in 9:27
'Ball of the Clipped Yew Trees' (1745)
    1:*94*
ballabile 9:100
ballad 9:100
    metre 9:103
ballad opera 10:53
    English 10:46
    most popular 10:46
    see also Singspiel
BALLADE 9:100
    see also Index of Music
BALLET 9:100
    composing for 3:44
    golden age of 3:96ff
    importance of ballerina 3:102
    for *intermedi* 10:8
    introduction of steps 3:99
    in opera 10:80
    'partnering' in 3:100
    Russian 3:102
    17th-century for 3:98-9
    with songs/choruses 10:43
    'types' of dances 3:99
    use of pointework 3:*100*, 101
    see also Index of Music
ballet d'action 3:99-100
ballet de cour 3:*96*, 96-8; 10:15
Ballets Russes 3:42, 44
Balletti, Manon 1: *105*
Balmoral, Scotland 8:73, 74, *75*
Balon, Jean 3:99
Baltimore, Tchaikovsky in 3:21

VOLUME 1
Mozart

VOLUME 2
Beethoven

VOLUME 3
Tchaikovsky

VOLUME 4
Albinoni, Corelli, Handel,
    Pachelbel, Purcell, Rameau,
    Telemann, Vivaldi

VOLUME 5
Bach, Haydn

VOLUME 6
Chopin, Liszt, Schubert

VOLUME 7
Brahms, Mahler

VOLUME 8
Berlioz, Mendelssohn, Schumann

VOLUME 9
A Guide to Classical Music

VOLUME 10
A Beginner's Guide to the Opera

Balzac 6:78
  Chopin and 6:67
  Eugénie Grandet 6:80
band 9:100
Banks, Sir Joseph 1:111, *112-13*
bar 9:100
Barbarina, La 5:*63*
barcarolle 9:100
Bargain, The Newrew 3:77
Barisani, Siegmund 1:44
baritone 9:100; 10:76
Baroque, origin of word 9:8, *8*
Baroque era
  in France 10:15ff
  Italian opera in 10:*12*
  landmarks of 9:10-11
  the organ in 5:39-40
  spirit of 9:8
    ingredients 9:8-9
Baroque music 9:100
  the age of 9:8ff
  beginnings of 4:47
  contrasts in 5:38
  counterpoint in 5:33
  effect of patrons on 9:9
  influence of Handel 4:84
  at a popular level 9:9
  selection of pieces from 4:15ff
'Baroque School', difficulty in defining 4:7
Barrington, the Hon. Daines, paper on
    Mozart 1:20
BARTOK, Bela *see Index of Composers*
Barwahser, Hubert 1:63
baryton 9:100
'Bäsle, the' (Maria Thekla Mozart) 1:40
bass 9:100; 10:76
  figured 9:106
  see also double bass
basset clarinet 1:56
bassett horn 9:95
basso continuo 5:33
bassoon 9:49, 100
  double 9:49
  timbre of 6:23
baton 9:100
Batoni, Pompeo 1:85
battaglia 9:100
battery 9:100
Bauer-Lechner, Natalie 7:*90*
  Mahler and 7:90, *90*
  and Mahler's marriage 7:93
Bauernfeld, Eduard von, on Schubert 6:7
Bäuerle, Adolf, *Die Burger in Wien* 6:56
Bavaria, population control in 7:61
'Bawdy House' 4:27, *27*
Bayreuth, Tchaikovsky in 3:52
Bayreuth Festival, Tchaikovsky on first
    3:21
Bazaine, Marshal 7:74
Beardsley, Aubrey, and *The Yellow Book*
    3:*28*
beat 9:100
beats 9:100
Beauchamps, Pierre 3:98
Beauclerk, Charles 4:27
Beaujoyeux, Balthasar de 3:97
Beaumarchais
  comment on *The Marriage of Figaro*
      (Wolfgang Amadeus Mozart) 10:54
  influence of the Commedia dell'Arte
      10:20

Le Barbier de Seville 1:13
Le Mariage de Figaro 1:13
Bechstein, and piano manufacture 7:41
Bedlam 4:*98-9*
Beecham, Sir Thomas, and Russian opera
    10:43
'Beechwood', Newport 3:109
Beer Street (Hogarth) 4:98
Beethoven, Karl von 2:13, *23*
  custody of 2:13, 22
  letter from 2:*23*
Beethoven, Caspar Carl van 2:22
  death of 2:13
Beethoven, Joanna van 2:13
  and custody of son 2:22
Beethoven, Johann van 2:22, *23*
  employment 2:26, *26*
  treatment of Beethoven 2:8-9
BEETHOVEN, Ludwig van *see Index of*
    Composers
Beethoven, Ludwig van (grandfather) 2:*26*
  employment 2:26, *26*
Beethoven, Maria Magdelena van 2:9
'Beethoven myth' 2:39
'Beethoven's Tenth' 7:47
Begichev, Vladimir, and *Swan Lake* 3:39
Behring, Emil 2:109
bel canto 5:71; 9:100; 10:39, 40
  influence on Glinka 10:42
  Rossini and 5:*72*
'Bel Napoli', Newport 3:106
Belgiojoso, Princess
  Liszt and 6:91
  and Liszt/Thalberg 'showdown' 6:108
Belgioso, Baldassarino *see* Beaujoyeux,
    Balthasar de
Belgium, revolution in 9:24, 25
Bellevue Avenue, Newport 3: 107-108
BELLINI, Vincenzo *see Index of Composers*
Bellotto, Bernardo 1:85
bells
  'magic' 3:55
  percussion 9:60
Benedictus 9:100
Beneficence (Masonic lodge) 1:35
'benevolent despots' 9:9
Bennett, William Sterndale, and Bach
    revival 8:55
Benois, Alexandre, setting for *The*
    Nucracker 3:44-5
Berceuse 9:101
BERG, Alban *see Index of Composers*
bergamasca 9:101
Berganza, Teresa 10:79, *79*
Bergonzi, Carlo 10:76
Berlin 5:*16-17*
  J. S. Bach in 5:12, 29
  W. F. Bach in 5:17
    style of music for 5:17
    blockade of 9:36
  Chopin in 6:63
  court harpsichord player 5:12
  Die Fledermaus in 10:54
  effect of potato blight in 7:62
  1846 description of 8:109
  Frederick the Great, King of Prussia, and
      5:61
  Glinka in 10:42
  Abraham Mendelssohn flees to 8:33-4
  Mendelssohn in
    as musical director 8:39

19th-century court life in 8:109
  revolution in 7:*70*
  the Schumanns in 8:93
  the theatre in 8:108
Berlin Academy
  Carstens and 2:78
  re-opening of 5:60
Berlin Philharmonic Orchestra 6:39, *39*
Berlinsche Musikalische Zeitung, on
    Hanswurst 10:30
Berlioz, Harriet
  collapse of marriage 8:12
  effect of death on Berlioz 8:13
BERLIOZ, Hector *see Index of Composers*
Berlioz, Louis 8:11
  death of 8:13
Bernacchi 4:72
Berenstaadt 4:*64*
Bernis, Cardinal de 1:*102*, 105
Bettziech, Heinrich, on Berlin 8:109
Biedermeier period 6:52ff, *52*
billiards 1:*31*
  Mozart's like of 1:31
Billroth, Theodor
  and Brahms's Symphony No. 2 7:32
  summer retreat 7:83
binary form 9:101
biographers (Beethoven's) 2:20, *20*, 34
  and criticism of his music 2:38
Biographie von Ludwig von Beethoven
    (Schindler) 2:20
biology, advances in 4:108-110
Birmingham, England by Mendelssohn
    8:*38*
Birmingham Music Festival, Mendelssohn
    and 8:*38*, 39
Bismarck, Otto von 7:68ff, *69*
  description of 7:71
  family background 7:70
  'iron and blood' policy 7:72-3
  and the National Assembly 7:71
  and unification of Germany 9:25
  and William I, King of Prussia 7:*69*
bisseurs 10:34
bitonality 9:101
BIZET, Georges *see Index of Composers*
Blacher, Boris, and variations 2:54
Black Death, symptoms of 5:76
'Black Friday' 7:104
Blake, William
  The Ancient of Days 9:*20*
  Vestibule of Hell 3:*53*
Blanc, H. Le, *The Art of Tying the Cravat*
    6:49-50
blank verse, sung *see* recitative
Blasis, Carlo 3:102
Blasiuskirche, Mühlhausen, organist at 5:9,
    25
'blazing buildings', Mazarin and 10:16
bleeding/blood-letting 2:103, *103*
Bloody Assizes 4:30
BLOW, John *see Index of Composers*
blues 9:101
Blüthner, and piano manufacture 7:41
Board of Ten, Venice 4:52
bocca chiusa 9:101; 10:85
BOCCHERINI, Luigi *see Index of*
    Composers
'body-snatchers' 2:104
Bogatyrev, Semyon, and Tchaikovsky's
    Symphony No. 6 3:58

Bohemia, 'national' composers 9:22
Böhm, Georg, and J. S. Bach 5:9
Böhm, Karl 6:39
Böhme, Kurt 10:77
BOIELDIEU, Adrien *see Index of Composers*
Boito, honorary doctorate from Cambridge 3:59
bolero 9:101
Bologna, Italy
    Corelli in 4:12
    Mozart in 1:23
Bolshevik revolution (1917) 3:84; 9:35
Bolshoi Theatre, Moscow 10:67, *67*
    première of *Swan Lake* 3:39
BONONCINI, Giovanni Battista *see Index of Composers*
Bonn, Germany 2:26-7
    masked ball in 9:8-9
Bordeaux, France, ballet in 3:100
Borkh, Inge 10:78
Born, Ignaz von 1:35, *36, 37, 38, 43*
    cantata performed for 1:36
Börner, Andreas 5:9
BORODIN, Alexander *see Index of Composers*
Boskovsky, Willi 1:*54,* 54-5
Boston Festival Orchestra, Tchaikovsky and 3:21
Boston Tea Party 5:68
Botanical Gardens, Kew, England 4:*106-107*
bouche fermée 9:101
Boucher, François 1:*89*
    response to Neo-Classicism 1:87
Bougainville, Louis Antoine de 1:110, *111*
    voyages of 1:113
Bouille, Marquis de 5:102
Bourbons, restoration of to the French monarchy 9:24
Bourrée 9:101
    use of in suites 5:46, 49
bows
    bowing technique 2:62
    invention of concave 2:62
BOYCE, William *see Index of Composers*
Boyer d'Argens, Marquis de 5:61
Boyhood and Youth (Tolstoy) 3:92-3
Boyne, Battle of the (1690) 4:30, *30*
brace 9:101
Bragadin, Senator 1:103
Brahms, Christiane 7:7
Brahms, Johann Jakob 7:7
BRAHMS, Johannes *see Index of Composers*
'Brahmsians' 7:24-5
    views on music 7:25
Brailov 3:*34*
    Tchaikovsky at 3:35
Brandenburg, Margrave of 5:*30*
    J. S. Bach and 5:29, *30*
bravura 9:101
break 9:101
'Breakers, the' Newport, USA 3:106, *106-107*
Brecht, Bertholt
    collaboration with Weill 10:51
    flees Germany 10:51
Breitkopf and Härtel 2:50
    and *Erlkönig* 6:20
Bremen, Germany

Brahms in 7:10
    emigration from 7:62
Brendel, Franz, and 'New Music' 7:29
Brentano, Antoine, and Beethoven 2:19-20
Breslau, University of
    Brahms and 7:13, 26-7
    work for 7:13
Bretagne 3:16
Breuning, Frau von 2:*26*
    and Beethoven 2:*26*
Breuning, Stephan von 2:9, *20*
    and Beethoven 2:20, *20*, 59
    on Symphony No. 3 2:13
Breuning family, Beethoven and 2:27
Brianza, Carlotta 3:*43*
bridge 9:101
bridges, iron 4:*109*
Brighella (in Commedia dell'Arte) 10:20
brillante/brilliant 9:101
brindisi 10:85
brio 9:101
brisé 9:101
Bristol, England 5:66
Britain
    annual opera seasons 10:46, 47
    coach travel in 8:44
    and Congress of Vienna (1814-15) 7:68
    contributions to Romantic era 9:19-20
    and French Revolution 5:106
    and Germany 9:35
    opera houses *see* individual names
    operetta in 10:55-6
    'people's opera' 10:47
    'public' schools 8:80-81, *81*
    rise of cotton industry 6:43
    rise as industrial power 9:18
    rise of the middle classes 7:105
    and Seven Years War (1756-63) 2:95
    Theatres Act (1843) 10:47
    and World War I 9:27
    see also England
British East India Company 5:70, 6:43
British Museum 9:*13*
British Union Catalogue 1:67
BRITTEN, Benjamin *see Index of Composers*
Broadwood, James
    Chopin and 6:67
    pianos 6:74
        factory 7:40
Broadway, New York 3:*17*
    Tchaikovsky on 3:18
Brock, von, and opera translations 10:29
Broglie, Marechal de 5:60
Broschi, Carlo *see* Farinelli
'Brotherhood of St Luke' 2:84
Brown, David 3:28
Brown, John 8:78
BRUCH, Max *see Index of Composers*
BRUCKNER, Anton *see Index of Composers*
Brummel Beau 6:47
Brunsvik, Countess Josephine von, and Beethoven 2:18, *19*
Brunsvik, Countesse Therese von 2:*10*, 18
    and Beethoven 2:18, *19*
Brunswick, Duke of 5:107
Brunswick Manifesto (1792) 5:107
bruscamente 9:101
Brustwerk 5:40; 9:101
Bryan, George 6:47
Brymer, Jack 1:63, *63*

Bubble Act (1727) 5:73
bubonic plague 5:76
    characteristics of 5:77
Büchner, Georg, use of work by Berg 10:50
Bucintoro, the, Venice 4:55, 56
Budapest, Brahms in 7:38, *40*
Budapest Opera *see* Royal Budapest Opera
buffo/buffa 9:101
Buffon
    Epochs of Nature 4:108
    Natural History 4:103
    Theory of the Earth 4:108
bugle 9:101
BULL, John *see Index of Composers*
Bullinger, Abbé 1:*44*
    Mozart and 1:*11*
        letter from 1:28
bulls, papal, banning Freemasonry 1:34
Bülow, Hans von 6:90
    and Brahm's music 7:13, 24, 29
        on Violin Concerto 7:30
    conducting 7:*28*
    death of 7:14
    influence of Wagner 7:29
    and Mahler 7:90
    marriage 7:29
    and 'New Music' 7:29
    post at Meningen 7:29
    Tchaikovsky and 3:67
    and Wagner's operas 7:29
    and the Weimar school 7:29
Bulwer Lytton, *The Last Days of Pompeii* 1:89
Buontalenti, Bernardo, ballet costumes by 3:96
Burgtheater, Vienna
    Haydn Concert in 5:93
    Mozart concert in 1:74, *76*
burlesques, English 10:46
burletta 9:101
Burlington House, Piccadilly, London 4:62, *63,* 69
Burney, Charles
    and the Bachs 8:55
    on Corelli's Concerto Grosso in G minor op. 6 No. 8 4:19

Composer	Volume
Albinoni	4
Bach	5
Beethoven	2
Berlioz	8
Brahms	7
Chopin	6
Corelli	4
Handel	4
Haydn	5
Liszt	6
Mahler	7
Mendelssohn	8
Mozart	1
Pachelbel	4
Purcell	4
Rameau	4
Schubert	6
Schumann	8
Tchaikovsky	3
Telemann	4
Vivaldi	4

Burroughs, Silas 2:109
Busoni, Ferruccio
    Mahler and 7:95
    style of piano playing 2:38
BUXTEHUDE, Dietrich *see Index of Composers*
BYRD, William *see Index of Composers*
Byrom, John, on Handel and Bononcini 4:71
Byron, Lord George 9:*20*
    impact on Europe 9:19-20
    and rebellion against society 9:19

C

cabala 1:*105*
cabaletta 9:101; 10:85
Caballé, Monsérrat 10:78
Caccini, Guilio
    and the Camerata 10:9
    influence on Baroque music 4:47
    Le Nuove Musiche 10:9
cadence 9:101
    perfect 9:113
cadenza 9:101
    Beethoven and 3:72
        for Violin Concerto 2:61
    in Brahms's Violin concerto in D op. 77 7:31
    in concertos 3:72
    'Fritz Kreisler' 2:61, 63
    Mozart's attitude to 1:76, 78; 3:72
        for Flute and Harp Concerto in C major 1:61
        for Piano Concerto No. 21, 1:76, 78
    operatic 10:85
    practice in Beethoven's time 2:63
caelsura 9:101
Caernarvon, Earl of, resident composer to 4:63, 70
café life 10:10
'Caffe degli Inglesi', Rome 1:85
Caffé Greco, Rome 8:*47*
calando 9:101
California, discovery of gold in 1848 7:*60*
Callas, Maria, and *bel canto* 10:40
Calov, Abraham, of Wittenberg 5:*22*, 27
Calov Bible, title page 5:*22*
calypso 9:101
Calzabigi, Raineiri, and Gluck's *Orfeo ed Euridice* 10:26
Camargo, Marie 3:*98*
Cambert, Robert
    collaboration with Perin 10:18
Cambrai, League of 4:53
Camerata 10:8-9
    and the importance of music drama 10:9
    lack of inventiveness in works 10:9
    objectives 10:9
    structure of operas 10:9
cambiare 9:101
Cambridge University Musical Society, and Brahms's Symphony No. 1 7:48
camera, da 9:101
campana/campane 9:101
campanology 9:101
Camus, Count Johann Georg von, and Beethoven 2:28
Canaletto, and the Grand Tourists 1:85
cancan 9:101

cancrizans 9:101
canon 5:33, 9:101
Canon and Gigue (Pachelbel) 4:19
cantabile 9:101
CANTATA 5:23-4; 9:101
    definition of 5:23
    first major exponent of 5:23
    see also Index of Music
cantatrice 9:102
cantelina 10:85
canticle 9:102
cantilena 9:102
canto 9:102
cantor 9:102
    see also Kantor
cantus firmus 9:102
canzona/canzone 9:102
canzonet/canzonetta 9:102; 10:85
    by Tchaikovsky 3:8
Capell, Richard, on Schubert 6:17
cappella 9:102
Capitol, Washington 3:*20-21*
Capitoline Museum acquisitions 1:84
capriccio/caprice 1:86; 9:102
Caracalla, Emperor of Rome 7:83
carbolic, Lister's use of 2:108
carillon 9:102
Carissimi, Giacomo 4:80
Carl Rosa Opera Company 10:47
Carl Theodor, Elector Palatine 1:19, 26
Carlisle House, Soho Square, Germany 1:*106*
Carlsbad, Germany
    Chopin in 6:66
Carlsbad Decrees (1819) 9:24
Carnegie, Andrew 3:*19*, 105
    Tchaikovsky and 3:18, 19
Caroline of Anspach 4:96
Carreras, José 10:76
Carstens, Asmus Jacob 2:77-8
    Night with her Children, Sleep and Death 2:*76*, 78
cartoons, use of classical music in 7:101
Casanova, Gaetano 1:101
Casanova, Giacomo 1:*100*, 100ff, *108*; 9:12
castanet 9:102
'castle of heaven', Weimar, Germany 5:*24-5*
castrato/castrati 6:*106*; 9:102
    in Italian opera 4:68
    last professional 10:13
    range of voice 10:13, 14
    in opera 10:13, *13*
        use in German 10:29
        in Gluck's 10:26
    and Royal Academy of Music 4:71
Catalogue of All My Works (Mozart) 1:72
    entry for Serenade in G major 1:*50*
    entry for K, 467 1:74
catalogues, thematic 1:67
cataloguing 1:67
catch 9:102
Cathedral of Christ the Redeemer, Moscow 3:49
Catherine the Great, Empress of Russia 1:*107*, 108; 3:*82*
    as patron of opera 10:41-2
    and Russian westernization 3:82, *82*
Catharinenkirche, Hamburg, organist at 5:9, *9*
CAVALLI, Pietro *see Index of Composers*
cavatina 9:102; 10:85

Cavour, Count
    and pact wih France 7:72
    and unification of Italy 9:25
Cecchetti, Enrico 3:102, *102*
cédez 9:102
celeste 3:55; 9:102
    Tchaikovsky and 3:45
cello 9:42, 102
Celsius, Anders 4:105
Cène, Le (publishers of engraved music) 4:37
censorship
    in Austria 6:56
    reintroduction in England 4:29
    Russian 3:86
cercar la notte 10:85
Cerrito, Fanny 3:*100*
CHABRIER, Emmanuel *see Index of Composers*
Chaconne in F minor, (Pachelbel) 4:22
Chadwick, James 9:30
Chaillot, Chopin in 6:69
chalumeau 1:56; 9:95
CHAMBER MUSIC 1:48, 58-9; 9:102
    Beethoven's contribution to 2:42
    contemporary 1:59
    for Versailles 1:97
    see also Index of Music
chamber opera *see* OPERA, chamber
chamber orchestra *see* orchestra, chamber
chamber symphony *see* SYMPHONIES, chamber
Chanel, Coco 7:84
chanson 9:102
chant
    Gregorian 9:107
        foundations of 5:42
    keeping the rhythm in 7:50
    Latin 5:42
Chapel Royal, Windsor
    composer to 4:64
    orchestra of 5:42
    Purcell and 4:13
'character pieces' 4:*11*
    La poule 4:*11*, 18-19
characteristic piece 9:102
Charcot, Dr Jan-Martin 2:*109*, 110
Charles II, King of England 4:*23*
    coronation procession 4:*24-5*
    creation of musical establishment 4:87
    and development of Church music 5:42
    and development of science 4:*104*
    and Purcell 4:14
    restoration of 4:23ff
    death of 4:40
Charles II, King of Spain 2:93
Charles III, King of Spain 1:83
Charles V, Emperor 2:92-3, *93*
    and Martin Luther 5:24
Charles VI, Emperor 2:93, 94
    death of 5:60
    musical recitals 9:9
    and Vivaldi 4:40
Charlotte, Queen of England 4:97; 5:*18-19*
    and Mozart 1:20
    and J. C. Bach 5:19, *19*
Charpillon, La 1:*107-108*
CHARPENTIER, Marc-Antoine *see Index of Composers*
'Château sûr Mer', Newport, USA 3:*106*
Chatelin, Covent Garden, London 4:29

Chatsworth, England
    head gardener at 8:23
    Lily House 8:23
chauffeurs 10:34
chef de claque 10:34
Cherevichki 3:13
Chernyshevsky, N. G. 3:*83*
Cherubini
    Chopin and 6:78
    and Mendelssohn 6:78
        criticism of 8:36
    and Paris Conservatoire 6:89
chest voice 9:102
child prodigy 1:18ff
childhood, 18th-century attitude to 1:18
children
    early 19th-century attitudes towards
        8:105
    clothes, early 18th-century 6:*43, 48-8,* 50
    literature for 8:105-106
    Queen Victoria and 8:72, *73*
Chigi collection (statues) 1:84
China, porcelain trade 5:70, *70*
chinrest, introduction of 2:62
chitarrone 9:82
chiuso 9:102
chloroform 2:106-107
chocolate, introduction of to Europe 5:67, *67*
choirs 9:102
    directing medieval 7:50
Chopin, Emilia 6:62
CHOPIN, Fryderyk *see Index of Composers*
Chopin, Isabella 6:62
Chopin, Justyna 6:*62*
Chopin, Ludwika 6:62
Chopin, Nicolas 6:*62*
    early life 6:62
choral 9:102
choral symphony *see* SYMPHONIES, choral
chorales 5:23; 9:102
    development of 5:42
    Luther and 5:23
    tunes in Church music 5:38
chord 9:102
    broken 9:101
    common 9:102
choreographers 3:100-101
    of *Apollo* 3:44
    early 3:98
    of *La Esmeralda* 3:*101, 102*
    of *La Fille mal Gardée* 3:100
    of *The Firebird* 3:44
    of *Giselle* 3:101
    of *The Nutcracker* 3:102
    of *Ondine* 3:102
    of *Pas de Quatre* 3:102
    of *The Sleeping Beauty* 3:42
    of *Swan Lake* 3:38, *38,* 40, 102
choreography 9:102
    innovations in 3:100-101
chorus 9:102; 10:72-3
    importance in Greek drama 10:8
'Christian awakening' (17th century) 5:22
Christian Church
    ban on women in music 10:13
    influence on development of opera 10:8
Christie, John, and Glyndebourne 10:48
Christina, Queen of Sweden 4:*104*; 9:*8*
    and Corelli 4:12

Christmas card, Victorian 8:*73*
Christofori, Bartolomeo, and the
        pianoforte 6:74
chromaticism/chromatics 1:52, 79; 9:102
    in Piano Concerto No. 22 (Mozart) 1:79
chronometer, development of 4:106
CHURCH MUSIC *see Index of Music*
Cibber, Susanna 4:*76*
    and *Messiah* 4:*76,* 76-7
Cimarosa, at Russian court 10:42
Cincinatti Volksblatt (newspaper) 7:65
cittern 9:84, 102
Civil constitution of the Church 5:103
Civil War, American, effect on imigration
        7:64
Claque, The 10:*34*
clarinet 9:48, 102
    bass 3:55; 9:48
    improvements to 6:23
    Mozart's use of 1:56
        in Symphony No 40 1:66
Classical/Classicism 9:9, 13ff, 102
Classical era
    concerto in 3:72
    landmarks of 9:10-11
    the symphony in 2:32
Classical music
    the age of 9:8ff Beethoven and 1:52
        revolutionizing of 2:15
    early development of 4:47
    effect of Baroque era on 9:8-9
    predominance of orchestra in 6:23
    what is the style? 1:76-7
Classicism, triumph of 1:82-90
clavichord 9:98, 102
    C. P. E. Bach and 5:17
    Handel and 4:60
clavier 9:102
Clay, Henry 4:100
clef 9:102
Clement, Franz 2:*59,* 59-60
    Beethoven and 2:60
    description of violin playing 2:60
CLEMENTI, Muzio *see Index of Composers*
Clermont, Rameau in 4:11
'clinics' (19th-century) 2:*102-103*
Clive, Robert 5:70, *70-71*
'cloud chariots' 10:16
close harmony *see* harmony, close
cluster 9:102
coach travel 8:44
Cocteau, Jean, operatic experiments
        10:50-51
coda 9:102
codetta 9:102
coffee, introduction of to Europe 5:67, 68
coffee houses 4:29, *97,* 97-9; 5:*73*
    debates in 9:12
    importance of 8:*104-105*
col legno 9:102
colascione 9:83
Colbert, Jean-Baptiste 1:*93,* 94
'cold war' 9:36
Coleman, Mrs 10:45
Coleridge, Samuel Taylor
    and Romantic era 9:19
    Lyrical Ballads 9:19
colla voce 10:85
colleganza 4:50-51
Collegium Musicum, Leipzig, Germany
        director of 5:12

and J. S. Bach's suites 5:47
Colete, use of work by Ravel 10:50-51
Collier, Jeremy, *A Short View of the
        Immortality and Profaneness of the
        English Stage* 10:45-6
Colloredo, Count Hieronymous 1:*11, 26*
    and the Mozarts 1:9-10, 11
    as a musician 1:25-6
    and Wolfgang 1:23, 25-6, 41
    dismisses 1:29
Cologne, Germany
    effect of potato blight in (1845) 7:62
Cologne, Elector of 2:8, 26, *26*
Colombina (in Commedia dell'Arte) 10:20
colonialism, effects of 9:34-5
coloratura 9:102; 10:85
    use in German operas 10:29
Coltellini, Mozart and 1:22
combination tone *see* tone, combination
come 9:102
Comédie-Française de Berlin, director 5:61
Comédie-Française, enforcement of
        monopoly 10:24
comedy, in opera *see* opera buffa
'comedy of character' 10:21-2
Comedy Opera Company 10:56
comic operas, English 10:46
    German equivalent of 10:29
    see also opera buffa
Commedia dell'Arte 4:54; 10:*20*
    characters 10:20, *20-21*
    French version 10:24
    influence on opera 10:19
    influence on Spingspiel 10:27
Commerson, Philibert de 1:11-12
Commissioner of Antiquities, Papal States
        1:84

VOLUME 1
Mozart

VOLUME 2
Beethoven

VOLUME 3
Tchaikovsky

VOLUME 4
**Albinoni, Corelli, Handel,
Pachelbel, Purcell, Rameau,
Telemann, Vivaldi**

VOLUME 5
Bach, Haydn

VOLUME 6
Chopin, Liszt, Schubert

VOLUME 7
Brahms, Mahler

VOLUME 8
Berlioz, Mendelssohn, Schumann

VOLUME 9
A Guide to Classical Music

VOLUME 10
A Beginner's Guide to the Opera

COMMISSIONS:
  Mozart's:
    for Archduke Ferdinand 1:23
    for carnival in Milan 1:23
    for Count Firmian 1:23
    for Duc de Guines 1:27, *60, 61*
    for Franz Ziegenhagen 1:38
    from Walsegg-Stuppach 1:15
  Tchaikovsky's 3:13
    from Imperial Theatre, Moscow 3:10
    from Mme von Meck 3:10, 32, 33
    from Vsesolozhsky 3:44
Committee of Public Safety, France (1793) 2:85; 5:109
commodo/comodo 9:102
'communism', in Germany in 1840s 7:62
compass 9:103
'Composer to the Island of Ceylon' 8:44
Composer-in-Ordinary, Westminster Abbey 4:14
composers
  Baroque (1653-1767) 4:7ff
  'fans' of 9:9
  and film music 7:101
  first 'professional' (Beethoven) 2:31
  impact of French Revolution on 10:31
  improvement in status of 6:16
  influence of gypsy music on 7:35
  influence of nationality on operas 10:8
  last for castrato voice 10:13
  and musical journals 8:101
  nationalist 9:22-3
    sources of inspiration 9:22
  output of 18th-century opera 10:12
  Romantic, sources of inspiration 9:22; 10:38
  Russian, first outstanding 10:42
    sources of inspiration 9:22; 10:42
  at Russian court 10:41-2
  sources of inspiration 3:62
  use of opera by 20th-century 10:52
  and *verismo* 10:40
composition 9:103
comprimario 9:103; 10:85
con 9:103
con spirito 9:103
concert master 9:103
concert pitch 9:103
Concert Spirituel 1:28
CONCERT SUITES *see Index of Music*
concertato style 9:103
  evolution of 4:47
Concertgebouw Orchestra 2:*56*, 65, *65*; 3:57
concertante 9:103
  French taste for 1:61
concertina 9:103
concertino 3:72; 5:30; 9:103
CONCERTO 2:72; 5:29; 9:103
  Baroque 4:17; 5:38; 9:9
  Concerto Without Orchestra 6:98
  crucial role of solo instrument 3:72
  number of movements 3:72
  orchestra's work in Romantic 6:98
  origin of word 7:30
  for particular virtuosos 3:72
  solo 3:72
  and sonata tradition 3:72
  triple 9:117
  what is a? 3:72
  see also Index of Music

'concert works' (Chopin) 6:70
concerto grosso 3:72; 9:103
  development of 4:47
CONCERTS
  in Jacobikirche, Lüneberg 5:9
  musicians' reliance on 6:104
  in Ospidale della Pietà, Venice 4:40
  in Palazzo Chigi, Siena 4:39
  publicising 6:105
  at Rheinberg 5:58
  by touring virtuosos 6:105
  Venetian 4:*36-7*
  J. S. Bach's:
    for Frederick the Great, King of Prussia 5:12
    in Cöthen 5:29
    in London 5:19
  Berlioz's:
    conducts his own works 8:12
    for Harriet Smithson 8:14
  Brahms's:
    in Budapest 7:38
    in Detmold 7:10
    in Hanover 7:38
    first solo 7:38
    in Leipzig 7:38
    playing Piano Concerto no. 1 7:38
    routine of tours 7:12
    of Violin Concerto 7:31-2
  Brahms/Joachim/C. Schumann 7:10
  Brahms/Reményi 7:27, 30
  Chopin's 6:82
    charity 6:69
    in Edinburgh 6:68, *68*
    first public 6:63, *63*
    in London 6:68
      at the Guildhall 6:69
    in Paris 6:65
      for French royal family 6:67
      last in 6:84
      pieces played 6:65
      at the Salle Pleyel 6:67, 68
      in salons 6:81
    in Rouen 6:67
    on 26 April, 1841 6:68
    in Vienna 6:63-4
  Handel's:
    in Foundling Hospital 4:77, 77
    of Oratorios 4:65
    for Queen Anne 4:61
  Haydn's:
    in London 5:91-2
    in Vienna 5:*92-3*, 93
  Herz/de Meyer 6:108
  Hoffnung, Gerard 3:55
  Joachim's:
    début 7:28
  Liszt's 6:*107*
    audience behaviour at 6:91
      clique of followers 7:28
    Beethoven at 6:88
    in Hungary 6:*92*
      in Budapest 6:89
    in Paris
      press reviews 6:89
      success of 6:91
    in Vienna 6:8-9
      for relief of homeless 6:91
  Liszt/Thalberg 'showdown' 6:108
  Mahler's:
    conducts last 7:95

Mendelssohn's:
  charity for Silesia 8:37, 44
  in Düsseldorf, frustration over 8:38
  at Gewandhaus 8:38
    programme for 8:*55*
    sponsors of 8:109
  in London 8:77
    at the Argyll Rooms 8:43
    greatest success in 8:44
Mozart's:
  amounts received for 1:30
  benefit-type 1:36
  freelance 1:30
  in England 1:20, *20-21*
  in Mannheim 1:26
  in Munich 1:18
  in Paris 1:27
    public 1:20
  subscription 1:*41*
    works for 1:72
  in Vienna 1:43; 5:91
    at Schönbrunn 1:18-19
Paganini's:
  in Paris 6:106
  in Vienna 6:13
Rubinstein's:
  in America 6:*109*
Schubert's:
  success of *Erklönig* at 6:20
  of 26 March 1828 6:13
C. Schumann's 7:19; 8:93
  programme for Gdansk 7:*19*
  see also C. Weick
R. Schumann:
  of Symphony no. 1 8:94
C. and R. Schumann:
  conflicting engagements 8:91-2
  eastern European tour 8:93
  in Leipzig 8:94
  in Russia 8:92
Tchaikovsky's:
  at Lyceum Theatre, Baltimore 3:21
  in Moscow 3:13
  for opening of New York Music Hall 3:17, 18
  Russian Music Society 3:56-7
  in St Petersburg 3:13
  in Washington 3:22
Telemann:
  in Hamburg 4:10
Vivaldi's:
  for Prince Frederick 4:40
Wagner's:
  criticism of 7:25
C. Weick:
  Grand Concerts 8:90
  tour with her father 8:89
concord 9:103
conductor 9:103
  growing prominence of 7:50
  role of the 7:50-51
conducting
  Handel and 4:61-2
  Tchaikovsky and 3:12-13
    conducts Pathétique Symphony 3:13
    tours in Europe 3:13
Congress of Vienna (1814-15) 2:98-9; 6:51; 7:68-9
  and re-establishment of absolute monarchs 9:23-4
  structure of Germany after 8:109

conservatory/conservatoire/conservatorio
9:103
castrati at 10:14
study routine at 10:14
popularity of Neapolitan 10:20
Consistory, Arnstadt, and J. S. Bach 5:9
console 9:103
consonance 9:103
consort 9:103
broken 9:101
Constantinople 6:92-3
Liszt in 6:93
Constituent Assembly, French 2:85
'constitutional monarchy' 4:24
contemporary music, re-creation of the
suite in 5:49
Conti, Prince de, musical salon 1:20, 20-21
continuo 1:58; 9:103
in Baroque music 4:7
disappearance of 7:50
'Continental system' 2:89
contra 9:103
contrabasso 9:103
contralto 9:103
contrapuntal principles 1:77; 9:103
contredanse 9:103
convent parlour, Venetian 4:37, 37
Cook, Captain James 1:110, 110ff
death of 1:117, 118, 118
Cook, Thomas 7:82
and The Great Exhibition (1851) 8:27
and organized travel 7:79-80
Copenhagen, C. Schumann in 8:92
Copernicus 4:104
coperato 9:103
COPLAND, Aaron see Index of Composers
Coppretta, Caterina 1:104
cor 9:103
cor anglais 9:47, 103
see also horn, English
Coralli, Jean 3:101
Coram, Thomas 4:77
CORRELLI, Arcangelo see Index of
Composers
cornet 9:103
cornetts 9:89
Correspondance littéraire (French journal)
1:19
Corsi, Jacopo
and the Camerata 10:8-9
and Dafne 10:9
and recitative 10:9
'Cossack Countess' 6:94-5
Cossel, Friedrich Wilhelm, and Brahms's
early training 7:7
Cossotto, Fiorenza 10:79
Cöthen, Germany, J. S. Bach in 5:29
Council of Trent (1545) 5:42
counterpoint 9:103
free 9:106
German love of 5:23
Schubert and 6:10, 13
Schumann and 8:101
R. Strauss's use of 10:50
use in Renaissance 5:33
what is it? 5:33
countertenor 9:103
country dances 9:103
COUPERIN, François see Index of
Composers
couplet 9:103; 10:85

courante, use in suites 5:46, 49
Court Chapel Choir, Vienna, Schubert in
6:10
Court Theatre, Vienna
Schubert at 6:12
success of Erlkönig at 6:20
Court Trumpeter, Eisenach (Ambrosius
Bach) 5:8, 15
courtesans, Venetian 4:54
'court of honour', Tchaikovsky and 3:13, 13
court organist, Salzburg, Mozart as 1:28-9
cowbell 9:103
Covent Garden, London 4:68-9, 94, 97
Handel and 4:64, 68
oratorio season at 4:65-6
Crabbe, George, use of work by Britten
10:48
craftsmen, during Baroque era 9:8
Cramer, J. B., and Beethoven's Piano
Concerto no. 5 2:50
cravats 6:47, 49-50
crescendo 9:103
Crimean War (1853-6) 3:76, 76
effect on Russian music 10:42
Cristofori, and invention of piano 4:47
Cromwell, Oliver 4:23, 23
crotchet 9:103
crumhorn 9:93, 103
Crystal Palace (for Great Exhibition)
8:22-3, 23ff
method of building 8:23
removal of 8:30
site for 8:23
Cubist movement 9:32
Cui, César 3:8
and 'The Mighty Handful' 10:43
on Tchaikovsky's Francesca da Rimini
3:55
cuivré 9:103
curtal 9:94
Curzon, Clifford 6:31, 31
Cuzzoni, Francesco 4:64, 70
and Guilo Cesare in Egitto 4:71
and Ottone 4:71
cycle 9:103
cyclic form 9:103
cymbal 9:56, 103
CZERNY, Carl see Index of Composers
Czerny, Joseph, and 'Trout' Quintet 6:24

D

da capo 9:103
Daguerre, Jacques, scenery for the Opéra
10:32-3
Dahn, Constanze 6:55
Damrosch, Walter 3:17
and Tchaikovsky 3:16, 17
dance
at the French court 10:15
importance in ancient Greek drama 10:8
dance rhythms, use of by Weill 10:51
dance-songs, Hungarian gypsy 7:34
dancers, professional 3:98ff
DANCES
inspiration for Schubert 6:18
used as themes 2:54
see also Index of Music
dancing masters 3:96
dandy, rise of in early 19th century 6:47

Danhauser
Beethoven's death mask 2:15
Dannreuther, Edward, and Tchaikovsky's
Piano Concerto No. 1 3:67
Dante 3:54
Tchaikovsky and 3:52
DARGOMIZHKY, Alexander see Index of
Composers
Darwin, Charles 2:105; 4:109
On the Origin of Species 4:109
Das Knaben Wunderhorn Mahler's use of
7:97
Dauberval, Jean 3:100
Davenant, Sir William
and The Siege of Rhodes 10:45
and theatre revival 4:26
David, Félicien 1:89
David, Ferdinand, and Mendelssohn's
Violin Concerto 8:52
David, Jacques-Louis
and Neo-Classicism 1:87
Oath of the Horatii 1:87-8, 89
Davidov, Bob 3:12, 61
Davidov, Lev 3:12, 16
Davidov, Vera, and Tchaikovsky 3:27-8
Davidov family 3:12
house of 3:12
Davidsbündler 8:90
Davis, Sir Colin 3:73, 73
Davy, Sir Humphrey 4:109
DEBUSSY, Claude see Index of Composers
début 9:103-104
declamando 9:103
Decline and Fall of the Roman Empire
(Gibbon) 1:84
decrescendo 9:104
DEDICATIONS
Albinoni:
to Maximilian Emanuel II 4:8
of 12 concertos 4:8
J. S. Bach's:
of Brandenburg Concertos 5:29
to Frederick the Great, King of Prussia
5:12
to the Margrave of Baden 5:29
of 'Musical Offering' 5:12

Composer	Volume
Albinoni	4
Bach	5
Beethoven	2
Berlioz	8
Brahms	7
Chopin	6
Corelli	4
Handel	4
Haydn	5
Liszt	6
Mahler	7
Mendelssohn	8
Mozart	1
Pachelbel	4
Purcell	4
Rameau	4
Schubert	6
Schumann	8
Tchaikovsky	3
Telemann	4
Vivaldi	4

Beethoven's:
to Archduke Rudolph 2:30, 50
to Count Razumovsky 2:*12*, 28, *69*
to Dorothea von Ertmann 2:*21*
of first sonatas 2:45
to Guilietta Guicciardi 2:18, *45*, 46
to Haydn 2:45
to Napoleon 2:13
of Piano Concerto No. 5 2:50
of Piano Trios op. 1 2:27, *27*
to Prince Lichnowsky 2:27, *27*, *43*, 46
to Prince Lobkowitz 2:20, *69*
of Sonata in A major op. 101 2:*21*
of Sonata in C minor op. 13 2:*43*, 46
   title page 2:*43*
of Sonata in C sharp minor 2:18, *45*, 46
of String Trios op. 9 2:28
of Symphony No. 1 2:28
of Symphony No. 3 2:20, *89*
of Symphony No. 5 2:20, *69*
of Symphony No. 6 2:20
to Van Sweiten 2:28
of Violin Concerto 2:59
to Von Breuning 2:59
to Von Camus 2:28
to Waldstein 2:9
Brahms's:
to Joachim 7:30
of Violin Concerto in D op. 77 7:30
Chopin's:
to Delfina Potocka 6:65
to Liszt 6:71
of op. 10 Etudes 6:71
of Piano Concerto No. 2 6:65
of Waltz op. 64 No. 1 6:65
Corelli's:
of first 12 trio sonatas 4:12
to Queen Christina of Sweden 4:12
Handel's:
to Earl of Burlington 4:62
of *Teseo* 4:62
Liszt's:
to Litolff 6:98
of Piano Concerto No. 1 6:98
Mahler's:
of Symphony No. 10 7:95
to his wife 7:95
Mendelssohn's:
of Scottish Symphony 8:76
to Queen Victoria 8:76
Mozart's:
to Anton Stadler 1:36
to Count-Archbishop of Salzburg 1:21
to Haydn 1:30, 72; 5:91
to Princess of Nassau-Weilburg 1:20
to Princess Victoire 1:20, *21*
to Puchberg 1:45
Purcell's:
to Charles II, King of England 4:14
of *Sonnata's of III Parts* 4:14
Schubert's:
to Goethe 6:20
Tchaikovsky's:
to Mme von Meck 3:12
of Piano Concerto No. 1 3:67
of *Romeo and Juliet* 3:71
of Symphony No. 4 3:33
of Symphony No. 6 3:61
to Von Bülow 3:67

Vivaldi's:
to Count Gambara 4:36
to Count Morzin 4:39, 41-2, *42*
to Charles VI, Emperor of Austria 4:39
to Ferdinand of Tuscany 4:37
to Frederick IV of Denmark 4:36
of *Il cimento dell'armonico* 4:39, 41-2, *42*
of *L'estro armonico* 4:37
of *La cetra* 4:39
of *La stravaganza* 4:37
to Vettor Delfino 4:37
of set of 12 sonatas 4:36
degree 9:104
Defoe, Daniel 1:110
   A Journal of the Plague Year 5:81
   Robinson Crusoe 1:110
dehors 9:104
Delacroix, Eugène 6:67, *78, 80*
   Chopin and 6:67
   Liberty Leading the People 9:15
DELIBES, Leo see *Index of Composers*
delicato 9:104
délié 9:104
delirante 9:104
delizioso 9:104
demi 9:104
demisemiquaver 9:104
Denmark
   prohibitions on tobacco 5:68
   and Schleswig-Holstein 7:*71*, 73
dentists (19th century) 2:106
descant 9:104
Descartes, Réné 4:104, *104*; 9:9
   philosophy 9:8
   and Queen Christina of Sweden 9:*8*
Dessoff, Otto 7:48
détaché 9:104
Detmold
   Brahms in 7:11
   Director of Music in 7:10
deus ex machina 10:85
deutscher Tanz 9:104
Deutsch, Otto Erich 1:67
   catalogue of Schubert's songs 6:18
development 9:104
Devil, 'pacts' with the 6:*104*, 107
Devonshire House, London, ball at 8:42
Diabelli, Anton 2:54
   and Schubert's works 6:12, 20
Diaghilev, Serge
   and development of ballet music 3:44
   and introduction of Russian opera in the West 10:43
   and *The Sleeping Beauty* 3:42
dialect, use of in comedies 10:19
dialogue-passages, in opéra comique 10:24
diatonic see scale, diatonic
Dichter, Misha 6:102
Dickens, Charles, *Little Dorrit* 7:84
Dickinson, A. E. F., criticism of Symphony No. 40 (Mozart) 1:68
Dictionnaire Raisonné des Sciences', des Arts et des Métiers see *Encyclopédie*
Didelot, Charles-Louis 3:100
Diderot, Denis 9:*12*
   attacks on the establishment 10:24
   on Bacon 4:104
   and the *Encyclopédie* 9:12, *12*
   influence on opéra comique 10:23
   on Winckelmann 1:88

Die Muskete, caricature of Mahler 7:*92*, 97
Dietrich, Albert, and Brahms's symphonies 7:49
Dijon, France, Rameau in 4:11
dilettante, Albinoni as 4:8, *8*
diminished 9:104
dimished seventh 9:104
diminuendo 9:104
'diminution' 5:33; 9:104
dioramas 10:32-3
director, of medieval chants 7:50
   see also conductor
Director of Church Music, Hamburg (Emanuel Telemann) 5:18
Directory, The (French) 2:86
dirge 9:104
Discobolus, discovery of 1:89
discord 9:104
disease/illness
   germ theory of, in 19th century 2:108-109
   improvements in diagnosing 9:32
Disraeli, Benjamin and The Great Exhibition (1851) 8:23
'dissidents', Russian 3:86
dissonance 9:104
   in 20th-century music 9:32
Dittersdorf 1:30
   on Mozart's Piano Concerto No. 21 1:75
divertimenti 4:87; 9:104
   development of 5:49
divertissement 9:104
DNA, discovery of 9:30, 32
D'Oyly Carte, Richard, and Gilbert and Sullivan 10:47, 56
dodecaphony 9:104
'Dog's Dinner' 3:107
dolce 9:104
dolente 9:104
Domanowecz, Baron Zmeskall von, and Beethoven 2:20, 28
dominant 9:104
Domkirche, Halle, Germany, organist at 4:60
DONIZETTI, Gaetano see *Index of Composers*
doppio 9:104
Doré, Gustav, *Paolo and Francesca* 3:*54-5*
Dorn, Heinrich, Schumann's nickname for 8:89
Dostoyevsky, Fyodor 3:90-92, *92*
   beliefs 9:27
   and Nationalism 9:22
   and 'Westerners' 3:86
   The Brothers Karamozov 3:91
   Crime and Punishment 3:91-2, *92*
   The Idiot 3:91
   Poor Folk 3:90-91
   The Possessed 3:91
   manuscript page 3:*92*
Dostoyevsky, Kichale 3:91
dot 9:104
Dottore, Il (in Commedia dell'Arte) 10:20
double bar 9:104
double bass 9:43, 104
   Mahler's use of 7:97
'double escapement' 6:74
double tonguing 9:104
'doubling' 6:23
doucement 9:104
Dover, Treaty of (1670) 4:25

DOWLAND, John *see Index of Composers*
downbeat 9:104
Downes, Edward, on Clarinet Concerto
    K. 622 (Mozart) 1:58
Doyle, Richard, *An Overland Journey to
    the Great Exhibition* 8:*24*
drama
    ancient Greek 10:9
    ingredients of 10:8
    used by Christian Church 10:8, *8*
    use of music in German 10:29
    at Versailles 1:96-7
dramatic 9:104
Dresden, Germany 6:*66*; 8:*90-91*
    J. S. Bach in 5:10
    W. F. Bach in 5:17
    Chopin in 6:64, 66, *66*
    cultural activity in 8:109
    Friedrich in 2:80-81
    Handel in 4:63
    rising in 7:27; 9:*92*, 93
    Schumann in 8:92
        on cultural activity in 8:109
        and gaining position in 8:93
Dreyshock, Alexander 6:104, *108*, 109
Drommer, Judith 4:9
drone 9:104
'dropping off' 8:44
drum roll 9:104
drums 9:57
    Mahler's use of 7:97
    toy 3:55
    see also kettledrums; timpani
Drury Lane Theatre, London, music/drama
    at 4:16
Dryden, John
    The Indian Queen 4:16
    'Tyrannic Love' 4:26
Du Bois, William 9:34
DuBose Heywood, Edwin, and Gershwin's
    Porgy and Bess 10:52
Dublin
    Handel in 4:65
    Messiah in 4:76-7
Dublin Journal, on *Messiah* 4:50
Ducal Theatre, Milan 1:*22-3*
ducat, Venetian symbolism of 4:50
Duden, Gottfried
    on conditions in America 7:62
    *A Self-Criticism Concerning His Travel
        Report to Warn Against Further
        Rash Emigration* 7:62
    *Report on a Journey to the Western
        States of America* 7:62
Dudevant, Aurore *see* George Sand
Dudevant, Casimir 6:67
duels/duelling 3:*26*-7; 8:*92*
DUETS 9:104; 10:73
    see also Index of Music
Duke of York's Theatre, London, founding
    of 4:26, *26*
dulcimer 9:76, 104-105
Dumas, Alexander (the elder), and *The
    Nutcracker* 3:45
Dunbar, Battle of (1650) 4:*23*
Dunbar Medal, the 4:*23*
Duncan, Isadora, and dance development
    3:44
duo 9:105
Duplessis, Mariette, Liszt and 6:91
duplet 9:105

Dupré, Louis 3:99
Dur 9:105
Durbach, Fanny 3:*23*
    and Tchaikovsky 3:25
Durchkomponiert 9:105
Dušek, Franz 1:13
    and Mozart 1:44
Dušek, Josefa 1:44
Düsseldorf, Germany 8:*92*
    Brahms in 7:9, 10
    municipal music director 8:93
    Mendelssohn in 8:38
    Schumann in
        with Clara 8:93
        lowering of artistic standards 8:93
        quarrels with authorities 8:93
Dutch East India Company 5:72
Dux Castle, Bohemia 1:108, *108*
DVOŘÁK, Antonín *see Index
    of Composers*
Dwight, John, on Tchaikovsky's Piano
    Concerto No. 1 3:67
dynamics 9:105

E

Eberlin, Louise 4:10
Ecole Polytechnique, Paris 8:*84*
écossaise 9:105
Edinburgh, Scotland
    Chopin in 6:68, *68*
    Mendelssohn in 8:44, *44*
education, 19th-century 8:79ff
    cadet school 8:83-4
    home tuition 7:82-3
Eichendorff, Wolf's use of works by 6:29
Eilmar, Archdeacon Georg, and J. S. Bach
    5:25-6
Einstein, Albert 9:30, *32*
Einstein, Alfred, on Mozart's Symphony
    No. 40 1:64
    on Schubert 6:33
Eisenach, Germany 5:*22-3*
    J. A. Bach in 5:15
    court trumpeter and director of music
        in 5:8, 15
    Lutheran connections 5:24
    Pachelbel in 4:9
Eisenstadt, Schubert in 6:13
Elbridge Gerry, Mrs 3:107
electronic music *see* music, electronic
elegy 9:105
ELGAR, Edward *see Index
    of Composers*
Eliot, George
    on girls' education 8:81
    on Weimar 7:81
Elizabeth of Brunswick-Wolfenbüttel 5:57,
    58
Ellis, Osian 1:63
Elsner, Josef, Chopin and 6:63, 70
Elssler, Fanny 3:101
Elssler, Johann, and Haydn 5:93
Elvira Madigan (film, 1967) 1:76
embouchure 9:105
emigration *see Auswanderung*
'empire' look 6:*42*, 43-5
empires, collapse of 9:30, 34-5
enchainez 9:105
encore 9:105; 10:85

Encyclopédie 9:12-13
Endeavour 1:114-15
Engert, von, choice of subject 6:*54*
Engels, Friedrich 9:*25*
    Communist Manifesto 9:25, 26
engineering, advances in 20th century 9:32
England
    arrival of opera in 10:44
    Bach revival in 8:55
    Casanova in 1:*106*, 107-108
    Church music in 5:42
    and Commedia dell'Arte 10:20
    criticism of the theatre in 10:45-6
    cultural revival in 4:25-6
    decline in operatic works 10:46
    in the early 19th century 8:102
        fashion 6:47
        literacy in 8:79
        painting 6:53
    exhibits at The Great Exhibition (1851)
        8:24
    influence of folk music in 9:33
    insurrection in 9:25
    iron industry in 4:109, *109*
    Mendelssohn in 8:37, 38, 39, 76-7
        climax of visits 8:39, 48-9
        crossing to 8:42
    Mozart's visit cancelled 1:13
    musical taste in 17th century 4:14
    'national' drink 5:68
    national opera in 10:44ff
        foundation of 10:48
    opera styles in 10:46
    performance of Brahms's Violin
        Concerto 7:31-2
    popularity of oratorios in 8:77
    prohibition on tobacco 5:68

VOLUME 1
Mozart

VOLUME 2
Beethoven

VOLUME 3
Tchaikovsky

VOLUME 4
**Albinoni, Corelli, Handel,
Pachelbel, Purcell, Rameau,
Telemann, Vivaldi**

VOLUME 5
Bach, Haydn

VOLUME 6
Chopin, Liszt, Schubert

VOLUME 7
Brahms, Mahler

VOLUME 8
Berlioz, Mendelssohn, Schumann

VOLUME 9
A Guide to Classical Music

VOLUME 10
A Beginner's Guide to the Opera

and Prussia/Austria-Hungary wars 5:62
religious differences in 4:*24*, 24-5, 30, 100
the Restoration (1660) 4:23ff
   sexual mores of the court 4:28-9
Tchaikovsky in 3:16, 59
trade with the East 5:69-70
traditional entertainments 10:44
war with Holland (1667) 4:24-5
see also Britain
English Chamber Orchestra 5:37, *37*
English horn *see* horn, English
enharmonic 9:105
Enlightenment, 18th-century 1:77, 110; 9:9, 12
art form during *see* Rococo
beliefs of a true representative 9:15
dictates of 10:22
'Grand Scheme' 9:15
interests 9:*12-13*
inspiration for 9:13
and opéra comique 10:23
theory behind 9:12-13
ensemble 9:105; 10:73-4
composition of 5:30
for *intermedi* 10:8
structure of Baroque 4:*20*
types of 1:58
ensemble music, W. F. Bach and 5:17
ensemble singing 10:13
entertainments,
   private, and development of opera 10:8
   public, and rise of opera 10:8
entr'acte 9:105; 10:85
by Lully 10:18
Entwurf-Katalog, Haydn and 5:93
episode 9:105
equal voices *see* voices, equal
equale 9:105
Erard, Sebastien
and piano development 6:74
grand piano 2:45
and Liszt 6:89
Erfurt, Germany
J. A. Bach in 5:15
Pachelbel in 4:9
Erkel 9:22
ernst 9:105
Ernst August, Elector of Hanover, and Handel 4:61
Ertmann, Baroness Dorothea von 2:*21*
and Beethoven 2:20; 8:38, 48
card from 2:*21*
Mendelssohn and 8:38, 48
escapist writing 9:33
Essays in Musical Analysis (Torey) 1:64
Esterhazy, Prince Paul Anton 5:89
Esterhazy, Prince Nikolai 5:*90*
death of 5:91
and Haydn 5:90
Esterhazy, Prince Nikolaus II, and Haydn 5:93
and Liszt 6:88
Esterhaza 5:*90*
Haydn at 5:90-91
estinto 9:105
étouffez 9:105
ETUDES *see Index of Music*
etwas 9:105
Eugènie, Empress of France, and Queen Victoria 8:78

euphonium 9:105
Europe
after World War II 9:36
age of unrest in 9:23-7
boundaries in the 1860s 9:*21*
Church dramas in 10:8
commodities from the East 5:70-71
common language during the Enlightenment 9:12
curbs on revolutionaries 9:24
development of trade links 5:67
dominance of Italian musicians/style in 4:47
domination of Romanticism in 9:20
effect of revolutions on music 10:30, 31
'gay' epoch (1890s) in 9:26
impact of Byron 9:19-20
insurgent nationalist forces in Eastern 9:27
insurrections in 9:*23*
map of (1871) 7:*73*
outlook for 9:36
potato blight in (1845) 7:62
poverty/prosperity in 9:26
'power vacuum' in 9:36
religions
   attitudes to 9:8
   divisions in 4:53
   effects of 9:8
revolutions
   in 1820s 9:24
   in 20th century 9:34
spread of opera in 10:8
spread of the plague in 5:76ff
tourism in 7:76ff
'unorthodox' religious feelings in 5:22ff
eurythmics 9:105
'Eusebius' 8:88, 89
Evelyn, John, diary 4:29
exercise 9:105
Exhibition of the Works of Industry of all Nations *see* Great Exhibition, The
exhibition tours (Mozart) 1:9
earliest 1:18
exploration
age of 1:109ff
and development of navigational instruments 4:103
exposition 9:105
extemporize 9:105
extravaganza 9:105
French 10:*16-17*

F

Fa 9:105
Faber, Eberhard 7:62
facile 9:105
fado 9:105
fagotto 9:105
Fahrenheit, Daniel Gabriel 4:105
Falieri, Doge Marino 4:50
FALLA, Manuel de *see Index of Composers*
false relation 9:105
falsetto 9:105
Familiengesetz law 7:88
family 9:105
fancy 9:105
fandango 9:105
fanfare 9:105

FANTASIA 9:105
free 9:106
see also Index of Music
fantasy 9:105
Faraday, Michael 4:110
farandole 9:105-106
Farinelli 4:*70*; 6:*106*; 10:*13*, 13-14
faruca 9:106
fashion
early 19th-century 6:43ff
effects on lower classes 6:50
the 'English' look 6:47
fashion accessories 6:45-6
influence of Goethe's work on 8:105
Queen Victoria and 8:78
in Romantic era 6:48
fashion plate, invention of 6:43
of 1824 6:*47*
'father of modern philosophy' (Descartes) 4:104
'father of science' (Bacon) 4:103-104
'Father of Singspiel' (Hiller) 10:29
FAURÉ, *see Index of Composers*
Favart theatre, Paris 10:32
'Feast of the Pheasant' 4:87
feierlich 9:106
female voice 10:78-9
see also individual singers; types of voice
feminine 9:106
Ferdinand, Archduke, commission for wedding of 1:23
Ferdinand, Emperor of Austria 2:*99*, 100
Ferdinand II, King of Naples, revolt against 9:24
Ferdinand VII, restored to throne of Spain 9:23-4
Ferdinand Maximilian, Count von Morzin and Haydn 5:89
fermata 9:106
Ferrand, Humbert, Berlioz and 8:10, 13
Fersen, Count 5:102
Festival Theatre, Bayreuth 10:37, *37, 64*
influence of style of presentation 10:37
festivals, Venetians 4:54-5, *55*
Fêtes Venetiennes 4:55, *55*
Fétis, on Chopin's Paris début 6:65
Feydeau theatre, Paris 10:32
fiddle 9:78, 106
FIELD, John *see Index of Composers*
fifth 9:106
Figaro
comment on Offenbach's theatre 10:53
criticism of Berlioz's Symphonie Fantastique 8:14
figure 9:106
'figured bass' 1:58
film industry, growth of 9:33-4
film music 7:101
fin 9:106
finale 9:106
fine 9:106
Fingal's Cave 8:*62*
Mendelssohn at 8:37, 45
fingering 9:106
continental 9:103
cross 9:103
Fink, Gottfried Wilhelm, and musical journalism 8:101
Finland, 'national' composer 9:22
first 9:106
Firmian, Count, opera 1:23

Fischer-Diskau, Dietrich 10:77
    on *Gretchen am Spinnrade* 6:18-19
Fisher, Kitty 1:107
Fitzgerald, Edward, on Mozart 1:64
flam 9:106
flamenco 9:106
Flamsteed, John 4:108
flat 9:106
    double 9:104
flat keys 9:106
flatterzuge 9:106
flautist 9:106
flauto 9:106
Flaxman, John 1:88, *88*
flebile 9:106
Fleming, Alexander 9:34
flexatone 9:106
flight, powered 9:*32-3*
Florence, Italy 8:*47*
    Albinoni in 4:8
    beginnings of opera in 10:8
    Handel in 4:60
        opera performed in 4:69
    by Hollander 3:*33*
    Mendelssohn in 8:47
    Mozart in 1:23
    Tchaikovsky in 3:*11*, 35
    and tourism 7:76
florid 9:106
flourish 9:106
flügelhorn 9:106
flute 9:45, 106
    Bach's use of 1:61-2
        in Suite No. 2 BWV1067 5:47
    early 9:86
    German 9:107
    Frederick the Great and 5:58, *59*
    Handel's use of 1:61-2
    improvements to 6:23
    Mozart's dislike of 1:60, 61
    timbre of 6:23
    transverse 5:47
Foire de Saint-Germain 10:23, 24
Foire de Saint-Laurent 10:23
Fokine, Michael 3:44
folkdance
    Austrian in 'Eine Kleine Nachtmusik'
        1:49-50
    Tchaikovsky's use of 3:68
folk melodies
    in German Church music 5:38
    Mahler's use of 7:97
folk/gypsy music 7:34-5
    Brahms's first contact with 7:*8*
    Chopin's use of 6:31, 61, 63
    Hungarian 7:34, 35
    influence on 20th-century music 9:33
    Mendelssohn and British 8:37
    Russian 7:35
    influence on Glinka 10:42
        influence on Russian opera 10:41
    Singspiel use of 10:29
folk songs
    Brahms's use of 6:28
    Lessing and 9:19
    revival during Romantic era 9:19
    Schubert's use of 6:15-16
folk themes, inspiration from 9:22
Fontenoy, Battle of (1745) 5:*60-61*, 62
forlana 9:106
form 9:106

Fontana, Domenico 1:83
Fonteyn, Margot 3:45
fortepiano 9:106
    see also piano
fortissimo 9:106
Foundling Hospital, London 4:35
    Handel concerts at 4:77, 77
Fouquet, Nicolas 1:92
'Four Hundred, The' 3:108-109
fourth 9:106
Fox, Charles 4:98
France
    battle between establishment and rebels
        10:24
    Berlioz's reputation in 8:12
    and Commedia dell'Arte 10:20
    court ballets 10:15
    creating a new 2:85ff
    development of Baroque music in 4:22
    development of Church music in 5:42
    18th-century 'character' pieces 4:18,
        18-19
    early 19th-century fashion 6:47
    early 19th-century painting 6:53
    first railways 7:77
    and Germany 9:35
    glorification of monarchy 10:24
    growing power in 17th century 4:25
    growing unrest in 6:83-4
    influence on Europe during the
        Enlightenment 9:12
    influences of late 17th-century music
        5:23
    invasion of England (1805) 2:88
    invasion of Europe (1794) 2:98
    Liszt tours in 6:89
    literacy in 19th-century 8:79
    monarchy restored in 9:24
    offer of French nationality 9:23
    opera
        attacks on 10:31
        changes in taste for 10:18
        founder of in 10:16, 18
        reception of Italian 10:15
        spread of opera to 10:14
        style in late 18th century 10:31
    predominant entertainment 10:15
    and Prussia/Austria-Hungary wars 5:62
    revolution in 9:24; 10:31ff
        July Revolution (1830) 9:*23*
    revolutionary fervour 9:18
    rise of the middle classes 7:105
    rise of musical comedy in 10:22, 25
    'September Massacres' (1792) 5:108
    and Seven Years War (1756-63) 2:95
    and South Seas exploration 1:113
    Tchaikovsky and 3:16
    tourism in 7:76-7
    trade with the East 5:69
    victories 2:88-9
    violin technique 2:62
    and war with Germany 7:74
    war with Russia 2:89-90, *89*
    and World War I 9:27
    see also French Revolution
Franchomme, Auguste 6:68
Francis I, Emperor of Austria 1:*35*; 6:*56*
    and Freemasonry 1:34, *35*
    and the Mozarts 1:18
    new laws of 6:51-2, 57
Francis II, Emperor of Austria 2:97-8, *99*

Francis II, King of Naples, deposition of
    9:26
Francis Joseph, Emperor of Austria 2:100
    and Bad Ischl 7:83
    and Lueger 7:106
    and 'Mayerling Affair' 7:104
    and Prussia 7:73
    silver wedding celebrations 7:*106-107*
Franck, Johann Matthias
    and Haydn 5:88
    teaching method 5:88
Franck, Salamo, and J. S. Bach's cantatas
    5:26
Frankfurt, Germany
    Telemann in 4:10
    travelling fair at 8:108
Frankfurt-on-Oder University, C. P. E. Bach
    at 5:17
Franklin, Benjamin 4:110
Franz Ferdinand, Archduke of Austria,
    assassination of 7:104; 9:27
Frederick IV, King of Denmark 4:*36*
    and Vivaldi 4:*36*, 36-7
Frederick Augustus II, painter to 1:85
Frederick the Great, King of Prussia
    2:94, *94*; 5:12, 18, 56ff, *56, 64*
    and Algarotti 5:60
    and Boyer d'Argens 5:61
    characteristics 5:61
    and culture/learning 5:57-8
    daily routine 5:62
    enthusiasm for music 9:9
    harpsichordist to 8:55
    humane reforms by 5:60
    relaxations 5:58
    sexuality 5:58, 60
    treatment of by father 5:56
    and Voltaire 5:58, 59, 60
    Anti-Machiavel 5:59-60
    see also CONCERTOS
Frederick William I, King of Prussia 5:56,
    57
    death of 5:60
    treatment of his son 5:56
free expression, individual 9:13
free verse 9:32

Composer	Volume
Albinoni	4
Bach	5
Beethoven	2
Berlioz	8
Brahms	7
Chopin	6
Corelli	4
Handel	4
Haydn	5
Liszt	6
Mahler	7
Mendelssohn	8
Mozart	1
Pachelbel	4
Purcell	4
Rameau	4
Schubert	6
Schumann	8
Tchaikovsky	3
Telemann	4
Vivaldi	4

GENERAL INDEX

Freemasons/Fremasonry 1:33ff, *33*
  Haydn and 5:91
  Mozart and 1:34-5, 40, 43
    music for 1:33, 36, 57
  spread of 1:33-4
  tribute to Mozart 1:40
French Revolution (1789) 2:85; 5:102ff
  Beethoven and 2:26-7
  collapse of 9:23
  counter-revolution allies 5:106-107
  effect on ballet 3:101
  effect on opera 10:30, 31
  effects on fashion 6:43
  effect on Singspiel 10:30
  nationalism and 9:23
  poster 5:*109*
  revized monarchy plans 5:103
  Romantic poets' view of 9:19
Freni, Mirella 10:78
frequency 9:106
fret 9:106
fretta 9:106
Freud, Sigmund 7:*95*
Fricken, Ernestine von, Schumann and 8:90
Friderick Christian, King of Poland, and
    Vivaldi 4:40
Friedrich, Caspar David 2:76, 80-83
  advice to painters 2:80
  by Kersting 2:79
  style of painting 6:54, *54*
  The Arctic Shipwreck 2:*82*
  Cross in the Mountains 2:*79*, 81
  Moon Rising Over the Sea 6:*54*
  Two Men Contemplating the Moon
    2:*80-81*, 83
  The Wanderer Above a Sea of Mist 9:*14*
Friedrich August, Elector of Saxony 5:*26*
  J. S. Bach and 5:27
  mourning period for 5:12
Friedrich August II, Elector of Saxony 8:109
  J. S. Bach and 5:12
Friedrichbad, Baden-Baden 7:83
'Friend of the People' (Marat) 9:*15*
Froebel, Friedrich, and education 8:*80*
Johann Jacob *see Index of Composers*
Frohne, Pastor Johan 5:25
frottola 9:106
fugato 9:106
FUGUE 9:106
  the art of the 5:33
  exposition of 5:33
  see also Index of Music
funerals, Austrian edict on 1:15
fuoco 9:107
furiant 9:107
Fürnberg, Karl Joseph von, and Haydn 5:89
Fuseli, Henry 1:86
  Artist in despair over the magnitude of
    Antique Fragments 1:*85* 86
'futurists' 7:29
FUX, Johann *see Index of Composers*
fz 9:107

G

G 9:107
Gabler, Barbara 4:9
GABRIELI, Giovanni *see Index of*
  Composers
galant 9:107

galanteries 9:107
Galilei, Vincenzo
  and the Camerata 10:9
  and recitative 10:9
Galileo Galilei 4:104-105
  Dialogues on the Two Chief Systems of
    the World 4:104-105
Gallenberg, Count Wengel Robert 2:18
galliard 9:107
  use in suites 5:49
galop 9:107
Galop Chromatique, Liszt playing 6:*92*
Galuppi, Baldassare
  collaboration with Goldoni 10:21
  at Russian court 10:42
Gama, Vasco da 4:52
gamba *see* viola da gamba
gambling, Mozart and 1:31
gamelan 9:107
gamme 9:107
Garden, Edward 3:70
garden design, Neo-Classical influence
  1:86
gardens
  principles of Enlightenment 9:15
  principles of Romantic 9:15
Garibaldi, Giuseppe 9:*24-5*, 26
Garrick, David, and Noverre 3:99
gartenlaube 8:106
Gasparini, and the Ospidale della Pietà
  4:37
GASSMANN, Florian Leopold *see Index of*
  Composers
Gautier, on the Englishman 6:47
gavotte 9:107
  use in suites 5:49
GAY, John *see Index of Composers*
Gebler, Tobias
  and Freemasonry 1:36
  and Mozart 1:34
Gelosie fortunate, Le (Anfossi) 1:70
Geltzer, Vassily, and *Swan Lake* 3:39
Geminiani, and violin virtuosity 4:47
Gemmingen, Otto von, and Freemasonry
  1:34-5
gemshorns 9:88
Geneva Conservatory, Liszt at 6:90
Genzinger, Maria Anna von 5:89
  death of 5:93
Georg Ludwig, Elector of Hanover, and
  Handel 4:61
  see also George I, King of England
George I, King of England 4:*94-5*, 96
  and Handel's music 9:9
  music for coronation of 4:87
  and Peace of Aix-la-Chapelle 4:84
George II, King of England, and Handel's
  music 9:9
George III, King of England 4:*95*, 96-7;
  5:93
  Cook and 1:*118*
  coronation of 4:87, *87*
  and Handel's music 9:9
  and Mozart 1:20
George IV, King of England, and Liszt 6:89
German Confederation, establishment of
  8:102
'German problem' 9:35-6
German theatre, founding of 8:107
German nationalists, and anti-Semitism
  7:104, 105

Germany
  agricultural improvements in 7:61
  Albinoni's operas in 4:8
  Bach family; dominance of musical posts
    in 5:13
  Bach revival in 8:55
  bankruptcy 7:61
  Baroque period in 9:8
  and Beethoven's centenary 2:34
  Church music
    basis of in North 5:38
    division in 5:42
    influences on 5:38
  Commedia dell'Arte in 10:20, *27*
  communication in 19th-century 8:102
  controversy over modern music 7:23
  cultural lead in Romantic era 9:18
  development of the cantata in 4:80
  development of oratorios in 4:80
  domination by Prussia 7:68
  drama
    development of 106-107
    dominant form of 8:107-108
    first major dramatist 8:106
  early 19th-century painting 6:53
  education in 19th-century
    eligibility for university 8:79-80
    obsession with the classics 8:80, *80*
  effect of potato blight on 7:62
  effect of *Zollverein* 7:70
  in 1816 7:57
  emigration *see Auswanderung*
  Emperor of 7:70, 74, *74*
  Federal Diet 7:69
  the fever of 1816 7:58-9
  foreign policy 9:35
  Heine on society in 8:109
  hospitality for the upper classes 8:109
  the 'hungry forties' 8:109
  idealized family life 8:81
  impulse for cultured life 8:109
  industrialization in 7:69-70; 8:109
  influences on Baroque music in 5:38
  insurrections in 9:25
  invasion by Napoleon 2:82
  leisure in the 19th century 8:102ff
  life in the royal courts 8:109
  literature in early 19th century 8:105-106
  middle classes in 8:*104-105*, 105-106
  Mozart in 1:19
  National Assembly 7:69, *70*
  national consciousness and Wagner
    10:37
  national traditions 8:55
  national style
    foundation for opera 10:27
    influence of Singspiel on 10:30
  native music dramas 10:27
  new composer 8:35-7
  opera in
    fight for 10:28
    foundation for 10:27
    Italian in 10:15, 27, 28-9
    response to opera seria 10:28-9
  Romantic period in 10:35ff
  opera houses *see* individual names
  pauperism/hunger in 7:109
  peasant household 6:*46-7*
  peasant life in 19th-century 8:102,
    104-105
  piano manufacture 7:41

the plague in 5:76
poetry in 6:17
railways 7:70, 72, 77
rebirth of culture 2:76
rivalry in music 10:28
structure of
    in 1815 7:68
    in 19th century 8:109
    in late 17th century 5:22
Sturm und Drang movement in 9:19
Tchaikovsky and 3:16
theatre tradition in 8:106-107
and Thirty Years War 5:22
    effects of 5:38
travel in early 19th-century 8:102
unification of 9:25
upper classes in 8:108-109
the visual arts in 2:76ff
violin technique 2:62
war with Denmark 7:71, 73
Year of Revolution (1848) 7:69
Ges 9:107
gesang 9:107
Gewandhaus, Mendelssohn and 8:38, *39*, 48, 109
Gewandhaus Orchestra 2:50
Geymüller, Johann von, Schubert and 6:53
Ghezzi, Pier Leone, caricature of Vivaldi 4:*33*, 33
Ghiaurov, Nicholai 10:77
Giant Grenadiers 5:60, *60*
Giant's Staircase, Doge's Palace, Venice 1:*104*
GIARDINI, Felice *see Index of Composers*
Giazotto, Remo, and Albinoni's works 4:16
gigue 9:107
    use in suites 5:46, 49
Gilbert, W. S. 9:26; 10:*56*
    collaboration with Sullivan 10:47, 55-6
    on French operetta 10:56
    humour in libretti 10:56
    influence on British and American
        theatre 10:56
    see also OPERETTA
'Gilded Age' 3:106
Gilels, Emil 7:45, *45*
giocoso 9:107
Giovanni de' Bardi, Count, salon of 10:8-9
Giraud, Anna 4:38, 40
Giraus, Paolina 4:38
girls, education of 8:81-2
gittern 9:77, 107
Giulini, Carlo Maria 1:71
giusto 9:107
Gladkowska, Konstancia, Chopin and 6:64
glee 9:107
Gleichenstein, Ignaz von 2:*18*
    Beethoven and 2:19
GLINKA, Mikhail *see Index of Composers*
glisando 9:107
glockenspiel 9:59, 107
    Mahler's use of 7:97
GLUCK, Christoph Willibald *see Index of Composers*
Glyndebourne Festival 10:48, 61
Gmunden, memorial to Brahms 7:*15*
Gneixendorf, Germany 2:*23*
    Beethoven in 2:14, 22
Goelet, May 3:110
Goethe, Johann Wolfgang von 6:*16-17*
    Berlioz's use of works by 8:10

Brahms's use of works by 7:15
and Classicism 1:88, 89
and creation of German Theatre 8:107
influence on 19th-century drama
    8:107-108
influence on Romantic movement 8:61
and Karlsbad 7:83
on Leipzig 8:109
love of classical music 8:35
manifesto against Classicism 9:19
Mendelssohn and 8:33, 34-5, *35*
    influence on 8:61
    last visit to Goethe 8:38
as a Romantic 9:20
Schubert's use of work by 6:11, 17, 19
    response to 6:20
and *Sturm und Drang* 9:19
on women's education 8:82
Wolf's use of works by 6:29
Faust 8:35
    Mendelssohn and 8:36
    on *The Magic Flute* 1:38
Sorrows of Young Werther 2:27; 8:105; 9:19
    and mood of Romantic era 9:19
Walpurgisnacht
    Mendelssohn and 9:47
Gogol, Nikolay 3:*90*
    The Government Inspector 3:*90*
    Taras Bulba 3:*90*
Goldberg, Gottlieb, J. S. Bach and 5:12
Goldberg, Johann, J. S. Bach and 3:62
Goldoni, Carlo 4:*35*, 49; 10:12, *20*
    collaboration with Galuppi 10:21
    development of social satire 10:21
    use of Commedia dell'Arte characters
        10:21
    and development of opera buffa 10:21-2
    and Vivaldi 4:35; *35*
gong 9:60, 107
Gordon, Colonel William, by Batoni 1:*86-7*
Gotha, Germany, Pachelbel in 4:9
Gottingen, Germany,
    Brahms in 7:11
    Joachim in 7:9
Gottschalk, Louis 6:104
GOUNOD, Charles *see Index of Composers*
governess, status of 8:*82*, 83
Goya, Francisco de
    as a Romantic 9:20
    3rd of May 1880 9:*18-19*
GP 9:107
grace-note 9:107
Gramont, Comte de 4:28
Granada, cholera outbreak in (1887)
    2:*104-105*
Grand Alliance, invasion of Germany
    (1690) 4:9, *9*
Grand Army (French)
    in Russia 2:89
    smashing of the 2:90
    victories 2:88-9
    in Vienna 2:*98-9*
'Grand Circular Tour of the Continent, A'
    7:79-80
Grand Council, Venice 4:52
Grand Lodge (Freemason), first 1:33
Grand Tour/Tourists 1:84-5, *84-5*; 7:76
    Mendelssohn's 8:41ff
    Mozart's 1:19-21
Grande Ecurie (Woodwind band) 4:20

Granville, Mary, and Handel 4:62
Grätz castle, Silesia 2:*25*
    Beethoven at 2:25
Graun, Johann Gottlieb
    adopts Italian style 10:28
    and W. F. Bach 5:16
grave 9:107
gracioso 9:107
Great Exhibition, The (1851) 8:22ff
    Berlioz and 8:12
    centrepiece of 8:27
    'chief attraction' 8:27
    closing of 8:30, *30*
    daily attendances 8:27
    exhibits
        classifying 8:24, 26
        description of some of 8:26-7
        Krupp's 7:72
    hostility towards 8:23-4
    official opening 8:24, *24-5*
    the 'pounds' and 'shillings' of 8:27-30
    refreshments at 8:*28*, 28-9
    sections of 8:26, *26-7*
    sheet music commemorating 8:*29*
    success of 8:27, 75
Great Southern Continent, The 1:110
Greece, ancient
    appeal of 9:13
    interest in 1:82ff
    keeping musical rhythm in 7:50
    roots of opera in 10:8
    revival of interest in classical 9:13
Greece modern, revolution in 9:24
Greenwich, Palace, London 4:*24-5*
Greenwich Observatory, London 4:*24-5*
Gregory the Great, Pope, and Church
    music 5:42

VOLUME 1
Mozart

VOLUME 2
Beethoven

VOLUME 3
Tchaikovsky

VOLUME 4
Albinoni, Corelli, Handel,
Pachelbel, Purcell, Rameau,
Telemann, Vivaldi

VOLUME 5
Bach, Haydn

VOLUME 6
Chopin, Liszt, Schubert

VOLUME 7
Brahms, Mahler

VOLUME 8
Berlioz, Mendelssohn, Schumann

VOLUME 9
A Guide to Classical Music

VOLUME 10
A Beginner's Guide to the Opera

GRÉTRY, André *see Index of Composers*
GRIEG, Edvard *see Index of Composers*
Grillparzer, Franz 6:57
    on Beethoven's death 2:22
    and Napoleon 6:58
    Schubert and 6:53
       epitaph to 6:13
Grimani, Abbé 1:101
Grimm, Baron Melchior 1:*20*
    and Mozart 1:11, 19-20
Grimm brothers 2:84
    Jakob and the Mendelssohns 8:34
Grisi, Carlotta 3:*101*
Grisi, Guilia and Giudetta 10:39
Grob, Therese, Schubert and 6:10, 11
Grosses Festspielhaus, Salzburg 10:66, *66*
Grossholz, Marie *see* Tussaud, Madame
Grosvenor family 6:*48-9*
Grotto, The (secret society) 1:35
Grotto of Aigen, Salzburg, Germany 1:*36*
ground 9:107
Grumiaux, Arthur 2:65, *65*
Guaneri family 2:62; 4:47; 9:9
Guerra, Antonio 3:*100*
Guettard 4:108
Guicciardi, Countess Giulietta 2:*45*
    and Beethoven 2:18, *19*
guidebooks 7:78, *81*
Guines, Duc de
    and Mozart 1:27
       commission for 1:*60*, 61
Guillotin, Dr 5:108
guitar 9:63, 107
    early 9:85
    Mahler's use of 7:97
Gumpendorf, Vienna, Haydn's house at 5:93
Gurk, Bishop of 1:9
Gymnasium 8:80
Gymnasium Poeticum, Regensburg, Pachelbel at 4:8
Gwynne, Nell 4:*27*, 27-8
gypsies, origin of 7:34
'gypsy bands' 7:34-5
gypsy music *see* folk/gypsy music

H

H 9:107
Habanera 9:107
Habeneck, François-Antoine 6:105
    Beethoven's Symphony No. 5 2:71
    and première of Berlioz's Symphonie Fantastique 8:14
Hadji Murad (Tolstoy) 3:93
Hagn, Charlotte von, Liszt and 6:91
Haibl, Sophie, on Mozart when composing 1:57-8
Hainburg, Haydn in 5:88, *88*
hairstyles, in Romantic era 6:47, *48*
Haitink, Bernard 2:*56*, 57; 3:57
Hall of Stars of the Queen of the Night (Schinkel) 2:*81*, 83
Halle, Germany
    and J. S. Bach 5:9-10
    W. F. Bach in 5:17
    the plague in 5:76
    religious developments in 5:25
Hallé, Charles, on Paganini 6:107
Halle University, Handel at 4:60

Halles, Les, Paris 6:*82*
Hamburg 4:*60*; 7:*90-91*
    Brahms in 7:10
       founds women's choir 7:11
       house of his own in 7:11
    emigration from 7:*60*, 62
    Handel in 4:60
    Mahler in 7:90-91
       efforts to leave 7:91-2
    musical director of main churches 4:10
    the plague in 5:76
    reaction to Italian opera 10:28
    refugees in 7:27
    second opera house 10:*28-9*
    Telemann in 4:10
Hamburg Opera, conductor with 7:90
Hamelin, Madame, and the 'empire' look 6:44
Hamilton, Gavin 1:87
Hamilton, Sir William 1:88-9
HANDEL, George Frideric *see Index of Composers*
Haugwitz, Count 2:95
Hanover, Germany
    Brahms in 7:11
    Handel in 4:61, 62
       conditions for taking post in 4:61
       population control in 7:61
Hanover Square Rooms, London 5:*18, 92, 96-7*
Hanoverian Legation, London, secretary to (Klingemann) 8:41
Hansen, Joseph, and *Swan Lake* 3:40
Hanslick, Eduard
    and Brahms's music 7:24
       and Symphony No. 1 7:48
    and musical criticism 8:101
    of Wagner 7:25, 8:101
Hanswurst 10:*28*, 29-30
'happiness, pursuit of' (USA constitution) 9:9
Hapsburg, Empire/House of 2:92ff
    insignia 2:*93*
    loss of power 9:27
    restoration of 9:23
    struggle for national identity in 9:22
    and Thirty Years War (1618-48) 5:22
harminoc 9:107
harmonica 9:107
    glass 3:55, 9:107
harmony/harmonies 1:52; 9:107
    close 9:102
    'colour' of 6:23
    open 9:112
    overthrow of 9:32
    pamphlet war over 10:26
Harper, Heather 4:83, *83*
harps 9:62
    early 9:75
    Mozart's dislike of 1:60, 61
harpsichord 9:67, 107
    accompaniment for recitative 10:13
    C. P. E. Bach and 5:17
    J. S. Bach and
       toccatas for 5:9
       use in Concerto No. 5 BWV1050 5:35
    Handel's ability on 4:61-2
    method of sound reproduction 6:74
    Pachelbel works for 4:22
    Purcell and 4:14

Rameau and 4:11; 10:18
    Scarlatti and 4:22
harpsichord competition, Bach and 5:10
Harrison, John 1:110; 4:106
Hart, Charles 4:27
Harvey, William 4:106
    De Motu Cordis 4:106
Hasse, adopts Italian style 10:28
Hatwig, Otto, and Schubert 'orchestra' 6:53
Hatzfeld, Count von 1:44
Hauptmann, Gerhard, Mahler and 7:93
Hauptwerk 5:40
Hawkins, Sir John, on Corelli's violin playing 4:12
Haydn, Anna Maria 5:88
HAYDN, Joseph *see Index of Composers*
Haydn, Mathias 5:88
HAYDN, Michael *see Index of Composers*
Haydn, Nicola, as Handel's librettist 4:71
head voice 9:107
headwear (1820s) 6:*45*, 45-6, 47-8
Hegel, C. W. F. 8:*84*
    and the Mendelssohns 8:34
    Mendelssohn studies under 8:36
Heidegger, J. J. 4:62, *70*
    and Handel 4:64, 69
    and King's Theatre 4:72
Heidelberg University, Germany
    Schumann at 8:89
    students at 8:*82-3*
Heiligenstadt, Vienna 2:*10-11*, 11, 13
    Beethoven in 2:*17*; 9:20
'Heiligenstadt Testament' 2:11, *11*, 17, 48
Heine 6:67
    on Berlioz 8:8
    on Dreyshock 6:109
    on German society 8:109
    on musicians in Paris 6:82
    Schubert's use of works by 6:17
    Schumann's use of works by 6:28
helicon 9:107
'Hell-Fire' Club 4:98
Helpmann, Robert 3:45
hemidemisemiquaver 9:107
Henrici, Friedrich, and J. S. Bach's cantatas 5:27
'Henriette', Casanova and 1:104
Henry III, King of France, ballet for 3:97
Henry IV, King of France
    and ballet 3:97
    opera for 10:9
Hensel, Wilhelm 8:38
HENZE, Hans Werner *see Index of Composers*
Herbert, Victor 3:21
Herculaneum, Italy 1:*82*, 82ff
Herder, Johann Gottfried
    and J. C. F. Bach 5:19
    and ballads 6:17
Hermann, Marie 7:*88*
    see also Mahler, Marie
Herschel, George, Brahms and 7:32
Herz, Henri 6:104, 108-109
    Chopin and 6:78
    rivalry with de Meyer 6:108
Herzogenberg, Elisabeth von
    Brahms and 7:13
    death of 7:14
hey(e) 9:108
Heyse, Dr Karl, and Mendelssohn 8:83

Hill, Aaron
on Handel's opera style 4:72-3
and Handel's *Rinaldo* 4:*64*
Hiller, Ferdinand
Chopin and 6:65, 78
letter from Liszt 6:65
Hiller, J. A., and Gay's *Beggar's Opera* 10:29
Hingeston, John 4:13, 14
Historicism 7:106
History of Ancient Art (Winkelmann) 1:87
'history painter', Carstens as 2:77-8
'hit' songs, in 18th-century England 10:46
Hoboken, Anthony van 1:67
hoe-down 9:108
Hofburg palace, Vienna 2:*96-7*
Redoutensaal masked ball 2:*30-31*
Hoffman House, New York 3:*18-19*
Hoffmann, Ernst Theodore Amadeus 2:71
on Beethoven's Symphony No. 5 2:*71*
criticism of Beethoven 8:101
and *The Nutcracker* 3:44
Schumann and 8:87
Tchaikovsky and 3:13
Hoffmann, Heinrich, *Struwwelpeter* 8:105
Hoffnung, Gerard 3:55
Hofkomponist, Dresden (Bach) 5:12
Hofmannsthal, Hugo, and R. Strauss's *Elektra* 10:50
Hoftrompeter 5:11
in Eisenach 5:8, 15
Hohenlohe, Prince Chlodwig, and upper-class hospitality 8:109
Hohenlohe-Ingelfingen, Prince Kraft von, and upper-class hospitality 8:109
Hohenzollerns 7:68
as emperors of Germany 7:74, *74*
Holdsworth, Edward, on Vivaldi 4:*39*
Holland
Mozart in 1:20-21
trade with the East 5:69
war with England (1667) 4:24-5
HOLST, Gustav *see Index of Composers*
Holy Roman Empire, crown of 2:*94*
Holy Alliance 9:24
homage 9:108
Homestead Act (American) 7:64
homophony 9:108
homosexuals, attitudes towards 3:*24*, 24-5
see also Tchaikovsky
HONEGGER, Arthur *see Index of Composers*
Hood, Admiral 2:86
Hooke, Robert 4:108
Horlsey, Dr William, on Mendelssohn 8:42-3
Horne, Marylin 10:79
horns 9:108
altering pitch of 1:72
development of 4:20
early 9:88
English 9:105
French 9:53
hand- 9:107
Haydn Symphony for 5:99
valve system 1:72
see also bassett horn; crumhorn; gemshorn; post horn; saxhorn
'hospitals', music training in 4:36
'house' musicians 3:10
household management, 19th-century 8:105

Howard, Sir Robert, *The Indian Queen* 4:16
Howe Elliott, Mrs Maud 3:108
Huberman, Bronislav, on Brahms's Violin Concerto in D op. 77 7:30
Hugo, Victor
Liszt's use of works by 6:100
Notre Dame de Paris 6:80
Humboldt, Alexander von 8:84
Humboldt, Wilhelm von 8:*84*
educational reforms 8:80, 84
and the Mendelssohns 8:34
HUMMEL, Johann *see Index of Composers*
humoresque 9:108
Hungary
folk/gypsy music in 7:34
invasion of 9:36
Liszt in 6:91, *92*
Mozart in 1:19
'national' composers 9:22
revolution in 9:24
Schubert in 6:13
hurdy-gurdy 9:80
Hüttenbrenner, Anselm 6:*11*
on Beethoven's death 2:15
and Schubert 6:12
and *Erlkönig* 6:20
and Symphony No. 8 6:*38*
Hütter, Leonhard, of Wittenberg 5:24
Hyde, Anne 4:28, *28*
hymn 9:108
Hynd, Ronald, and *The Nutcracker* 3:*46-7*

I

I Musici ensemble 4:*22*, 48
idée fixe 9:108
of Berlioz's Symphonie Fantastique 8:14, 16
'Idle Hour', Long Island 3:105-106
Il trionfo del tempo e del disinganno (Handel) 4:12
Illuminati 1:34
meeting place 1:*36*
Mozart and 1:35
Illustrated London News, The, obituary to Mendelssohn 8:*49*
'Immortal Beloved, The', Beethoven's letter to 2:13, 19, 20
Imperial Choir School, Vienna, and Schubert's Symphony No. 1 6:33
Imperial family, Austrian 1:*26*
see also Hapsburgs
Imperial and Royal School, Vienna 6:*8*
regime at 6:10
Schubert at 6:*8*, 10
uniform 6:10, 50
Imperial Theatres, Moscow 3:10
director of 3:42
Imperial Vienna Opera
director of 7:91, *92*
Mahler at 7:97
resignation from 7:94
impromptu 9:108
improvization 9:108
J. S. Bach and 5:12
Chopin and 6:62-3
on Polish drinking song 6:63
German organists and 5:14
by melody instruments 5:14

Mendelssohn and 8:49, 77
Schubert and 6:12
in modo di 9:108
Inamorata (in Commedia dell'Arte) 10:20
indeterminacy 9:108
India
British trade with 5:69-70
Industrial Revolution 4:*108*, 110
rise of cotton industry during 6:43
industrialization, the Enlightenment and 9:15
Inferno (Dante) 3:52
fifth canto 3:53
instrumental parts, solo 1:56
instrumentation 9:108
INSTRUMENTS 9:108
in Balkan states/Turkey 7:34-5
in Baroque era
development of 4:47
potential of individual in 4:7
description of *timbre* of 6:23
early 9:71ff
Hungarian gypsy 7:34
improvements to
18th-century 4:20
and orchestration 6:23
introduction of new 4:20
limitations of 2:34-5
Monteverdi's use of 4:20
'painting' with combinations of 6:23
solo 9:61ff
unusual 3:55
Telemann and 4:17-18
Wagner, and development of 3:55
Brass 9:50ff, 101
development of valves 6:23
Mahler's use of 7:97
in Mozart's Day 1:72
Electronic 3:55
Keyboard:
C. P. E. Bach and 5:17, 18
character pieces for 4:18
number of pieces for by Telemann 4:10
see also clavichord; harpsichord; piano

Composer	Volume
Albinoni	4
Bach	5
Beethoven	2
Berlioz	8
Brahms	7
Chopin	6
Corelli	4
Handel	4
Haydn	5
Liszt	6
Mahler	7
Mendelssohn	8
Mozart	1
Pachelbel	4
Purcell	4
Rameau	4
Schubert	6
Schumann	8
Tchaikovsky	3
Telemann	4
Vivaldi	4

Percussion 9:55ff, 113
  early 9:73
Reed 9:114
  see also Woodwind
Stringed 9:41ff, 62ff, 116
  C. P. E. Bach and 5:17, 18
  early 9:75ff, 96ff,
  use of by Baroque composers 9:9
  use of in 18th-century orchestra
    6:23
Woodwind 9:44ff
  early 9:86ff, 91ff
  Gabrieli's use of 4:20
  Mahler's use of 7:97
  technical advances in 6:23
  see also individual instruments
instruments, scientific (17th and 18th
    centuries) 4:103, 104, 105-106
interlude 9:108
intermedi 4:87; 10:8
  costume design for 10:9
  reaction against 10:8-9
  themes for 10:8
INTERMEZZO/INTERMEZZI 9:108;
    10:14, 14
  humour banished to 10:19
  most popular 10:20
Pergolesi
  La Serva Padrona 10:18
    performances in Paris 10:25
    popularity of 10:20
    title page 10:21
Ristori, Calandro 10:41
international trade, rise of 5:66ff
interval(s) 9:108
  consecutive 9:103
  simple 9:115
intonation 9:108
inversion 9:108
Iron Chancellor see Bismarck, Otto von
Italy
  J. C. Bach in 5:19
  Baroque music in 4:47; 9:8
  Berlioz and 8:10
  Church drama in 10:8
  development of ballet in 3:96
  development of Church music in
    5:42
  emergence of opera buffa 10:19
  first railways 7:77
  Glinka in 10:42
  leading composer in 1815 10:38
  Liszt in 6:90
  Mendelssohn in 1:9, 18, 22-3
  Mozart in 1:9, 18, 22-3
  musical influences
    on Brahms's music 7:38
    of late 17th-century 5:23
    on Europe 5:38
  operatic centre of 10:20
  pact with France 7:72
  private entertainments in 10:8
  revolution in 9:24
  rise of opera in 10:9, 10ff
  Tchaikovsky and 3:16
  tourism in 7:76-7
  unification of 9:25-6
  verismo opera 10:40
  violin technique 2:62
  war with Austria 7:104
Ivanov, Lev, and Swan Lake 3:40

J

Jacobikirche, Lübeck, Germany, concerts
    in 5:9, 9
Jacquin, Nicolas von 1:43, 45
Jagemann, Karoline, and theatre in Weimar
    8:107
James, Duke of York 4:28, 28
JANÁČEK, Leoš see Index of Composers
Janina, Olga, and Liszt 6:94-5
Janowitz, Gundula 10:78
Japan, Dutch trade with (17th century) 5:69
jazz 9:33, 34
Jeanrenaud, Cécile 8:38
  see also Mendelssohn, Cécile
Jeffries, Judge 4:30
Jena, Battle of (1806) 8:84
Jenger, Johann 6:11
Jennens, Charles 4:76
  and Handel's works 4:75
    and Messiah 4:76
  letter from Handel 4:65
Jenner, Edward 2:104, 109
Jenny, Mme, Schubert and 6:11
Jerome Bonaparte, King of Westphalia 2:29
Jerome, Jenny 3:109, 110
Jeunehomme Concerto (Mozart) 1:10
jew's harp 9:108
jig 9:108
Joachim, Joseph 2:62, 62; 7:27, 32
  and Beethoven's Violin Concerto 2:60
  and Brahms 7:8, 9
    cadenza in Violin Concerto 7:31
    conducts first performance of Piano
      Concerto No. 1 7:11
    denounces him 7:13
    description of 7:15
    and Double Violin Concerto 7:13
    impact of Brahms's music on 7:30
    revisions of Violin Concerto 7:30-31
  concerto written for 7:30
  letters
    to Clara Schumann 7:28
    to Liszt 7:29
  and Liszt 7:28
    criticism of his music 7:29
  and 'New Music' 7:29
  posts
    in Hanover 7:28
    in Weimar 7:28
  and tribute to Schumann 7:30
  see also CONCERTOS
Johannskirche, Lüneberg, Germany
    organist at 5:9, 39-40
Johnson, Dr Samuel 4:97
  on Italian opera 4:68
  on London 4:100
Jones, Gwyneth 10:78
Jones, Inigo, and stage design 10:45, 45
Joseph II, Emperor of Austria 1:10;
    2:96-7, 97; 10:29
  death of 1:14
  founds theatre of German musicals 1:12
  and Freemasonry 1:34, 35
  and German national opera 10:30
  and the Illuminati 1:34
  and Mozart 1:12, 22
  and Salieri 10:30
  and Singspiel 10:29, 30
    founds national theatre of 10:30

Josephine Bonaparte, Empress of France
    2:87
Journal des Débats, Berlioz writes for 8:12
Judson, Stanley 3:45
'July Revolution' (1830) 6:78
'July Monarchy' in France 6:78, 83-4
Junkers; in 19th century Prussia 7:70
Jurgenson 3:61
  and Swan Lake Suite 3:40
  Tchaikovsky and 3:59, 61

K

Kalkbrenner, Friedrich 6:61
  Chopin and 6:70, 78
  6-piano extravaganza 6:65
Kammermusicus, Austrian, Mozart as
    1:26, 30
Kamsko-Votkinsk, (Tchaikovsky's
    birthplace) 3:7
Kantor 5:10
  of Arnstadt 5:25
  importance of post of 5:38
Kapelle 9:108
Kapellmeister 9:108
  Bonn 2:26, 26
  of Cöthen 5:10, 26
  to Count von Morzin 5:89
  to the Esterhazy's 5:90-91, 93
  importance of post of 5:38
  Salzburg 1:11
  Saxe-Weissenfels 5:12
  to Stadttheater, Leipzig 7:88-9, 89
  Viennese 1:13; 6:10
  Westphalian 2:29
Karajan, Herbert von 7:52-3
Karl Theodor, Elector Palatine 1:10; 4:20
  and Mozart 1:11
Karlsbad, Germany
  Brahms in 7:14
  and tourism 7:83
Karlsschule, Stuttgart, Germany 2:78
Kassel, Prussia, Mahler in 7:88
Kaunitz, Wenzel Anton von 2:95
Keats, John, and rebellion against society
    9:19
keen 9:108
keeper and assistant of the Royal
    instruments 4:13, 14
Keiser, Reinhard, and Handel 4:60
Kell, Reginald 1:63
Keller, Ferdinand, Chopin 6:70
Keller, Maria Anna, and Haydn 5:89
Keller, Therese 5:89
Kelly, Michael 1:51
Kemble, Charles 8:10
Kempff, Rudolf 1:79
Kempff, Wilhelm 2:49, 49
Kerll, Johann Kaspar, and Pachelbel 4:8
Kersting
  Caspar David Friedrich in his Studio
    2:79
  The Embroiderer 8:109
key(s) 3:62; 9:108
  changes in variations 2:54
  flat 9:106
  modulations 1:52
  Mozart's use of 1:72
    use of C minor 1:79
  organization in Classical music 1:77

relationships between 1:52; 9:114
in 16th/17th centuries 2:54
Schubert's use of unrelated 1:52
sharp 9:115
of Tchaikovsky's symphony No. 6 3:58
key signature 9:108
keyboard 9:108
keyboard instruments *see* INSTRUMENTS, keyboard
Keyserlingk, Count von, and J. S. Bach 5:12
Kielmansegg, Baron, on Handel's *Water Music* 4:88
Killigrew, Thomas, and theatre revival 4:26
Kind, Friedrich, and Weber's *Der Freischütz* 10:35-6
Kindergarten 8:80
King, A. Hyatt, on Clarinet Concerto K.622 (Mozart) 1:60
King's Company, the 4:26
    King's Theatre, Haymarket 4:65, 69
    Handel and 4:63, 64, 72
    Royal Academy of Music and 4:70
Kinsky, Prince 2:29
    contract with Beethoven 2:89-9, 29, 30
Kipchak Khan 5:76
Kirnberger, Johann Philipp
    and J. S. Bach 8:55
    and W. F. Bach 5:17
klavier 9:108
klavierauszug 9:108
klein 9:108
Klimt, Gustav 7:108
    and the Secession 7:108-109
    style of painting 7:106-107
Klingemann, Karl 8:42
    on English food 8:41-2
    letters, on English way of life 8:42
    travels with Mendelssohn 8:37
    visit to Sir Walter Scott 8:44-5
Knabe Piano Company 3:17
    testemonial for 3:21
Knobelsdorff, Georg Wenzeslaus von 5:58
knowledge, 20th-century explosion in 9:30
Koch, Joseph Anton 2:78-9
    The Schmadribach Falls 2:76-7, 78-9, 80
Koch, Robert 2:109
Köchel, Ludwig Ritter von 1:67
    cataloguing Mozart's music 1:67
Köchel (K) numbering system 1:67
KODÁLY, Zoltán *see Index of Composers*
Kohlmarket, Vienna 2:31; 5:88
Königgrätz, Battle of (1866) 7:72, 73
Konzertmeister
    Salzburg 1:9, 22, 26
    Weimar 5:9-10
Körner, K. T., Schubert and 6:17
kornett 9:108
Korompa castle, Hungary 2:18
koto 9:108
Krause, Tom 10:77
Kreisler, Fritz 2:64
    and Beethoven's Violin Concerto 2:63, 64
    invitation from Mrs Vanderbilt 3:109
Kremlin, Moscow 3:86-7
Kreutzer, Rodolphe 2:62
Krupp, Alfred 7:72
Krzyzanowska, Justyna *see* Chopin, Justyna
Kubelik, Rafael 7:103
KUHNAU, Joseph *see Index of Composers*
Kupelwieser, letter from Schubert 6:12-13

L

laboratory, early 4:106-107
Laennec, René 2:104
Lafayette, General 5:104, 105
Lafontaine, Mademoiselle 3:99
Lamartine, Alphonse de 6:79, 80
lament/lamento 9:109; 10:85
lancers 9:109
ländler 9:109
landscape
    Friedrich and 2:79, 80-81, 81-2
    'heroic' 2:78
    'improvement' of 9:15
Lang, P. H., on Classicism 9:13
Lange, Joseph 1:11
    portrait of Mozart 1:14, 25
largamente 9:109
larghetto 9:109
largo 9:109
Larrey, Baron 2:106
Last Days of Pompeii, The (Lytton) 1:89
lauda 9:109
laughing gas 2:106, 106
lavolta 9:109
Le Havre, France 3:16
leader 9:109
Lear, Evelyn 10:78
ledger (leger) line 9:109
Leewenhoek, Anton Van 4:105, 109
legato 2:62; 9:109
LEHAR, Franz *see Index of Composers*
Lehmann, Johann Georg, and W. F. Bach 5:17
Leibnitz, Gottfried 4:108
leicht 9:109
Leipzig, Germany 5:12, 14-15
    J. S. Bach in 5:11-12, 12, 27
        disputes with Church council 5:27
        examination for job in 5:27
        first major work in 5:27
        position on return to 5:12
    Brahms in 7:10
        plays Piano Concerto No. 1 7:11
    Chopin in 6:66
    cultural activity in 8:109
    Mahler in 7:88-9, 89
        scandal in 7:89
    marketplace 8:90
    Mendelssohn in
        and cultural activity 8:109
        and Gewandhaus 8:38, 39, 101
        repertoire in 8:38
    opera in 10:28
    and publishing industry 8:109
    reaction to Italian opera in 10:28
    Schumann in 8:89, 91-2
    Singspiel in 10:29
    Telemann in 4:10
Leipzig Conservatory
    first professor of composition 7:23
    foundation of 8:109
    foundation of teaching 7:25
    founder 7:23; 8:39
    Mendelssohn and 8:39
    and 'New Music' 7:23
Leipzig University
    C. P. E. Bach at 5:17
    Schumann at 8:89

Leipziger Musikalische Zeitung, on Paganini 6:107
'leisure', in Schumann's Germany 8:102ff
Leiter, Mary 3:110
leitmotiv 9:109; 10:85
    in Wagner's operas 10:37
Lely, Peter 4:26
    painting of Nell Gwynne 4:26-7
Leningrad Philharmonic Orchestra 3:62
lento 9:109
LEONCAVALLO, Ruggero *see Index of Composers*
Leopold, Archduke 2:97, 97
Leopold, Grand Duke of Tuscany 1:23
Leopold, King of Belgium, and Queen Victoria and Prince Albert 8:75-6
Leopold, Prince 5:11, 29
Leopold II, Emperor of Austria
    and French Revolution 5:102
    and Mozart's family 1:15
    coronation of 1:14
    work for 1:15
Leppard, Raymond 5:37, 37
Lermontov, Mikhail 3:88-9, 89
    A Hero of Our Time 3:88, 89
Lessing, Gotthold Ephraim 8:106
    literary recommendations 9:19
lesson(s) 5:49; 9:109
LESUEUR, (or Le Sueur), Jean-François *see Index of Composers*
'Letheon' 2:106
Leutgeb, Anton 1:15
Levi, Hermann, and Brahms's symphonies 7:49
'libertines', in 18th century 9:12

VOLUME 1
Mozart

VOLUME 2
Beethoven

VOLUME 3
Tchaikovsky

VOLUME 4
Albinoni, Corelli, Handel, Pachelbel, Purcell, Rameau, Telemann, Vivaldi

VOLUME 5
Bach, Haydn

VOLUME 6
Chopin, Liszt, Schubert

VOLUME 7
Brahms, Mahler

VOLUME 8
Berlioz, Mendelssohn, Schumann

VOLUME 9
A Guide to Classical Music

VOLUME 10
A Beginner's Guide to the Opera

librettists 10:74
    influence of nationality on operas 10:8
    restraints of opera seria on 10:13
    see also individual librettists
libretto/libretti 9:109
    of Baroque operas 10:12
    18th-century subjects 10:12
    publishing 10:12
    use of by other composers 10:12
licenza 9:109
Lichnowsky, Prince Karl 2:*25*
    and Beethoven 2:9, 26, 27, *27*, 46
    and Mozart 1:36
Lichnowsky, Princess Christian 2:27
Lichtenthal, Brahms in 7:12
Liebfrauenkirche, Halle 5:*15*
    organist at 4:60; 5:*15*, 16
lieblich 9:109
Liebniz, Gottfried 5:26
LIED/LIEDER 6:28-9; 9:109
    development of 2:84
    strophic 6:28
    through-composed 6:28
    see also Index of Music
liedertafel 9:109
ligature 9:109
Lincoln's Inn Fields, London 4:*70-71*
Linley, Thomas 1:*22*, 23
Linnaeus, Carl 1:111, *112*; 4:109-110
Lippershey, Hans 4:104
Lister, Joseph 2:108
Liston, Robert 2:103, 105
Liszt, Adam 6:88
    ambitions for son 6:88
    last words to Liszt 6:89
    and Liszt's music training 6:88
Liszt, Cosima 6:90
    on Liszt's 'marriage' 6:93
    marriages 7:29
        to von Bülow 6:93
        to Wagner 6:95
LISZT, Franz *see Index of Composers*
Liszt-Wagner movement 7:25
'Lisztomania' 6:91
litany 9:109
    Mozart's settings for 1:9
literature
    dismissal of Classical 9:19
    during Romantic era 9:18
    in early 19th-century Germany 8:105
    inspiration from in Romantic era 8:61
    in Tchaikovsky's Russia 3:86ff
Litolff, Henri, Liszt and 6:98
Liverpool, England emigration from
    7:62
L'Orchestre de la Suisse Romande 3:48
Lobkowitz, Prince 2:*29*, 69
    and Beethoven 2:20, 69
    contract with 2:28-9, *29*, 30
Locatelli, Pietro 2:62
    and violin virtuosity 4:47
loco 9:109
London, England 4:*94-5*; 8:*41*
    J. C. Bach in 5:*18*, 19; 8:55
    J. C. F. Bach 5:19
    W. F. Bach in 5:19
    Berlioz in
        conducts at Drury Lane Theatre 8:12
        for The Great Exhibition 8:12
    'carriage trade' 4:100
    Chopin in 6:67, 89

clubs 4:97-9
food in 8:41-2
Great Fire of (1666) 4:29; 5:*83*
Great Plague (1665) 4:29; 5:80-1
Handel in 4:62, 65-6
    first visit 4:61-2
in Handel's time 4:94ff
Haydn in 5:91-2
    symphonies for 5:99
Liszt in, début 6:89
manners and morals in 4:97
Mendelssohn in 8:37, *37*
    attachment to 8:37, 39, 41
    behaviour in 8:42-3
    début 8:37
    greatest success in 8:44
    introduced to society 8:42
    lodgings 8:42
    number of visits to 8:41
    performances in 8:43
Moscheles in 8:42
Mozart in 1:20; 5:19
new churches in 4:109
opera in
    introduction of Russian 10:43
    Italian in 10:*44*, 46-7
    as opera centre 4:63-4, 68; 10:46
    season in 4:61-2
parks 4:99
Restoration of Charles II in 4:25-6
salons 10:10
C. Schumann in 7:*20*
society in 8:*43*
    Mendelssohn introduced to 8:42
stock exchange 5:73
style of stage productions 10:45
tea drinking in 5:68
theatre revival in 4:*26*, 26-7
theatres in 10:44
shops 4:100
sports 4:99
'London Bach, the' 5:19
London Philharmonic Orchestra 5:101
London Symphony Orchestra 8:67
Loos, Adolf
    Ins Leere Gesprochen 7:110
    Ornament and Crime 7:107
Loredan, Leonardo, Doge of Venice 4:*50*
Lorengar, Pilar 10:78
Lorenzkirche, Altdorf, organist at
    (Pachelbel) 4:8
Lorraine, Duke of, and Lully 10:16
Lorraine, Maurice de, Comte d'Elboeut
    1:83
lotteries 1:*105*
Lotz, Theodor, and basset clarinet 1:56
Louis XIII, King of France 1:92
    and ballet 3:97
Louis XIV, King of France 1:*92* 92ff, 95;
    10:*15*
    and Académie Royale de Musique 10:18
    attitude to Italian opera 10:18
    and ballet 3:97
    and Charles II, King of England 4:25
    day in the life of 1:96
    love of dance 10:15, *17*
    and Lully 10:16, 18
    musicians of 4:20
    as *Le Roi Soleil* 3:97
Louis XV, King of France 1:*96*, 97-8
    and Vivaldi's 'Spring' concerto 4:41

Louis XVI, King of France 1:98; 5:102-103
    execution of 2:85, 86, 106, *106-107*
    and French Revolution 5:102ff
    and revized monarchy 5:103
Louis XVII, King of France, death of (1793)
    5:109
Louis XVIII, King of France 9:24
Louis Napoleon 9:*24*
Louis Philippe, King of France 6:78, 83-4
Louise of Saxe-Coburg Gotha, Princess 8:71
Louvre's Grand Gallery in Ruins, The
    (Robert) 1:86
Lübeck, Germany
    J. S. Bach in 5:25
    conditions for post of organist 4:60
Ludwig II, King of Bavaria, and Wagner
    2:31; 10:37
Lueger, Karl, and Christian Socialists 7:106
'Lullistes' 10:18
LULLY, Jean-Baptiste *see Index of*
    Composers
Lupu, Radu 8:100, *100*
lustig 9:109
lute 9:64, 109
    Dowland and 4:72
    number of pieces for by Telemann 4:10
Luther, Martin 5:22, 38
    J. S. Bach and 5:27
Luther Bible 5:27
Lutherans
    and the *cantata* 5:23-4
    in Eisenach 5:22-3, 24
Lyell, Charles 4:108-109
    Principles of Geology 4:*109*
Lyceum Theatre, Baltimore 3:21
Lyceum, Warsaw, Chopin at 6:63
Lyons, France, Rameau in 4:11
lyre 9:74, 109
lyric 9:109

M

Ma/Maj 9:109
McAllister, Ward 3:108-109
McCracken, James 10:76
MACDOWELL, Edward see *Index of*
    Composers
McDowell, Ephraim 2:105
MACHAUT, Guillaume de *see Index of*
    Composers
McIntyre, Donald 10:77
MacNeil, Cornell 10:77
Macpherson, James, 'translation of Ossian'
    9:18
'mad scene', in *Lucia di Lammermoor*
    (Donizetti) 10:39, *39*
Madame Elizabeth of France 5:102
    execution of 5:109
Madrigal(s) 9:109
    for intermedi 10:8
maestoso 9:109
maestro 9:109
maestro di capella, Russian 10:41
maestro di capella da camera, Mantua 4:38
maestro de concerti, Ospedale della Pietà
    4:37
maestro di violine, Ospedale della Pietà
    4:35
maestro in Italia, Count Morzin's 4:39
Maeterlinck, Maurice, use of work by

Debussy 10:49
magazines, early 19th-century 8:106
    see also musical journals
maggiore 9:109
'magnetism therapy' 1:29
Magnificat 9:109
Mahler, Alma
    demands changes in Mahler 7:95
    and *Kindertotenlieder* 7:94
Mahler, Anna Justine 7:94
Mahler, Bernhard 7:88
Mahler, Emma 7:91
MAHLER, Gustav *see Index of Composers*
Mahler, Justine 7:91
    marriage 7:93
Mahler, Maria Anna, death of 7:93, *93*
    death of 7:94
Mahler, Otto
    suicide of 7:91
    works by 7:91
Maintenon, Madame de 1:96
Mainwaring, Captain John, on Handel's
    Messiah 4:76
Majorca, Chopin in 6:67
Makart, Hans 7:106-107
    style of painting 7:*106-107*
male voice 10:76-7
    see also individual singers; types of voice
Malfatti, Anna 2:*18*
Malfatti, Giovanni, and Beethoven 2:*18*
Malfatti, Therese, and Beethoven 2:19
malguena 9:109
Malibran, and Beethoven's Symphony
    No. 5 2:71
Malibran, Madame 8:*43*
Malibran, Marie 10:39
    Mendelssohn and 8:*43*
    Manchester, Duke of, and Handel 4:61
mandola 9:109
mandolin(e) 9:64, 109
    Mahler's use of 7:97
Manelli, Francesco, and first public opera
    house 10:9
Mangot, Marie-Louise 4:11
manifesto against the 'New Music', Joachim
    and 7:29
Mann, Thomas 7:99
    Death in Venice 7:78, *99*
mannequin dolls 6:43
Mannheim, Germany 1:*28-9*
    influence on 18th-century European
        music of Court musicians 4:20
    Mozart in 1:11, 26
    orchestra 1:19
    orchestra development in 4:20
Mannheim, Court of
    commission for J. C. Bach 5:19
    music at 2:*34*, 35
'Mannheim School' 2:*34*
Mantua, Italy, Vivaldi in 4:38
Mantua, Duke of, court musicians to 10:9, *9*
manual 9:109
maracas 9:110
Marat 9:*15*
'Marble House', Newport 3:106, *106-107*
marcato 9:110
Marchand, Louis, and the harpsichord 5:10
MARCH (or MARCHE, MARCIA)
    see also Index of Music
Marek, on Beethoven 2:59
Maria Amalia, Queen of Spain 1:83

Maria Hermenegild, Princess 5:*93*
    Haydn and 5:93, *93*
Mary of Modena, Queen of England 1:23
Maria Theresa, Empress of Austria 1:*35*;
    2:93-5, *95*; 5:60, *61*
    and Freemasonry 1:34, *35*
    letter to Marie-Antoinette 5:104
    and the Mozarts 1:18, 22
    operatic performances 9:9
Mariage de Figaro, Le 1:13
Marie-Antoinette 1:19, *97*, *98*; 5:103-105
    execution of 2:86; 5:*107*, 109
    and French Revolution 5:102ff
    on Mirabeau 5:104
Marie-Thérèse, Princess 5:109
marimba 9:110
marine chronometer 1:*113*
    invention of 1:110
marionette theatre, Eszterhaza 5:90
Markova, Alicia 3:45
Marlborough, Duke of 3:109
Marriner, Neville 4:91; 5:53, *53*
Marseilles, the plague in 5:76
Martelé 2:62; 9:110
Martini, Giovanni Battista 1:*22*
    J. C. Bach and 5:19
    Mozart and 1:23; 5:19
Martinsschule, Lüneberg, Germany,
    J. S. Bach at 5:24-5
Marx, Karl 9:*25*
    Communist Manifesto 9:26
Mary II, Queen of England 4:14, *29*, 30
Maryinsky Theatre, St Petersburg 3:102
    The Sleeping Beauty at 3:*43*
Marxsen, Eduard 7:*40*
    Brahms and 7:7, 38
marziale 9:110
masque 9:110; 10:44-5, *45*
mass production 9:*33*
    of textiles 6:43
MASSENET, Jules *see Index of Composers*
MASS (or MESSA, MESSE, MISSA) 9:110
    see also Index of Music
'Master Archive', National Library of Vienna
    1:67
Master of the King's Music, French (Lully)
    10:18
Mathias, William, and occasional music
    4:87
Mattheson, Johann
    on J. S. Bach 5:10
    and German national opera 10:28
    and Handel 4:60
mattinata 9:110
Maupertuis, Pierre Louis de 5:60
Maximilian Emanuel II, Elector of Bavaria,
    and Albinoni 4:8
Maximilian Joseph II, Elector of Bavaria,
    Mozart and 1:*18*
Mayer, Ferdinand, and Tchaikovsky 3:17-18
'Mayerling Affair' 7:104-105, *105*
Mayrhofer, Johann, Schubert's use of
    works by 6:17, 19
Mazarin, Cardinal Jules
    and introduction of opera to France
        10:14, 15
    and Torelli 10:16
MAZURKA 9:110
    see also Index of Music
Mazzini, Guiseppe 9:*25*

measure 9:110
Meck, Karl von 3:*32*
    country estate 3:*34*
    financial disaster 3:13
    on *The Sleeping Beauty* 3:42
    and Tchaikovsky 3:10, 29, 31ff
        on end of friendship with 3:31, 32,
            34-5
mediant 9:110
Medici, intermedi for 10:*8*
Medici, Catherine de', Queen of France,
    and ballet 3:96-7; 10:15
Medici, Duke Ferdinand de', impact of
    wedding music for 4:87
Medici, Marie de', Queen of France, opera
    for 10:9
medicine in the 19th century 2:102ff
    diagnosis 2:103, 104
    tools of the trade 2:103-104
medieval revival in art 2:83-4
Meiningen, director of the court orchestra
    (Von Bülow) 7:29
melisma 9:110
mellophone 9:110
melodies, structure of, in Clarinet
    Concerto K. 622 (Mozart) 1:58
melodrama 9:110
    in French opera 10:31
melodramma 9:110
melody/melodie 9:110
    overthrow of 9:32
    pamphlet war over 10:26
    R. Strauss's description of 10:50
membrophone 9:110
Mendelssohn, Abraham 8:33
    and defence of Prussia 8:34
    and education of his children 8:81-2
    effect of lifestyle on children's
        development 8:83
    flees to Berlin 8:33-4
Mendelssohn, Cécile
    meets Fanny Mendelssohn 8:39
    on Mendelssohn's death 8:39
Mendelssohn, Fanny 8:*37*
    birth of 8:33
    and composing 8:33

Composer	Volume
Albinoni	4
Bach	5
Beethoven	2
Berlioz	8
Brahms	7
Chopin	6
Corelli	4
Handel	4
Haydn	5
Liszt	6
Mahler	7
Mendelssohn	8
Mozart	1
Pachelbel	4
Purcell	4
Rameau	4
Schubert	6
Schumann	8
Tchaikovsky	3
Telemann	4
Vivaldi	4

death of 8:*37*, 39
education expectations 8:81-2
marriage 8:37
relationship with brother, Felix 8:37-8
MENDELSSOHN, Felix *see Index of Composers*
Mendelssohn, Lea
and Fanny's fingers 8:33
on Mendelssohn 8:34
Mendelssohn, Moses 8:33, *34*
Mendelssohn, Paul 8:33
Mendelssohn, Rebekka 8:33
Mengelberg, Willem, and Mahler 7:90
Mengs, Anton Raffael 1:87
MENOTTI, Gian Carlo *see Index of Composers*
mental health, progress with 2:*109*, 110
Mercure de France, on Vivaldi's 'Spring' Concerto 4:41
Méry, Joseph 1:89
Mesmer, Dr Franz Anton 1:*29*, 34
and Mozart 1:29
messa di voce 10:85
MESSIAEN, Olivier *see Index of Composers*
Metastasio, Anton 10:*11*
and absurdity of opera plots 10:13
and comic interludes 10:13, 19
as librettist 10:*11*, 12
Metastasio, Pietro 5:*89*; 10:12
and Haydn 5:89, *89*
mesto 9:110
mèta 9:110
metamorphosis 9:110
Methodism, rise of in 18th century 4:100
Metropolitan Opera, New York 10:52, 58
Mahler at 7:94-5
Mettenchor, Lüneberg, J. S. Bach and 5:8-9
Metternich, Prince 2:99; 6:51, *56*; 7:68-9
and Freemasonry 1:34
use of censorship 6:56
'system' 9:24
metre 9:110
common 9:103
metronome 9:110
Meyer, de 6:104
rivalry with Herz 6:108
MEYERBEER, Giacomo *see Index of Composers*
Mezzetino (in Commedia dell'Arte) 10:*21*
mezzo/mezza 9:110
Mi/Min 9:109
Michaeliskirche, Ohrdruf, organist at 5:8
Michaelisschule, Lüneberg, J. S. Bach at 5:8, *9*
Michelangelo, Wolf's use of works by 6:29
Mickiewicz, Adam 6:67
Lithuanian Ballades 6:*73*
microscope, development of 4:105, *105*
microtone 9:110
middle C 9:110
'Mighty Five', or 'Mighty Handful' 3:8; 10:42-3
Milan, Italy
J. C. Bach in 5:19
burning of 2:*100*
Mozart in 1:23
opera house 10:69, *69*
Rameau in 4:11
Mildenburg, Anna von, Mahler and 7:91
Mildmay, Audrey 10:48
Military Hospital, Scutari, Crimea 2:*108*

Military School, Warsaw, Poland, N. Chopin at 6:62
Miller 7:64
Milyukov, Antonina 3:10, 29
and Tchaikovsky 3:*10*, 11, 33
divorce from 3:34-5
letter from 3:33, 34
minim 9:110
minstrel 9:110
Ministry of Justice, Tchaikovsky and 3:26
Minuet/Menuet/Menuett 9:110
use in concertos 3:72
use in suites 5:49
Mirabeau, Honoré-Gabriel 5:104, 105
mirliton 9:110
miserere 9:110
misura 9:110
Modena, Mary of, Queen of England 4:28
Modern era, influence of J. S. Bach on 5:16
see also Contemporary era
modes 9:110-11
modes de Paris (early 19th century) 6:43
modo 9:111
modulation 9:111
Molière 1:*94, 95*, 96
and ballet-plays 3:97-8
influence of Commedia dell'Arte 10:20
and Lully 10:18
Les Fâcheux 3:97
Molinari, Bernardo 1:71
Mölk, Count von 1:*44*
moll 9:111
Moltke, Helmut von 7:73, 74
molto 9:111
Moniusko 9:111
Monmouth, Duke of 4:30
monochord 9:111
monodrama 9:111
monody 5:33; 9:111
monophony 9:111
monothematic 9:111
Montague, Duke of, on Handel 4:84
Montaigne, and Venice 4:53-4
Monte Carlo, Monaco
and tourism 7:84
casino 7:*82*
postcard from 7:*82*
Montespan, Madame de 1:96
MONTEVERDI, Claudio *see Index of Composers*
Montez, Lola 6:*93*
Liszt and 6:91, *93*
Montpensier, Mlle de 10:16
Monville, Monsieur de, garden at Retz 1:86
'Moors, the' 7:28
Mops (Masonic order) 1:*35*
morality plays, German 10:27
morbido 9:111
morceau 9:111
morendo 9:111
Moreschi, Alessandro 10:13
Morning Chronicle letter on Great Exhibition catering 8:29
Morton, William 2:106
Moscheles, Ignaz 6:61, *108*
and Bach revival 8:55
on Chopin's music 6:67, 71
on Liszt 6:89
and Mendelssohn in London 8:37

on *A Midsummer Night's Dream* 8:36
as touring virtuoso 6:105
Moscow, Russia 8:*13*
Berlioz in 8:13
influence on Russian music 10:43
opera house 10:67
Saint-Saëns in 3:29
the Schumanns in 8:92
Tchaikovsky in 3:8-9, 27
conducts concerts in 3:13
flat in 3:9
Moscow Conservatoire 3:8
Tchaikovsky at 3:31
Moscow Exhibition of Industrial Arts 3:49
mosso 9:111
MOTET 9:111
see also Index of Music
motif/motiv 9:111
motion 9:111
moto 9:111
motto 9:111
movements 9:111
movimento 9:111
Mozart, Anna Maria 1:8, *11, 28*
death of 1:11
effect on Mozart 1:28, 41
the genius of children 1:18
travels with Mozart 1:11
Mozart, Franz Xaver 1:*13*
Mozart, Karl Thomas 1:*13*
Beethoven and 8:48
Mozart, Leopold 1:8, *28*
'business' 1:9
and Colloredo 1:9
dismissed by 1:26
death of 1:13, 44
finances 1:18, 19
and Freemasonry 1:35-6
on French musical taste 1:*60*
and genius of his children 1:18
gifts to 1:21
made *Kapellmeister* 1:11
made *Konzertmeister* 1:9
and Mozart's education 1:9
future aims for 1:18
and Mozart's operas 1:22
and novel sound-effects 3:55
post in Salzburg 1:8, *9*
Versuch gründlichen Violinschule 1:*9*
view of contemporaries 1:52
visits Vienna 1:10
visits Mozart in 1:43
Mozart, Maria Anna (Nannerl) 1:8, *9, 19, 28*
exhibition tours 1:9
illnesses 1:20, 21, *31*
'cures' in Baden 1:14, 30, *31*
on Mozart's finances 1:30
musical talent of 1:18
Mozart, Maria Thekla ('the Bäsle') 1:40, *40*
Mozart, Theresa, death of 1:64
MOZART, Wolfgang Amadeus *see Index of Composers*
'Mozart of the Champs Elysées' (Offenbach) 10:53-4
Mravinsky, Evgeni 3:64, *65*
muffle 9:111
Mühlhausen
J. S. Bach in 5:9, 25, 39
conflict with employers 5:25-6
first compositions in 5:25
resigns post in 5:26

Muller, Wenzel, and development of
    Singspiel 10:30
Müller, Wilhelm 6:*19*
    Schubert's use of works by 6:17, *19*,
        20-21
Munich, Germany
    Albinoni in 4:8
    carnival 1:11
    Mendelssohn in 8:48
    Mozart in 1:11, 18, *18*, 26
        concert tours (1762) 1:18
        opera for carnival in 1:*10*
        preview tour to 1:18
        success in 1:29
Municipal Council, Berlin 8:34
Murat, Marshal 2:50
'Murlship', badge of 7:28
Museo Pio-Clemento, Rome 1:84
Musette 9:111
    use in suites 5:49
MUSIC
    abstract (absolute) 9:100
        difference from programme music
            8:17
    Baroque *see* Baroque music
    Beethoven and 18th-century 2:34
    in 'Biedermeier' households 6:*52*, 53
    Byzantine 9:101
    Classical *see* Classical music
    'colour' in 6:23
    concrete 9:103
    conductors and 'interpretation' 7:50
    contrapuntal 1:52
    dispute over 'Modern' 7:24, 25
    effect of publishing boom on 4:7
    electronic 9:105
    'empty/full' 6:23
    engraved 4:37, *38*
    experimentation with 9:32
    as form of personal expression 9:20, 22
    imitation of natural sounds in 8:17
    importance of performing in Venice 4:49
    influence of gypsy on 7:35
    influence of Purcell on English 4:13
    instrumental in late Renaissance 4:20
    the Italian influence 4:47
    keeping rhythm in 7:50
    major form in late 17th-century German
        5:23
    Mozart's
        emotional range of 1:72
        humorous 1:51
        Masonic 1:57
        polyphonic 1:52
    naming pieces 3:62
    Nationalist, as form of protest 9:22
    occasional 4:87
        'outdoor' element in 4:87
    popular 9:33
    popularity of pieces 4:15
        of Baroque in 20th century 4:15
        most popular in 18th century 4:15
    printed from type 4:37, *38*
    prohibition on Telemann's secular 4:10
    qualities of Baroque 4:15
    re-appraisal of 9:32
    reconstructed Baroque 4:15
    Romantic, emphasis in 9:20
    Romanticism in, ideals 9:20
    17th-century descriptive 8:17
    'serial' 9:32

    transferring to film soundtracks 7:101
    20th-century
        experiments with 9:32
        influences on 9:32-3
        influence of African and Asian 9:33
        inspiration in 9:33
        new styles in 9:32
        understanding 1:52, 58-9, 67, 76-7;
            2:44-5, 54, 62, 72-3; 3:44, 55, 62, 72;
            4:20, 47, 80, 87; 5:33, 42, 49, 99;
            6:23, 28-9, 74-5, 100; 7:34-5, 40-41,
            50-51, 101; 8:17, 55, 63, 101
    use of the imagination in 9:20
    utility 9:117
    at Versailles 1:96-7
    written by early members of the Bach
        family 5:14
    written for films 7:101
    see also CHURCH MUSIC; folk/gypsy
        music; 'New Music'; programme
        music
'music become stone' (Baroque
    architecture) 9:8
music-copying, J. S. Bach and 5:8
music critic/criticism 8:101
    Berlioz and 8:*11*, *12*, 13
    role in early 19th century 8:101
'Music Director, The' 8:89
music director, Laibach 6:11
MUSIC DRAMA 9:111; 10:85
    native German 10:27
    popularity in England 10:45
    see also Index of Music
    see also Wagner
music festival, al fresco 4:*15*
Music Festival, Düsseldorf, Germany,
    Mendelssohn conducts 8:38
Music Hall, New York 3:16, 17, *19*
    Tchaikovsky at opening of 3:17, 18
music journals
    contents 8:101
    first 8:101
    spread of 8:101
    see also individual names
music publishers/publishing
    C. P. E. Bach and 5:18
    Brahms publishes Schumann
        manuscript 7:21
    Brahms's 7:13
    Chopin and 6:63
    Corelli and 4:12
    and Handel's works 4:*62*
    Haydn's 5:90
    Schubert and 6:12, 13, 20
        of *Complete Works* 6:20
        of 'Trout' Quintet 6:24
        and 'Verbunkos' mode 7:35
    Vivaldi's 4:37-8
'musica prattica', J. S. Bach and 5:27
'musica theorica', J. S. Bach and 5:27
musical box 9:111
musical comedy 9:111
    see also opéra comique
musical societies, and Beethoven 2:31
Musicalisches Lexicon, frontispiece 5:*27*
musicians, change in social status 6:91
musicology 9:111
Musikverein, and Schubert's Symphony in
    C major 6:13
Musikvereinsaal, Vienna 7:*53*
Musil, Robert 7:109

musique concrète see music, concrete
Musset, Alfred de 6:67, *79*, *80*
    and George Sand 6:80
MUSSORGSKY, Modest Petrovich *see Index
    of Composers*
muta 9:111
mute 9:111
Müthel, Johann Gottfried 5:12
Mysliveček 1:40
Mystery Plays 10:8, *8*
myth-makers, Beethoven's 2:34
mythology/folklore, during Romantic era
    9:18

N

nachtanz 9:111
Nachtmusik 9:111
Naples, Italy
    J. C. Bach in 5:19
    development of comic opera in 10:19,
        20-21
    Garibaldi enters 9:*24-5*
    Mendelssohn in 8:47-8
    as operatic centre 10:20, 28
    the plague in 5:*76-7*
    spread of opera to 10:9
Naples, King of, and Haydn 5:91
Napoleon I, Emperor of France (Napoleon
    Bonaparte) 2:*35*, *85*; 5:*109*; 10:*31*
    Beethoven symphony to 2:13
    at Borodino 2:89
    burial in Les Invalides, (1840) 6:*83*
    and control of French opera 10:*31*, 32
    coronation of 2:*88*
    defeat at Waterloo (1815) 9:23

VOLUME 1
Mozart

VOLUME 2
Beethoven

VOLUME 3
Tchaikovsky

VOLUME 4
**Albinoni, Corelli, Handel,
Pachelbel, Purcell, Rameau,
Telemann, Vivaldi**

VOLUME 5
Bach, Haydn

VOLUME 6
Chopin, Liszt, Schubert

VOLUME 7
Brahms, Mahler

VOLUME 8
Berlioz, Mendelssohn, Schumann

VOLUME 9
A Guide to Classical Music

VOLUME 10
A Beginner's Guide to the Opera

and the 'empire' look 6:43, 44, 47
on HMS *Bellerophon* 2:90
invasion plans 2:88
legacy to Paris 6:83
and Marie Louise of Austria 2:98, *98*
rise of 2:86ff; 5:109
and *The Sorrows of Young Werther*
    (Goethe) 8:105
and Spontini's *Fernando Cortez* 10:32
unconditional abdication 2:90
and Venice 4:56
Napoleon III, Emperor of France (Louis
    Napoleon Bonaparte) 6:84
    and Prussia 7:74
Napoleonic Age 2:85ff
Napoleonic Wars, effect on Russian music
    10:42
Nassau-Weilburg, Princess of, and Mozart
    1:20
National Assembly, Frankfurt, Germany
    7:69, *70*
National Theatre, 'German' opera for 1:41
Nationaltheater, Munich, Germany 10:65
Nationalist era 9:21ff
    landmarks of 9:28
    nationalism
    origins of 9:22
    parallels of Romantic era 9:21
        differences in attitude 9:21-2
    as revolutionary movement 9:22
    rise of 9:35
    use of folk heritage 9:22, 23
nature, Romantic preoccupation with
    9:19, 20
naturale 9:111
Naval, Franz 7:92
'Nazarenes' 2:84; 6:54
    leaders of 2:83
Neapolitan Opera School, Scarlatti and
    4:69
neck 9:111
Neefe, Christian Gottlob, and Beethoven
    2:9
Nelson, Horatio 2:87
    death of 2:86-7
neo 9:111
Neo-Classicism 1:82ff
    elements of 1:90
Neri, Sir Isaac 4:103, 107-108
Netherlands, emigration to 7:59
Neue Zeitschrift für Musik 8:101
    Schumann and 8:87
    editorial on Brahms 7:18
Neumeister, Pastor, and the *cantata* form
    5:23
New Braunfels 7:65
'New Music'
    Brahms's battle against 7:23ff
    headquarters of rivals 7:23
    Manifesto against 7:29
        signatories 7:29
    schools of thought on 7:25
    Schumann and 8:101
New York, Mahler in 7:94-5
New York Morning Journal, Tchaikovsky
    article in 3:21
New York Symphony Society 3:17
Newly Crowned Hope (Masonic lodge)
    1:34, 37
    cantata for 1:38
    songs for 1:36

Newport, Rhode Island
    casino 3:*107*
    decline of 3:110
    hostesses 3:107
    houses 3:106-107, *106-107*
    the Season in 3:106
Newton, Isaac, and 'de-coding' the Bible
    9:8
Niagara Falls 3:*20*
    Tchaikovsky at 3:19, 21
Nice, France 7:*84*
    Berlioz in 8:10
    and tourism 7:84
Nielsen, Carl, style of piano playing 2:38
niente 9:111
Nietzsche, Friedrich
    influence of Wagner on 10:36
    on Brahms's music 7:11
Nightingale, Florence 2:107-108, *108*
    Notes on Hospitals 2:108
Nikolaikirche, Berlin, Kantor at 5:17
Nikolaikirche, Leipzig 5:*25*
Nile, Battle of the (1798) 2:87
ninth 9:111
No 45 Alser Gasse, Vienna 2:27
'noble savages' 1:118
NOCTURNE (or NOTTURNO) 9:111
    see also Index of Music
Nohant, France 6:66
    Chopin at 6:67
nonet 9:111
Norman, Jessye 10:78, *79*
North, Roger, on *The Indian Queen* 4:16
notation 9:111
note(s) 9:111
    changed 9:102
    half- 9:107
    leading 9:109
    non-harmonic 9:111
    passing 9:113
    sixteenth- 9:115
see also grace-note
'note row', Berg's use of 10:50
Notre Dame, Paris, music development at
    5:42
Nourrit, Adolphe 10:*32-3*
novels (Russian), late 19th-century 3:86ff
NOVERRE, Jean-Georges *see Index of
    Composers*
numbers, added 10:85
Nuremburg, Germany, Pachelbel in 4:9
nut 9:111
Nymphenburg palace, Munich, Germany
    1:*18*

O

obbligato 9:112
oboe 9:46, 112
octave(s) 9:112
    broken, in Piano Concerto No. 22
        (Mozart) 1:79
OCTET 2:72; 9:112
    see also Index of Music
ODE 9:112
    see also Index of Music
Oberwerk 5:40
Odescalchi collection (statues) 1:84
OFFENBACH, Jacques *see Index of
    Composers*

Ohe, Adele aus der 3:21
    and Tchaikovsky's Piano Concerto No. 1
        3:19
Ohrdruf, J. S. Bach in 5:24
'Old Arpeggio' (Thalberg) 6:108
Old Vic, London, 'people's opera' at 10:47
Olkhovsky, Viktor 3:26
Olmütz, Germany Mahler in 7:88
O'Morphy, Louise 1:*110-11*
Omai 1:*118*
Ondes Martinot 3:55
open form 9:112
OPERA 9:112
    the *Abbati* and 10:11
    ballad- 10:29
    ballet in 10:80
    in Baroque period 4:7; 5:38
    birth of 10:8ff
    breakdown of barriers in 10:34
    challenge to tragedy 10:18
    chamber 9:102
    circus-like atmosphere 4:68, *68-9*
    classification of 'comique' 10:34
    comic interludes 10:14, *14*
        Metastasio and 10:13
    competition to 10:10
    complexity of directing 7:50
    decline of comedy in 10:40
    development in Romantic era 9:20
    earliest surviving 10:9
    early 3:98
        money spent on 10:11-12
    early translations 10:28
    effect of French Revolution (1789) on
        10:31ff
    essential ingredients 10:9
    first 'Grand Style' *see* opera seria
    first great 10:9
    first with recitative 10:9
    formalizing/standardizing 10:13
    funding 18th-century 10:12
    in Germany 5:38
    Gluck's reform of 10:*25*, 26
    'Golden Age' 10:8, 22, 38ff
    grand 9:107
    importance of score 10:13
    inspiration for heroic 4:*72*
    in London 4:63-4, 68ff
    national influences on 10:8
    'natural' language for 10:46
    for opening of Royal Academy of Music
        4:71
    origins of 4:47
    parodies of 10:53
    for the people *see* Singspiel
    plots for 10:12
        subservient to spectacle 10:13
    popular taste and 10:11
    post-World War II experimentation
        10:52
    stylized 10:8
    verismo 10:40, 49
    see also Index of Music
Opéra, Paris
    Aladdin at 10:32
    Berlioz and 8:9
        rejection of work by 8:12
    closure of 10:31
    and establishment of Grand Opera 10:33
    foundation of 3:98
    Napoleon and 10:32

opened 'for the people' 10:31
patronage of 10:31
revolutionary works at 10:31
royalties 8:12
Russian opera at 10:43
special effects at 10:32-3
see also Palais Garnier
opera bouffe 9:112
opera buffa 10:18, 19ff, 53
birthplace of 10:20-21
characteristics 10:20-21
culmination of 10:22
Donizetti and 10:40
effect on French audiences 10:25
elements of Neapolitan 10:20
influence abroad 10:22
influence of Goldoni on 10:21-2
influence on opéra comique 10:23
Mozart and 1:70
parallel to 10:22
performance of first 10:20
rise of 10:14
Rousseau and 10:24-5
stock characters 10:21
style 10:19
see also INTERMEZZI
opéra comique 9:112
audience reaction to 10:33
birth of 10:22, *23*, 23-4
elements of 10:24, 53
greatest master of 10:26
mature 10:26
most important 10:33-4
parallel to 10:22
romanticism in 10:34
Rousseau's influence on 10:24
Opéra-Comique, Paris
foundation of 10:32
production of *Carmen* 10:34
types of work at 10:32, 33, 34
opera houses
in Baroque era 9:9
and the 'classics' 10:52
description of early 10:10
Eszterhaza 5:90
great 10:57-70
opening of first public 10:9
use of orchestra in 6:23
Vienna 7:*92*
curtain of 7:*94*
Opera of the Nobility 4:64, 73
musical director 4:*71*, 73
'opera-oratorio' 10:43, 50
opera seria 1:41; 9:112; 10:12-13
conventions 10:13
German response to 10:28-9
intermezzi in 10:14, *14*
Metastasio and 10:*11*
period of dominance 10:19
rival to 10:23
operating theatre, St Thomas's Hospital,
London 2:*106*
OPERETTA 9:112; 10:*26* 53ff
parody in 10:53
problems with texts 10:54
see also Index of Music
opus 9:112
opus numbers 1:67; 3:62
ORATORIO 4:80; 9:112
see also Index of Music
orchesis 4:20

ORCHESTRAL WORKS *see Index of Music*
orchestra 9:112
Beethoven's enlargement of 2:35
chamber 9:102
of the Chapel Royal 5:42
of Count Morzin 5:89
disbandment of 5:89-90
at court of Detmold 7:10
demand for in Vienna 10:30
development of during Baroque era
9:8-9
development of symphony 2:35
18th-century 2:35
early practice of directing 7:50
effect of musicians on sound of 6:23
Handel's combinations in 4:20
how it began 4:20
influence of Mannheim composer-
musicians on 4:20
Liszt's use of 6:96, 98
of the Lyceum Theatre, Baltimore 3:21
Mahler's use of 7:97
light and shade 7:97
in Mozart's day 1:72
novel sound-effects in 3:55
organization at Mannheim 2:35
placing of in Festival Theatre, Bayreuth
10:37
predominance in Classical/Romantic
music 6:23
Prince Esterhazy's 4:39
disbandment of 5:91
Haydn's first symphonies for 5:99
role of principal soloist 7:50
role in 'Romantic' concertos 6:98
of St Mark's, Venice 4:*33*, 35
standard of the Metropolitan Opera's
7:94-5
symphony 9:39
see also individual orchestras
orchestration 6:23; 9:112
changes in 6:23
Chopin and 6:23
18th-century 6:23
19th-century 6:23
Order of the Golden Spur, conferred on
Mozart 1:23
Ordres 5:49
ORFF, Carl *see Index of Composers*
organ 9:69, 112
historical role of 5:*40-41*
mechanical 3:55
parts of a Baroque 5:40
potential for Baroque music 4:7
working bellows for 5:*40*
Wurlitzer 3:55
organ building 5:39-40
J. S. Bach and 5:8
organ grinder 8:*106*
organ maker and keeper of the king's
instruments *see* Purcell, Henry
organ mass 9:112
ORGAN MUSIC *see Index of Music*
organistrum 9:112
orgel/orgue 9:112
*Origin and Foundation of Inequality
among Men* (Rousseau) 1:115
Orlowski, Chopin and 6:67
ornament 9:112
orrery 4:*102*
Osborne, Chopin and 6:65

Osborne, Isle of Wight 8:73, *74-5*
Ospedale della Pietà, Venice 4:35-7
figilie di coro 4:35-6
ossia 9:112
Ossian 9:*19*
fraud of 9:18
ostinato 9:112
Ottoboni, Cardinal Pietro
and Corelli 4:12
and Vivaldi 4:38
'outsiders' 8:63
ouvertures 5:46
overblow 9:112
overtones 1:52; 9:112
OVERTURE 9:112; 10:74-5
to comic operas 8:63
concert 8:63
dramatic 8:63
origin of work 8:63
as self-contained work 8;60
structure of French and Italian 8:63
to tragédies-lyriques 10:18
see also Index of Music
Overbeck, Friedrich 2:84
Franz Pforr 2:*82-3*
Oxford, England
Handel in 4:64
invitation to Pachelbel 4:9

P

p 9:112
Pabst 7:64
PACHELBEL, Johann *see Index of
Composers*
PACINI, Giovanni *see Index of Composers*
painting
abstract 9:32
during Biedermeier period in Austria
6:*53*, 53-4
Palais Garnier, Paris, France 10:68
see also Opéra, Paris
Palazzo Chigi, Siena, concert at 4:39
PALESTRINA, Giovanni Pierluigi da *see
Index of Composers*

Composer	Volume
Albinoni	4
Bach	5
Beethoven	2
Berlioz	8
Brahms	7
Chopin	6
Corelli	4
Handel	4
Haydn	5
Liszt	6
Mahler	7
Mendelssohn	8
Mozart	1
Pachelbel	4
Purcell	4
Rameau	4
Schubert	6
Schumann	8
Tchaikovsky	3
Telemann	4
Vivaldi	4

Pálffy, Count, and the Mozarts 1:19
palindrome 9:112
Pamphili, Cardinal
    and Corelli 4:12
    and Roman musical life 4:12
Pan-Germanism 9:27
pan-pipes 3:55; 9:86, 112
Pan-Slavism 9:27
Panharmonicon 3:55
Panini, Giovanni Paolo 1:85-6
Pantalon (in Commedia dell'Arte) 10:20
pantomime 9:112
pantonality 9:112
Pape, Jean-Henri, and piano development
    6:74
Paris, France 1:27, 60-61; 6:64-5, 82-3
    annual fairs in 10:23-4
    ballet in 3:99
    beginnings of opera in 10:15
    Berlioz in 8:11
        studying medicine 8:9
    cafés 5:68
    Casanova in 1:105-106
    Chopin in 6:64, 65, 82-3
        début 6:65
        lodgings in 6:65, 65
        musical associates 6:65
    in Chopin's time 6:78ff
    coffee introduced to 5:68
    Der Fledermaus in 10:54
    division over Lully/Rameau 10:18
    douceur de vivre 9:12
    during the Enlightenment 9:12
    early 19th-century fashions 6:43
    entertainments in 6:80, 81
    introduction of Russian opera 10:43
    Liszt in 6:89
    literary/artistic circle in 6:65, 78ff,
        78-9
    markets 6:82-3
    Mendelssohn in 6:78; 8:48, 48
    Mozart in 1:11, 19-20, 27, 27 60-61
        disillusioned with society in 1:41
    opera houses see individual names
    'ordinary' people in 6:82-3, 83
    Prussian troops in 7:73
    Rameau in 4:11; 10:18
        works produced in 4:11
    revolution in 9:24-5
        revolutionary theatres 10:32
    riots in 6:84, 84, 90
    salons 10:10
    Shakespeare performances in 8:10
    siege of (1871) 7:74
    transport in 6:83
    20th-century operatic experiments
        10:50-51
Paris Conservatoire
    Berlioz at 8:9
        performance of Symphonie
            Fantastique at 8:14
    director of 8:36
    Liszt at 6:89
    and modern violin technique 2:62
    rejects Mendelssohn symphony 8:48
garlando 9:112; 10:85
'parliament', French 5:104-105
part 9:112
partials 9:112-13
Partita 5:49; 9:113
passage-work 9:113

PASSION 9:113
    See also Index of Music
Pasta, Giuditta 10:39, 40
    role written for 10:39
Pasteur, Louis 2:106, 108-109
PASTICHE (or PASTICCIO) 9:113
    see also Index of Music
pastoral 9:113
patrons
    Beethoven's 2.20, 25ff
        attitude to 2:25
    effect on Baroque music 9:9
    Wagner's 2:25
patter song 9:113; 10:85
Paumgartner, Sylvester, and Schubert's
    'Trout' Quintet 6:24
pausa 9:113
pause 9:113
Pavan(e) 9:113
    use in suites 5:49
pavillion 9:113
Paxton, Joseph
    bursary 8:29
    conservatories 8:23
    and Crystal Palace 8:23
Paxton's Palace see Crystal Palace
'pea-soupers' (London fogs) 8:42
Peabody Institute, Baltimore 3:21
Péan, Dr 2:107
Pears, Peter 10:47, 47
pedal 9:113
pedal-board 9:113
pedal-piano 9:113
Pedrolino 10:20
Pellégrin, Abbé, and Rameau 4:11
pendulum clock, development of 4:105
penillion 9:113
pentatonic 9:113
'people's opera' 10:47
Pepusch, J. C. and Gay's The Beggar's
    Opera 10:29
Pepys, Samuel, 4:27
    diary of 4.29
    and London 4:29-30
        on the Plague in 5:80-81
    on Nell Gwyne 4:27
    and tea drinking 4:68
percussion
    Mahler's use of 7:97
        in Symphony No. 6 7:92
perfect 9:113
PERGOLESI, Giovanni Battista see Index of
    Composers
PERI, Jacopo see Index of Composers
perpetuum mobile 9:113
Perrault, Charles 3:42
Perrin, Pierre
    and Académie Royale 10:18
    collaboration with Cambert 10:18
Perrot, Jules 3:101, 102
Pertl, Anna Maria see Mozart, Anna Maria
pesant 9:113
Pesne, Antoine 5:58
Peter the Great, Tsar of Russia 3:82
    and Russian Westernization 3:82,
        82
Petipa, Marius 3:38, 38, 102
    and The Nutcracker 3:45
    and The Sleeping Beauty 3:42, 44
    and Swan Lake 3:38
pezzo 9:113

Pforr, Franz 2:84
    by Overbeck 2:82-3
Philadelphia, Tchaikovsky in 3:21
philharmonic 9:113
Philharmonic Society
    founder of 8:37
    and Mendelssohn 8:43
Philharmonic Society, Budapest, Hungary
    7:40
Philip V, King of Spain
    and Farinelli 10:13
    and musical entertainment 10:55
Philipp von Hessen-Darmstadt, Prince 4:38
philosophy, 18th-century 4:106-107
phrase 9:113
phrase-mark 9:113
physics, 20th-century progress in 9:30
piacere 9:113
piacevole 9:113
piagendo 9:113
pianino 9:113
pianissimo 9:113
pianists, 19th-century demand for 6:104
    virtuosos 6:104ff
        contests between 6:108
piano 9:113
    adequacy for Beethoven 2:45
    'American System' 7:41
    C. P. E. Bach and 2:35
    Beethoven's 2:14, 45
    in Brahm's time 7:40-41
    Broadwood 6:75
    Chopin's 6:75
    in Chopin's time 6:74-5
        playing techniques in 6:71
    development of 2:34-5
    'escapement' on 6:74
    grand 7:40; 9:65
    improvements to 6:74
    invention of 4:47
    manufacturing 7:40
    method of sound reproduction 6:74
    'new testament' of 2:44-5
    as part of social life 6:104
    prepared 9:114
    range of 6:74
    'square' 7:40
    Steinway 7:40, 62, 64, 64
    string length in 7:40, 41
    Tchaikovsky's preference in 3:21
    tone in Mozart's day 1:72
    type played by Liszt 2:62
    upright' 7:41, 9:66
    see also pedal-piano; player piano
piano contests/duels 1:12, 30
    Beethoven's 2:10
PIANO WORKS
    see also CONCERTOS; SONATAS, etc.
    see also Index of Music
Piazzo S. Marco, Venice, Italy 4:54
Piazzetta, Venice, Italy 4:52-3, 54
'Picander' 5:27
Piccini 1:11
    and Gluck 1:28
Piccioli, Luigi, and Tchaikovsky 3:8
piccolo 9:45
Pichler, Caroline, on Freemasonry 1:34
picnics, 19th-century 8:108
Pietists 5:22-3, 23
    and the cantata 5:23-4
Pilnitz Declaration (1791) 5:107

Pinel, Dr 2:*109*, 110
Pinto, George, and Bach's work 8:55
pipe 9:113
Piranesi, Giovanni Battista 1:85, *85*, 86
Pisarer, Vasily, Tchaikovsky and 3:27
piston 9:113
pitch 9:113
piu 9:113
Place Vendôme, Paris, France 6:*69*
plagiarism, the *abbati* and 10:11
plague 5:76ff
    burial of the dead 5:82-3
    causes of 5:84
    'cures' for 5:78
    scapegoats for 5:79, *79*
plague doctor 5:*79*
plainchant/song 1:52; 9:113
player piano 9:68, 113
Playfair, Lyon, and classifying The Great
    Exhibition 8:24, 26
plays
    music in 4:87
    Purcell and 4:14
pleasure gardens
    in Baroque era 9:9
    in London 4:97, 98, *98*, 99
plectrum 9:113
pleureurs 10:34
Pleyel, Camille
    Chopin and 6:67
    Liszt and 6:91
    salon of 6:81
    see also Salle Pleyel
Pleyel, Ignaz
    Joseph and Beethoven's Violin Concerto
        2:60
    as rival attraction to Haydn 5:92
plots, in 18th-century opera 10:12-13
pochette 9:78
poco 9:113
Poetua, Princess 1:*117*
Poland:
    Chopin leaves 6:64
    'national' composer 9:22
    revolution in 9:*23*, 24
    at time of Chopin's birth 6:61
Polish National Opera 6:63
police
    Austrian, and closure of theatres 6:56
    reliance on secret 9:24
    Russian political 9:24, 25
    secret 3:86
polka 9:113
Pollini, Bernhard, Mahler and 7:91-2
Polo, Marco 4:*50*
POLONAISE 9:113
polymodal 9:113
polyphony/polyphonic 9:113
    change from 4:47
    development in Church music 5:42
polyrythmic 9:113
polytonal 9:113
Polzelli, Luigia, and Haydn 5:89, 90-91
Pompadour, Madame de 1:*96*-7, 98;
    4:*106*
    and Mozart 1:98
Pompeii, Italy 1:*82*, 82-4, 88-90
    excavation of 1:83-4
    Mozart visits 1:89
    tourism to 7:76
    wall paintings 1:*83*, 90

Ponte, Lorenzo da 1:13; 10:*74*
    collaboration with Mozart 1:13, 14
    and *The Marriage of Figaro* 1:43; 10:22
Pope, Alexander 4:62
    on Newton 4:108
'Popish Plot' 4:*24*, 25
Porpora, Nicolo 4:*71*
    and Haydn 5:89
    and Opera of the Nobility 4:73
Porta, Giovanni
    and Royal Academy of Music 4:71
    Numitore 4:71
portamento 9:113
Pörtschach, Austria, Brahms in 7:30,
    30, 31
Portugal
    French invasion of 2:89
    revolution in 9:24
Porubsky, Bertha
    Brahms and 7:11
        song written for 7:11
position 9:113
post horn 9:114
postcards 7:78, *82*
postlude 9:114
Potoka, Delfina, Chopin and 6:65
potpourri 9:114
Potsdam, harpsichordist 8:55
POULENC, Francis *see Index of Composers*
Power, Hiram, 'Greek Slave' 8:27
praeludium 9:114
Praetorius, *Theatrum instrumentorum*
    5:*40*
'Pragmatic Sanction' 2:93, 94
Prague, Czechoslovakia 1:*44*
    Mahler in 7:88
    Mozart in 1:13, 30, 43-4, *44*
    revolutionary movement in 9:25
    the Schumanns in 8:93
pre-Raphaelites, Austrian version of 6:54
Predigerkirche, Erfurt, Germany organist
    at 4:9
PRELUDE
    to suites 5:49
    see also Index of Music
Prentz, Kaspar, and Pachelbel 4:8
Prés, Josquin de 5:42
Pressburg, (Bratislava) Mozart in 1:19
pressez 9:114
prestissimo 9:14
presto 9:114
Previn, André 6:*102*, 102-103
Previtali 1:71
Prey, Hermann 10:7
prima/primo 9:114
prima donna 4:68; 10:80
    most famous 19th-century 10:39
primo uomo 4:68
'Prince of Enlightenment' 5:25
principal 9:114
Prix de Rome
    Berlioz wins 8:10
        works submitted 8:10
producer, rise of the 10:52
professional concerts organization, and
    Haydn 5:92
programme, for Berlioz's Symphonie
    Fantastique 8:14, 16, 17
programme music 6:100; 8:17; 9:114
    Berlioz's Symphonie Fantastique as
        8:13-14

first Romantic 8:17
new dimensions to 7:101
requirements of 8:17
20th-century attitude to 8:17
Vivaldi's 4:39
progression 9:114
PROKOFIEV, Serge *see Index of Composers*
prologue, to tragédies-lyriques 10:18
Prussia
    Abraham Mendelssohn and defence of
        8:34
    and Congress of Vienna 7:68
    early 19th-century travel in 8:102
    education in 19th-century 8:79
    emigration from 7:62
    and French Revolution 5:106-107
    and Seven Years War (1756-63) 5:63
    state functions in 8:109
    and unification of Germany 9:25
    wars
        victory over France 7:73, *73*
        with Austria-Hungary 5:60-62; 7:104
Prussia, Crown Prince of 2:82
Prussia, King of
    death of 8:39
    and Mendelssohn 8:49
psalm 9:114
psalter 9:114
psaltery 9:76, 114
public entertainments, in Baroque era 9:9
publishing, during the Enlightenment 9:12
    18th-century libretti 10:12
    see also music publishing/publishers
PUCCINI, Giacomo *see Index of Composers*
Puchberg, Michael 1:14
    dedications from Mozart 1:45
    letters from Mozart 1:30, 36, 64

VOLUME 1
Mozart

VOLUME 2
Beethoven

VOLUME 3
Tchaikovsky

VOLUME 4
**Albinoni, Corelli, Handel,
Pachelbel, Purcell, Rameau,
Telemann, Vivaldi**

VOLUME 5
Bach, Haydn

VOLUME 6
Chopin, Liszt, Schubert

VOLUME 7
Brahms, Mahler

VOLUME 8
Berlioz, Mendelssohn, Schumann

VOLUME 9
A Guide to Classical Music

VOLUME 10
A Beginner's Guide to the Opera

Pulcinella (in Commedia dell'Arte) 10:20
Punch, on the Crystal Palace 8:23
Purcell, Edward 4:14
PURCELL, Henry *see Index of Composers*
Pushkin, Alexander 3:87-8, *88*
    Tchaikovsky and 3:13
    use of work by Mussorgsky 10:42
    Boris Godunov 3:87
    The Bronze Horseman 3:87
    The Captain's Daughter 3:87
    Eugene Onegin 3:87-8, *88*
    The Queen of Spades 3:87

Q

Quadrille 9:114
quadruplet 9:114
Quantz, Johann Joachim 5:*58*
    and Frederick the Great, King of Prussia,
      5:*58*
quarter-note 9:114
QUARTET 9:114
    see also Index of Music
quasi 9:114
'Queen of the Night' 2:22, *22*
Querelle des Bouffons 10:*24*, 25-6
Quinault 97
    and J. C. Bach's *Amadis de Gaule* 5:19
QUINTET(S) 9:114
    origin of name *59*
    see also Index of Music
quodlibet 9:114

R

Raaff, Anton, and *Idomeneo* 1:41
Racine, Jean 1:96
rackett 9:94
radicals, Russian 3:*83*, 83-4
radio 9:34
Radziwill Palace, Warsaw, Poland, Chopin
    concert in 6:63, *63*
Raff, Joachim 6:*98*
    and Liszt's orchestration 6:*98*
ragtime 9:114
railways
    development in Germany 7:70, 72
    effect on 19th-century tourism 7:77-8
    royal travel on 8:74, *74*
    through the Alps 7:84
Raimund, Ferdinand 6:55, *55*
    Das Mädchen aus der Feenwelt 6:55
rallentando 9:114
Ramdohr, Freiherr von 2:81
RAMEAU, Jean-Phillipe *see Index of*
    Composers
'Ramistes' 10:18
Ranelagh Gardens, London 4:99
'raree-show' 8:23
rasch 9:114
rattle 9:114
RAVEL, Maurice *see Index of Composers*
Razumovsky, Count, 2:*28*. 69
    and Beethoven 2:*12*, 28, *28*, 69
Razumovsky Palace, Vienna 2:*12-13*
realization 9:114
rebec 9:78
Récamier, Madame, and the 'empire' style
    6:*42*, 44

recapitulation 9:114
Recio, Marie 8:*13*
    and Berlioz 8:12
    death of 8:13
recitative 9:114; 10:9, 75
    convention of 10:13
    first works with 10:9
recorder 9:92, 114
recruiting song, Hungarian 7:35
Red Cross Convention 2:108
'red priest' *see* Vivaldi, Antonio
'Red Shirts' 9:*24-5*, 26
Redlich, Josef, on Austrian rulers 7:104-105
Redon, Odilon, *Evocation of Butterflies*
    3:*60*
Redoutensaal
    dances for carnival in the 1:51
    Haydn conducts concert in 5:93
reel 9:114
Reformation, German 5:22; 9:8
refrain 9:114
register 9:114
REICHA, Antoine *see Index of Composers*
Reichardt, Johanne Friedrich 6:*16*
    Schubert and 6:*16*, 18
Reichter, Anton, on Beethoven's piano
    playing 2:45
Reign of Terror (during French
    Revolution) 2:77, 85-6; 5:108-109
Reincken, Adam, 5:*9*
    J. S. Bach and 5:9
Reisinger, Wenzel, and *Swan Lake* 3:39
Reiss, Joanna *see* Beethoven Joanna van
relative 9:114
Rellstab, Ludwig, and Beethoven's Sonata
    in C sharp minor op, 27 No. 2 2:*44*, 46
Reményi, Eduard 7:*41*
    Brahms and 7:27, 30, *35*
      concert tour with 7:8
      ends association with 7:9
      meeting with Liszt 7:9
Renaissance, court entertainments in
    3:96-7
Renaissance music, use of counterpoint in
    5:33
Reno, Morris, and Tchaikovsky 3:17
Reno's, New York 3:18
repeat 9:114
répétiteur 9:114
reprise 9:114
requiem 9:114
'rescue' drama 10:26, 31
    developed in Germany 10:35
resolution 9:114
Resolution (ship) 1:*114*, 114-15
rest 9:114
retrograde 9:114
Reuter, *Kapellmeister* von, and Haydn
    5:88, *88*
rhapsody 9:114
Rheisberg 5:57-8, *58*
Rheinland, Schumann 8:*88-9*
rhythm 9:114
    experiments with 9:32
Rialto bridge, Venice 4:*52*
ricercar 9:114
Ricci, Ruggiero 8:51, *51*
Ricciarelli, Katia 10:79
Richter, Jean Paul 8:*89*
    popularity of novels 8:105
    Schumann and 8:87

Richter, Johanna, Mahler and 7:88
Richter, Karl 5:45, *45*
Richter, Franz Xaver 2:*34*
Ridotto, The, Venice 1:*103*
Ries, Ferdinand 2:*20*
    and Beethoven 2:20, *20*
Ries, Franz 2:*60*
    and Beethoven 2:59
riff 9:114
Rimondi, Margherita 4:8
RIMSKY-KORSAKOV, Nicholay
    Andreyevich *see Index of Composers*
'Ring a ring a roses' (song) 5:78, *84*
Ringstrasse, Vienna 7:106, *106*
Ringstrasse era 7:106-107
Rinuccini, Ottavio, and the Camerata 10:9
    and *Dafne* 10:9
ripieno 3:72, 5:29
Risorgimento 9:25
ritardando 9:114
ritenuto 9:114
ritmo 9:114
ritornello 9:114
Roberts, Hubert 1:86
    The Louvre's Grand Gallery in Ruins
      1:*86*
robes en chemises 6:*43*
Robespierre, Maximilien 2:85; 5:*108*, 109
Rochlitz, Friedrich, and musical journals
    8:101
Rockefeller, John D. 3:105
Rococo 1:82, 87, *89*; 9:13
Rode 2:62
RODERIGO, Joaquin *see Index of*
    Composers
Rodeztvensky Boulevard, Moscow 3:31
Roger, Etienne, commissions for Vivaldi
    4:37-8
'Roi Soleil' (Louis XIV, King of France)
    3:97, *97*
roll 9:114
Roller, Alfred, Secession Exhibition Poster
    7:*108*
Rolli, Paoli, and Royal Academy of Music
    4:71
'Rom' 7:34
ROMANCE 9:114
    see also Index of Music
'Romantic', degeneration of term 9:15
Romantic art, German 2:76ff
Romantic composers 1:52
Romantic era 9:15ff
    basic ideal of 9:20
    Britain's contribution to 9:19-20
    concerto in 3:72
      best loved 8:98
    development of symphonic poem in
      6:100
    and 'devilish talent' 6:*104*, 107
    effect on ballet 3:101-102
    effect on status of virtuoso 6:105
    expression of religious fervour in 5:42
    fashions 6:47-9
    influence of J. S. Bach in 5:16
    inspiration for songs in 6:17
    interest in past during 8:55
    landmarks 9:16-17
    literary initiative 9:18
    parallels the Nationalist era 9:21
    popular idealism in 10:40
    programme music in 8:17

and Schumann's music 8:93
  the symphony in 2:72
    best loved 8:94
Romantic harmony 1:52
Romantic movement
  founders of 6:17
  German, most important composers
    10:35
  great literary figures in 6:80
  impetus to 8:60-61
  in Paris 6:65
  Italian 10:38-40
  'pictorial' inspiration for 8:61
  predominance of orchestra in 6:23
  preoccupations of 10:38-9
  Schumann and 8:87
  20th-century reaction to 10:50-52
  revolt against rigidity of form 6:98
Romantic music/emphasis in 9:20
  influence of J. S. Bach on 5:39
  quintessence of 3:66
Romantics/Romanticism
  applying the term 9:20
  beliefs 9:15
  decline of 9:20
  and democratic revolution 9:15
  'high priest' of 9:19
  literary hero 9:19
  and music 9:20
  natural development of 9:21
  as revolutionary movement 9:22
  ultimate expression 9:20
Rome, Italy 3:50-51; 8:46
  appeal of Republican 9:13
  Berlioz in, emotional crisis in 8:10
  Carstens in 2:78
  Corelli in 4:12
  excavations in 1:84
  Goethe in 8:48
  Handel in 4:61
    employment in 4:61
  interest in ancient 1:82ff
  Koch in 2:78
  Liszt in 6:93
  Mendelssohn in 8:46
    apartment in 8:46-7
  Mozart in 1:23
  'Nazerenes' in 2:84
  revival of interest in classical 9:13
  spread of opera to 10:9
  Sunday academies 4:12
  Tchaikovsky in 3:50-51, 51
  Vivaldi in 4:38
rondeau 9:114
rondo 9:114
Roosevelt, Theodore 3:108, 110
root 9:114
Rosebery, Lord, on Balmoral, Scotland 8:74
Rosen, Charles, on Mozart's Clarinet
    Concerto K.622 1:57
Rosen, Gisbert, Schumann and 8:89
Rosicrucians 1:34
  Casanova and 1:106-107
Rossi, Giacomo, and Handel's *Rinaldo* 4:69
ROSSINI, Gioacchino *see Index of
    Composers*
Rothschilds, and Chopin 6:65
Rotunda, Ranelagh Gardens 1:20-21
Roubiliac, monument to Handel 4:66
Rouen, France, Chopin in 6:67
round 9:114

ROUSSEAU, Jean-Jacques *see Index of
    Composers*
Royal Academy of Music, London 4:63, 71
  caricature of singers 4:64
  decline of 4:64-5, 71-2
  first musical director 4:63
  Handel and 4:70-71
  raising funds for 4:70
royal band of violins, Purcell and 4:14
Royal Budapest Opera
  Mahler and 7:89
    leaves 7:90
Royal Opera House, London 10:60
  commission for Weber 10:37
  opening of 10:47
  original 10:46
  permanent national company at 10:48
Royal Society, English 4:104, 106-107
royalties, for libretti 10:12
rubarto 9:114
Rubinstein, Anton 6:109
  'Historical Recitals' 6:109
  and Liszt 6:109
  Tchaikovsky and 3:8
    and Symphony No. 1 3:8
RUBINSTEIN, Nikolay *see Index of
    Composers*
Rückert, Friedrich
  Mahler's use of works by 7:93
  Schubert and 6:17
Rückspositiv 5:40
Rudin 3:89
Rudolph, Archduke 2:29, 50
  and Beethoven 2:20
  contract with 2:28-9, 29, 30
Rudolph, Crown Prince of Austria 7:105
  suicide 7:104
Rudolph II, Emperor of Austria, crown of
    2:95
Rugby School, England 8:81, 81
Runge, Phillip Otto 2:79-80
  Fall of the Fatherland 2:82
  The Huelsenbeck Children 2:78, 80
  'Times of Day' 2:77, 79
    Morning 2:77, 79-80
Ruspoli, Marquis Francesco, and Handel
    4:61
Russia
  abolition of serfdom 9:22
  beginnings of ballet in 3:100
  Berlioz in 8:13
  Casanova in 1:107, 108
  and Commedia dell'Arte 10:20
  and Congress of Vienna 7:68
  crisis after Crimean War 3:76
  curbs on revolutionaries 9:24
  education in 3:80-81
  emigration to 7:59
  exhibits for The Great Exhibition 8:24
  exploitation of Pan-Slavism 9:27
  farming system 3:77
  first railways 7:77
  folk gypsy music in 7:34
  foreign artists in 10:41, 42
  and Germany 9:35
  and Holy Alliance 9:24
  inspiration for composers 9:22
  internal problem 3:76-7
  invasion of Turkey 3:56
  landlords 3:77ff
  Nationalism 9:22

  number of opera houses 10:43
  opera in
    arrival of 10:41
    formative period of 10:42
    national style in 10:41, 42
    style of early 10:42
  the plague in 5:76
  political police 9:24, 25
  post-revolutionary music 10:43
  public health in 3:80-81
  reforms in the 1860s 3:81-2
  and revolt in Poland 6:65; 9:23
  revolution in 9:24, 25
    effects on music 10:43
  revolutionary activities in 3:83, 83-4
  the Schumanns in 8:92
  struggle for national identity 9:22
  Ukrainian costumes 9:26
  under the Tsars 3:76ff
  and World War I 9:35
  see also literature; serfs/serfdom; Soviet
    Union
Russian Music Society 3:8
  founder of 3:49
Rutherford 9:30
R.V. 9:114
Ryabov, Stepan, and *Swan Lake* 3:39

S

Sabata, Victor de 1:71
sackbut 9:90
Sackville, Charles, Lord Buckhurst 4:27
Sacre Rappresentazione 10:8
SACRED MUSIC *see Index of Music*
Sadler's Wells, London 4:99; 10:47
  'people's operas' at 10:47
  productions of British operas at 10:47
St Johannis, Zittau, organ in 5:41
St Lawrence, Altdorf, organist at 4:8
St Léon, Arthur 3:101
St Mark's, Venice, Italy 4:33, 50
  and development of Church music 5:42
St Nicholas's Church, Hamburg, Germany,
  organ of 5:39-40

Composer	Volume
Albinoni	4
Bach	5
Beethoven	2
Berlioz	8
Brahms	7
Chopin	6
Corelli	4
Handel	4
Haydn	5
Liszt	6
Mahler	7
Mendelssohn	8
Mozart	1
Pachelbel	4
Purcell	4
Rameau	4
Schubert	6
Schumann	8
Tchaikovsky	3
Telemann	4
Vivaldi	4

St Paul's Cathedral, London 4:29
St Petersburg, Russia
    ballet in 3:100, 102
    ballet-master 3:38, *38*
    building of 3:82
    as music centre 10:43
    Tchaikovsky in 3:7-8, *12-13*
        conducts concerts in 3:13
    workers' living conditions in 3:*81*
St Petersburg Conservatoire 3:8
    Tchaikovsky at 3:27
St Philip and St James, Hainburg, organist
        at 5:88
St Rock 5:77
St Sebald, Nuremburg, Germany, organist
        at 4:9
St Stephen's Cathedral, Vienna, Austria
        5:*88-9*
    Haydn at 5:88, *88*
    organist 4:8-9
St Thomas's, Leipzig, Germany, Kantor at
        5:27
Saint-Cricq, Caroline de, Liszt and 6:90
'Saint-Foix, Georges de, on Mozart's
        Symphony No. 40 1:64, 68
SAINT-SAËNS, Camile *see Index of
        Composers*
Ste Croix-de-la Bretonnerie, organist 4:11
S. Angelo, Venice, Italy, Vivaldi and 4:40
S. Maria della Rotonda, Rome, Italy, Corelli
        anniversaries in 4:12
San Martino, Venice, Italy, 4:*34-5*
San Moisé theatre, Venice, Italy, Vivaldi
        and 4:38
S. Petronio, Bologna, Italy, music in 4:12
S. Samuele theatre, Venice, Italy 4:*53*
Sala, and Vivaldi 4:36
SALIERI, Antonio *see Index of Composers*
Sallaba, Dr 2:103
Sallé, Marie 3:*99*; 4:*73*
    and *Alcina* 4:73, *73*
Salle Pleyel, Paris 6:65
    Chopin concerts at 6:68
        last 6:84
Salomon, Johann and Haydn 5:91, 99
salon(s), musical 10:8-9, 10
    Beethoven and 2:46
    Parisian 6:81-2; 9:12
    of Prince de Conti 1:*20-21*
    Viennese 1:42-3; 2;46
'salon' music 1:*60*, 61
'salon pieces', Chopin 6:70
Salten, Felix, on Klimt 7:109
Salzburg, Germany
    18th-century 1:*8*
    Mozart in 1:29
        dismissal from 1:29
        gala of *Cosi fan tutte* 7:94
        resignation from 1:11
        return to 1:22
        salary in 1:29
        working conditions 1:11
Sand, George 6:67, 78; 7:*26*
    Chopin and 6:*66*, 66-7
    first successes 6:80
    Cosima 6:67
    Indiana 6:80
    Leila 6:80
Sand, Maurice 6:67, *67*
    and Chopin 6:68
Sanquirico, set for *Psamos* 3:99

Sans Souci, Potsdam, Germany 5:62, *62, 63*
Sarabande 2:54; 9:115
    use in suites 5:46, 49
Sarastro 1:*38*
    model for 1:35
Sassnitz, (Baltic island), Brahms in 7:32
·SATIE, Eric *see Index of Composers*
Savoy Operas 9:27; 10:56
saw, musical 9:111
Saxe-Weissenfels, Handel at court of 4:60
saxhorns 9:115
Saxony, Elector of 5:*26*
saxophone 9:70, 115
Sayn-Wittgenstein, Princess Carolyne 6:*94*
    Liszt and 6:92-3
    *The Interior Causes of the External
        Weaknesses of the Church in 1870*
        6:93
scale 9:115
    diatonic 9:104
    gapped 9:107
    major 9:109
    major/minor, basis of 1:52
    whole-tone 1:52; 9:118
SCARLATTI, Alessandro *see Index of
        Composers*
SCARLATTI, Domenico *see Index of
        Composers*
scena 9:115
Schachtner, Johann Andreas
    and Mozart 1:9
    on Mozart and concertos 1:72
Schaumberg-Lippe, Counts of, and
        J. C. F. Bach 5:18
Scheffer, Ary, portrait of Chopin 6:*70*
Scheibe, Johann Adolf, attack on J. S. Bach's
        composition method 5:27
Schellmann, Dr 6:24
scherzando 9:115
SCHERZO 9:115
    see also Index of Music
Schikaneder, Emanuel
    and *The Magic Flute* 1:31, 37
    and Mozart 1:15
Schiller, Friedrich 2:77
    on education of women 8:82
    and image of society 2:77
    influence on 19th-century German
        drama 8:107-108
    Liszt's use of works by 6:100
    Schubert's use of works by 6:17
    *Letters on the Aesthetic Education of
        Mankind* 2:77
    Ode to Joy 2:77
Schimon, Ferdinand, portrait of Beethoven
        2:*13*
Schindler, Alma Maria 7:*93*
    Mahler and 7:93
    marriage to 7:93
    see also Mahler, Alma
Schindler, Anton
    appropriates Beethoven's documents
        2:21
    Biographie von Ludwig von Beethoven
        2:*20*, 21
Schinkel, Karl Friedrich 2:82-3
    Gothic Cathedral by a River 2:*80*, 82
    *The Hall of Stars of the Queen of the
        Night* 2:*81*
    View in the Prime of the Hellenic Epoch
        1:*89*

Schlegel, August, influence on
        Mendelssohn 8:61
Schlegel, Friedrich 2:79, 83
    Schubert's use of works by 6:17
schleppend 9:115
Schleswig–Holstein, war over 7:*71*, 73
Schlosinger, and *Gazette musicale de Paris*
        8:101
Schlozer, Dorothea, educational
        achievements 8:82
Schmelling School, St Petersburg, Russia
        3:7
Schmidt, J. C. Handel and 4:63
Schnieder, Friedrich 2:*52*
    and Beethoven's Piano Concerto No. 5
        2:50, *50*
Schneider, Max, and *Alt-Bachisches Archiv*
        5:14
schnell 9:115
Schnitger, Arp 5:39
Schnitzler, Arthur 7:78, 109
Schober, Franz von, Schubert's use of
        works by 6:11, 17
SCHOENBERG, Arnold *see Index of
        Composers*
Schoenberg, Harold, on Tchaikovsky's
        music 3:23
Scholz, Bernhard, and Manifesto against
        'New Music' 7:29
Schönbrunn, Vienna, Austria 1:*18-19*
    Mozart at 1:18-19
Schönerer, Georg von, and German
        nationalists 7:106
School of Jurisprudence, St. Petersburg,
        Russia 3:7, *26*
    homosexual activity at 3:26
    Tchaikovsky at 3:7, 8, 26, *26*
schoolmistresses 8:83
schools, 19th-century village 8:*80-81*
Schopenhauer, Wagner and 7:26
schottische 9:115
Schouwburg Theatre, Amsterdam,
        Holland, centenary 4:40
Schrattenbach, Sigismund Christoph von,
        Prince Archbishop of Salzburg
        1:8, *8*, 9
    death of 1:25
Schubart, Christian Friedrich Daniel 6:*27*
    and *Die Forelle* 6:17, 24
Schubert, Ferdinand 6:9
Schubert, Franz Carl 6:9
SCHUBERT, Franz Peter *see Index of
        Composers*
Schubert, Franz Theodor 6:8
    and Schubert's career 6:10
Schubert, Ignaz 6:9
'Schubertiaden' 6:*10-11*, 12, *15*
    songs at 6:19-20, *20*
Schücking, Schubert's use of works by 6:18
Schultz, Johann, and Beethoven's Piano
        Concerto No. 5 2:50
Schumann, August, 8:88, *88*
Schumann, Clara, 7:*13, 17, 21, 27, 49*
    and Baden-Baden 7:82
    and Brahms
        on first meeting with 7:17
        and Julie Schumann 7:21
        misunderstandings with 7:21
        and his music 7:10
        and piano pieces 7:12, 46
        on relationship with 7:18

and Symphony No. 1 7:12, 48
   on his talent 7:9
and Brahm's mother 7:10
career conflicts with Schumann's 8:91-2
death of 7:14, 21
on difference between Liszt/Mozart
      7:28-9
effect of Schumann's illness on 7:10
forbidden to see her husband 8:93
and the 'futurists' 7:29
ideas on Schumann's music 8:94
letters
      to Brahms 7:18
      on Brahms joining her in London 7:20
      on Brahm's symphonies 7:47
      to Joachim 7:47
      on Liszt and Wagner 7:28
   on *Lohengrin* (Wagner) 7:29
and Liszt's piano playing 7:24
public enthusiasm for 8:92, 93, 94
reconciliation with father 8:92
rejection of Liszt's music 7:28-9
style of concerts 6:107-108
success in Russia 8:92
travel *see* individual countries, cities
      towns
Schumann, Elise, 7:*19*
Schumann, Emil, death of 7:21
Schumann, Emilie, suicide of 8:8
Schumann, Eugénie 7:*19*
Schumann, Felix 7:19, *19*
Schumann, Ferdinand 7:*19*
   death of 7:21
Schumann, Julie 7:19, *19, 20*
   death of 7:*20*, 21
Schumann, Ludwig 7:*19*
   illness 7:21
Schumann, Marie 7:*19*
SCHUMANN, Robert *see Index of*
      Composers
Schunke, Lugwig, information on
      Schumann 8:90
SCHÜTZ, Heinrich *see Index of Composers*
'Schwammerl' *see* Schubert, Franz Peter
Schwarz, Gustav, and Mahler's training
      7:88
Schwarzenberg, Prince 6:56
Schwartzenberg Palace, Haydn concerts at
      5:93
Schwind, Moritz von 2:84
   on Schubert 6:7-8, 9, 49
   Das Knaben Wunderhorn 6:*29*
   The Symphony 2:84, *84*
science
   birth of modern 4:102ff
   20th-century progress in 9:30, 32
'Sclerosenkavalier' 10:50
scoop 9:115
score 9:115
   full 9:106
   miniature 9:110
SCORING
   traditional 18th-century 6:23
   J. S. Bach:
      of Concerto No. 2 5:30
      of Concerto No. 3 5:32
      of Concerto No. 5 5:35
      of Suite No. 2 5:47
   Beethoven's:
      for Piano Concerto No. 4 2:51
      for Piano Concerto No. 5 2:51

Mozart:
   Clarinet Concerto K.622 1:57
   Flute and Harp Concerto in C major
      K.229 1:61
   Piano Concerto No, 21 in C K.467 1:74
   Piano Concerto No. 22 1:78-9
   Serenade in G major K.525 1:57
   Symphony No. 40 in G minor 'Tragic'
      1:66
   Symphony No. 41 in C Major 'Jupiter'
      1:69
scorrevole 9:115
Scotland 8:*45*
Mendelssohn travels in 8:37, 44-5
Scott, Sir Walter
   influence of novels on opera 10:38, 39
   Mendelssohn and 8:44
Scriabin, style of piano playing 2:38
Scribe, Eugene
   collaborations 10:33
   type of work 10:33
scuoli 4:51
Sebald, Amalie, and Beethoven 2:19
Secession/Secessionists 7:108-109
   members of 7:*108*
   1902 exhibition 7:109
second 9:115
Second Viennese School 1:52; 10:50
   first masterpiece of 10:50
Seddon, George 4:100
Seefried, Irmgard 10:79
segno 9:115
segue 9:115
Seidl, Anton, 'A Defence of Wagner' 3:21
semibreve 9:115
semiquaver 9:115
semitone 9:115
semplice 9:115
Senesino 4:*64*, 72, 73
   and Handel's *Guilio Cesare in Egitto*
      4:71
Senn, Johann, Schubert and 6:12
senza 9:115
septet 9:115
sequence 9:115
SERENADE 9:115
   development of 5:49
   see also Index of Music
serenata 9:115
serfs/serfdom (Russian) 3:77, 77
   abolition of 3:79, 79-81
   manifesto on 3:*79*, 80
Serialism 1:52; 9:115
series 9:115
'serious opera' *see* opera seria
serpent 9:89
Servandoni, Giovanni Niccolo, and
      Handel's 'Royal fireworks' 4:84-5
service 9:115
Seven Years War (1756-63) 2:95; 5:63
seventh 9:115
Sèvres porcelain 1:97
SEXTET 9:115
   see also Index of Music
sextuplets 9:115
Shakespeare, William
   influence of Commedia dell'Arte 10:20
   influence on Romantic movement 8:61;
      10:38
   inspiration of words of 6:17
   Lessing and 9:19

revival during Romantic era 9:19
'Shakespeare of the Dance' 3:100
'Shakespeare of Italian Opera' 10:*11*
Shalyapin, Feodor 10:*42*, 43
sharp 9:115
   double 9:104
shawms 9:91
Sheldonian Theatre, Oxford,
   England 4:64
Shelley, Percy and rebellion against society
      9:19
sherzando 9:115
Shilovsky, Vladimir, Tchaikovsky and 3:28
ships, propeller-driven 7:62
Shirley-Quirk, John 4:83, *83*
shoes 6:45
SIBELIUS, Jean *see Index of Composers*
Sicily, Italy, revolution in 9:24
Siebold, Agathe von
   Brahms and 7:11, 21
   Clara Schumann and 7:21
sight read 9:115
Silbermann, Gottfried 5:39
   organ by 5:*41*
Silesia
   charity concert for 8:37
   seizure of 5:60-62
Silote, Alexander
   and Tchaikovsky's Piano Concerto No. 1
      3:67
   and *The Sleeping Beauty* 3:42
simile 9:115
Simplon Pass 7:84
Simpson, James 2:105, 106
Simpson, Robert
   influence of Beethoven 2:39
   influence of Haydn 2:39

VOLUME 1
Mozart

VOLUME 2
Beethoven

VOLUME 3
Tchaikovsky

VOLUME 4
Albinoni, Corelli, Handel,
Pachelbel, Purcell, Rameau,
Telemann, Vivaldi

VOLUME 5
Bach, Haydn

VOLUME 6
Chopin, Liszt, Schubert

VOLUME 7
Brahms, Mahler

VOLUME 8
Berlioz, Mendelssohn, Schumann

VOLUME 9
A Guide to Classical Music

VOLUME 10
A Beginner's Guide to the Opera

Simrock,
    and Beethoven's Violin Concerto 2:60
    and Brahms 7:13
SINFONIA 8:63, 9:115
    see also Index of Music
sinfonia concertante 9:115
sinfonietta 9:115
Singakademie, Leipzig, Germany
    Director of 8:38
    performance of Bach's *St John Passion*
        8:55
singers
    demand for 10:12, 30
    at Russian court 10:41
    virtuosity of in Italian opera 4:68
    works for specific 10:39
singing, superior language for 10:26
singing schools, Albinoni's 4:8
singing technique, the *abatti* and 10:11
Singspiel 10:27ff, 53
    decline in Austria 10:30
    first work of 10:29
    influence on German music 10:30
    most popular character 10:*28*, 29-30
    Salieri's influence on 10:30
    supreme example of 10:27, 30
    tradition behind 10:29
    types of heroes 10:29
    in Vienna 10:29, 30
    'vulgarity' of 10:*28*, 29
sixth 9:115
sketch 9:115
sketchbooks, Beethoven's 2:37, 66
    Piano Concerto No. 5 in 2:51
    Symphony No. 5 in 2:*68*
SKRYABIN, Alexander *see Index of*
    Composers
slave trade 5:71-2
    ship for 5:*71*
'Slavophils' in Russia 3:82-3, 86-7
slentando 9:115
slide 9:115
slur 9:115
Smart, Sir George
    Mendelssohn and 8:37, 38
    and the Philharmonic Society 8:37
SMETANA, Bedřich *see Index of Composers*
Smith, John Christopher 4:*64*
Smith, Joseph 1:85
Smithson, Harriet 8:*10*
    and Berlioz 8:10, *10*, 14
        marriage to 8:11-12
    in Paris 8:10
    see also Berlioz, Harriet
soave 9:115
social satire, development of 10:21
Social Register 3:108
Socialism, rise of 9:35
'Socialist realism' 10:43
Societas Regia Scientiarum (Germany)
    4:106-107
Société des Concerts du Conservatoire,
    Paris 6:105
Society for the Improvement of the
    Labouring Classes (British) 8:75
Society for the Protection of German
    Emigrants in Texas (American) 7:65
soirées 10:10
    Chopin's 6:81
    early 19th-century 8:*105*
    Parisian 8:*49*

Solms-Braunfels, Prince Karl of 7:65
solo 9:115
soloists
    convention with arias 10:13
    development of music for 9:9
    distinction from orchestra 1:72
    and embelishments 10:13, 14
    and ensemble singing 10:13
    pre-eminence in opera seria 10:13, 14
Solomon, Maynard, on 'The Beloved
    Immortal' 2:19
Solti, Sir Georg 8:100, *100*
SONATA 9:115
    attitude to names of 2:34
    Baroque 1:58; 4:7
        development of during 9:9
    Classical music and 1:76-7
    development of 4:47
    in the 18th century 2:72
    elements of form 2:*73*
    given titles 9:20
    principles of form 9:20
    structure of 1:52
    title in 20th century 3:62
    trio 1:58
        use of counterpoint in 5:33
    variations on form of 2:72
    see also Index of Music
sonata da camera 1:58; 4:18
sonata da chiesa 1:58
    structure of 4:19
    Telemann and 4:18
sonatina 9:115
SONG 9:116
    for *intermedi* 10:8
    popular in German Church music 5:38
    spinning-room 8:104
    see also Index of Music
    see also LIEDER
song-cycle 9:116
Sonnenfels, Joseph von 1:43
Sonnleithner
    on Schubert 6:9, 12
        and *Erlkönig* 6:20
Sophia Dorothea, Queen of Prussia 5:*57*
Sophienkirche, Dresden, Germany
    organist at 5:12, 16
Sophie of Bavaria 2:100
sopranino 9:116
Sorau, Telemann in 4:10
sordun 9:94
sostenuto 9:116
sotto voce 9:116; 10:85
soubrette 10:85
South Seas, exploration of 1:113ff
souvenirs 7:78
Soviet Union, after World War I 9:35
Spain
    and Commedia dell'Arte 10:20
    French invasion of 2:89
    restoration of monarchy in 9:23-4
    revolution in (1820) 9:24
traditional version of operetta 10:55, *55*
Spangler, Michael, and Haydn 5:89
Spanish Inquisition 4:103
Spanish Succession, War of the 2:93
Spaun, Josef, von
    Schubert and 6:11
    songs of 6:18, 20
Spectator, The, criticism of Handel's
    Rinaldo 4:69

speech song 9:116
Spencer-Churchill, Lord Ivor 3:*104*
Spener, Philipp Jakob 5:22, 23
Spielmusik 5:32
Spieltenor 10:85
Spies, Hermine 7:*12*
    Brahms and 7:*12*
spinet 9:97, 116
spinto 10:85
spinning room 8:*104-105*
    importance of 8:102, 104
    denunciation of 8:104
    inspiration for Wagner 8:104
SPOHR, Louis *see Index of Composers*
Spontini, Chopin and 6:63
sprechgesang 10:85
Staatsoper, Vienna, Austria 10:62
Stabat Mater 9:116
staccato 9:116
Stadler, Albert, Schubert and 6:12
Stadler, Anton 1:*56*
    and basset clarinet 1:56
    character 1:56
    Mozart and 1:36
        pieces for 1:56
Stadttheater, Leipzig, Germany 7:*89*
Stael, Madame de, *Corinne en L'Italie*
    1:89
staff (stave) 9:116
stage effects: cost of 10:12
    17th-century 10:15-16, *16-17*
    19th-century 10:32-3
stage machinery 10:15-16, *17*
stage manager, outstanding 17th-century
    10:16
stage settings, for *intermedi* 10:8, *8*
Stamitz, Johann, and Mannheim
    composer-musicians 4:20
STANFORD, Sir Charles *see Index of*
    Composers
statues, demand for Greek/Roman 1:83, 84
Steiler, Joseph Carl, portrait of Beethoven
    2:*9*
Steiner, Max
    and film music 7:101
Steiner, Sigmund Anton 2:20
Steinway pianos *see* pianos, Steinway
Steinweg, Heinrich 7:62, *64*
    and piano manufacture 7:40
    see also pianos, Steinway
Stendhal, *Le Rouge et le Noir* 6:80
stethoscope, development of 2:104
Stewart, Frances 4:28
Steyr, Schubert at 6:24
Stifter, Adalbert, on family life 6:53
Stirling, Jane 6:68
    and Chopin 6:68, *68*
stock markets/speculation 5:72-3
Stockhausen, Julius
    and Brahm's songs 7:12
    on Mahler 7:97
stockings 6:44
Stoller, Herr von 6:24
Stoller, Josephine von, and Schubert's
    'Trout' Quintet 6:24
stop 9:116
    double 9:104
Stopes, Marie 9:*32*
Storace, Nancy 1:*45*
    farewell aria for 1:45
    sings Susanna 1:45

Storace, Stephen 1:45
storm and stress *see Sturm und Drang*
Story of My Life, (Casanova) 1:100
Stöttrup, A. 5:*16*
Stradivari, Antonio 2:62
Stradivari family at 4:47; 9:9
'straight' theatre 10:10
STRAUSS, Johann (the Younger) *see Index of Composers*
STRAUSS, Richard *see Index of Composers*
STRAVINSKY, Igor *see Index of Composers*
Streich, Rita 10:79
stretta/stretto 5:33; 10:85
string
    open 9:112
    sympathetic 9:116
string ensembles 1:58
student uprising, Viennese 6:57
study 9:116
Strungk, Nikolaus, and German national
        school 10:28
Sturm, Pastor 5:*16*
    C. P. E. Bach and 5:16
Sturm und Drang 2:35-6
    Haydn and 5:99
    movement 9:19
        most notable member 9:19
Stuttgart, Germany
    Chopin in 6:65
    French troops enter 4:9, *9*
    Pachelbel in 4:9
Stuyvesant Fish, Mrs 3:*108*, 110
style rocaille see Rococo
subdominant 9:116
submediant 9:116
subscribers, Mozart's 1:44
    Viennese 1:43
sugar, growing demand for in Europe 5:67
suicides, during Romantic era 9:19
SUITE 5:49; 9:116
    in Baroque period 4:7
    movements in 5:46
    other titles for 5:49
    see also Index of Music
    see also CONCERT SUITES
SULLIVAN, Sir Arthur *see Index of Composers*
Sun, studying eclipse of 4:*103*
supertonic 9:116
surgery, agony of in 19th century 2:104-106
Surrealist movement 9:32
Süssmayer, finishes Mozart's Requiem 1:15
Sutherland, Dame Joan 10:79
    and *bel canto* 10:40
Sweden, prohibition of tobacco in 5:68
swell 9:116
Swieten, Baron Gottfried von 1:43, *43*, 44, 45
    and Bach revival 8:55
    and Haydn's *Creation* 5:93
    and Haydn's *The Seasons* 5:93
Swift, Jonathan, and Handel's *Messiah* 4:77
Switzerland
    Liszt in 6:90
    insurrection in 9:25
    Mendelssohn in 8:48, *48*
        with family 8:35
    tourism in 7:78-9
    taking the waters 7:*83*
Sydney Opera House 10:70
SYMPHONIC POEM 6:100; 9:116

difference from programme music 6:100
    nationalist movements and 6:100
    see also Index of Music
SYMPHONY 9:116
    attitude to names of 2:34
    Beethoven's contribution to 2:42
    chamber 9:102
    choral 9:102
    contrast in 1:74
    first four-movement 1:65
    free-form *see* SYMPHONIC POEMS
    of nature 2:*76-7*, 79
    size of orchestra for 2:35
    structure of 2:72-3
    three-movement 1:65
    title in 20th century 3:62
    what is a? 2:72-3
    see also Index of Music
syncopation 9:116

T

tacet 9:116
Tafelmusik 9:116
Taglioni, Marie 3:*100*, 101; 6:81
Tahiti 1:*116*, 116-17
    war fleet 1:*115*
tailors, importance of 6:48-9
tambour 9:116
tambourine 9:56, 116
tam-tam, Mahler's use of 7:97
Taneyev, Sergei, Tchaikovsky and 3:67
tango 9:116
tanz 9:116
tapageurs 10:34
tarantella 9:116
Tarnovsky, Mufka, Tchaikovsky and 3:27
'tartanitis' 8:74
Tartini 2:62; 6:*104-105*
    at Russian court 10:42
    and violin virtuosity 4:47
    Devil's Sonata 6:*104*
Tauber, Richard 10:5
Tausig, Carl, and Liszt 6:109
Taust, Dorothea 4:60
Taylor, John, and J. S. Bach 5:12
Taylor family, Mendelssohn and 8:45, *45*
Tchaikovsky, Anatoly, and P. Tchaikovsky 3:11
Tchaikovsky, Modest 3:*28-9*
    and *Francesca da Rimini* 3:52
    and *The Queen of Spades* 3:13
    and *Swan Lake* 3:40
    on Tchaikovsky and Symphony No. 6 3:61
    and Tchaikovsky's papers 3:24
TCHAIKOVSKY, Pyotr Il'ych *see Index of Composers*
Tchaikovsky, Sacha 3:7, *16*
    death of 3:13
    see also Davidov family
tea, introduction of to Europe 5:67-8
Teatro alla Scala, Milan, Italy 10:69
Teatro S. Angelo, Venice, Italy, Vivaldi and 4:38
tedesco 9:116
TELEMANN, Georg Philipp *see Index of Composers*
telephone 9:34
telescope, development of 4:104, 105

television 9:34
temperament 9:116
tempo 9:116
tenor 9:116; 10:76
    heroic 9:107
ternary form 9:116
Terra Australis Incognita 1:110
tessatura 9:116; 10:85
tetrachord 9:116
Tetschen, altarpiece for 2:*79*, 81
textile shop 6:*44*
textiles, effects of imports on fashion 6:43
Textor, Maria Katharina 4:10
Thackeray W. M., *Vanity Fair* 7:80
Thalberg, Sigismond 4:61, 107-109, *109*
    and Liszt 6:104
        'showdown' with 6:108
    technique 6:108
Theater an der Wien, Vienna, Austria 2:*70*
    Beethoven concert in 2:66
    Clement and 2:60
    Die Fledermaus at 10:54
theatre
    early 19th-century 8:106-108
    in Restoration England 4:*26*, 26-7
    Viennese 6:54-5, *55*
    see also individual theatres
Théâtre des Bouffes-Parisiens 10:53
Théâtre Dramatique, Paris 6:81
Théâtre de la Foire 10:*23*, 24
    influence on opera 10:22
    laws against 10:24
Théâre Italien, Paris 10:32
Théâtre Lyrique, Paris
    decline of 10:34
    founding of 10:33
    and opéra comique 10:33-4
Theatre of Machines, Paris 10:16
Théâtre des Nouveautés, Berlioz and 8:10
Theatre Royal, London 4:26
    riot over French ballet 3:99
Theatro San Cassiano, Venice 10:9, 10
theme song 9:116
themes 2:54
theorbo 9:83
'Thermidoreans' 2:85

Composer	Volume
Albinoni	4
Bach	5
Beethoven	2
Berlioz	8
Brahms	7
Chopin	6
Corelli	4
Handel	4
Haydn	5
Liszt	6
Mahler	7
Mendelssohn	8
Mozart	1
Pachelbel	4
Purcell	4
Rameau	4
Schubert	6
Schumann	8
Tchaikovsky	3
Telemann	4
Vivaldi	4

Thibaut, Anton, Schumann and 8:89
third 9:116
Third Estate, French 5:*104-105*
'Third Section' police 9:22, 24
Thirty Years War (1618-48) 5:22, 38
Thomaskirche, Leipzig, Germany
    Kantor in 4:10
    Telemann work performed in 4:10
Thomasschule, Leipzig, Germany 5:*10*
    C. P. E. Bach at 5:17
    J. S. Bach and 5:*10, 25*
    Bach family and 5:15
Thorwaldson, Mendelssohn and 8:47
'Three Knocks' 1:36, 37
through-composed 9:116
thought, classical 9:13
Thun, Count Joseph 1:13, *43*
Thun, Wilhelmine, Countess, Mozart on
    1:43
Tiflis 3:*34-5*
timbre, of instruments 6:23
time 9:116
    compound 9:103
    duple- 9:105
    simple 9:115
    triple 9:117
time signature 9:116
Times, The, on the opening of the Great
    Exhibition 8:24
timpani 9:58, 116
TIOMKIN, Dimitri *see Index of Composers*
TIPPETT, Sir Michael *see Index of*
    Composers
tobacco 5:67
    tobacco evenings 5:*56-7*
toccata 8:63; 9:116
    see also FUGUE
Tolstoy, Leo 3:92-4, *94*
    and nationalism 9:22
    Anna Karenina 3:93, *93*, 94
    Boyhood and Youth 3:*92-3*
    Childhood 3:92
    The Contemporary 3:92
    The Cossacks 3:93
    The Death of Ivan Ilyich 3:93
    Hadji Murad 3:93
    The Power of Darkness 3:93
    Resurrection 3:93
    Sebastopol Sketches 3:93
    War and Peace 3:93, *93*, 94
Tomaschek, Johann, on touring 6:105
ton 9:116
tonal language, development of Baroque
    4:47
tonality 1:52
    experiments with 9:32
    'Second Viennese School' and 10:50
tone 1:52; 9:116
    combination 9:102
    covered 10:85
    fractional 9:106
    Gregorian 9:107
    quarter- 9:114
tone colour 9:116
tone poem 9:116
    Mendelssohn's overtures as 8:60
tonic 9:116
tonic sol-fa 9:116
Torelli, Giacomo, and stage effects 10:16
Tost, Johann, Haydn and 5:91
Tourte, François 2:62

Tovey, Sir Donald
    on Beethoven's Piano Concerto No. 5
    2:50
    on Mozart's last symphonies 1:64
tourism
    continental (1800-1900) 7:76ff
    organized 7:79-80
Towneley, Charles 9:*13*
trade/power, 17th and 18th centuries
    5:73-4
trade routes, 18th-century 5:70-71
tragédies-lyriques 10:18
    culmination of 10:18
    period of popularity 10:23, 26
    pamphlet war over 10:25-6
    Rousseau's influence on 10:24
    subject matter 10:18
'train bleu' 7:84
transcribe 9:116
translation
    of *The Beggar's Opera* 10:29
    of *The Devil to Pay* 10:29
    of *Die Zauberflöte* 10:30
    difficulty of 10:28
    Hiller and 10:29
    Von Brock and 10:29
transpose/transposing 9:116
    instrument 9:117
travel
    by coach 8:*44*
    in early 19th-century Germany 8:102
    first class 7:*79*, 80-82
    see also tourism
treble 9:117
Treitschke, Heinrich von
    on German emigrants 7:62
    History of German 7:62
tremolo 9:117
triangle 9:60
trill 9:117
TRIO 9:117
    see also Index of Music
trio sonatas *see* SONATAS: trio
triplet 9:117
tritone 9:116
tromba marina 9:79
trombone 9:52, 117
troppo 9:117
True Harmony (Masonic Lodge) 1:35
Trueman, President Harry S., on the atomic
    bomb 9:36
trumpets 9:51, 117
    altering pitch on 1:72
    early 9:90
    toy 3:55
    valve system 1:72
Truxa, Frau 7:14
'Tsar Liberator' *see* Alexander II, Tsar of
    Russia
tuba 9:54
Tuilleries, Paris, storming of 2:85;
    5:*106-107,* 107; 6:84
Tunbridge Wells, England Handel in 4:*66*
Turgenev, Ivan 3:89-90, *91*
    and 'Westerners' 3:86
    Father and Sons 3:89, 90
    A Month in the Country 3:89-90
    A Nest of Gentlefolk 3:89
    On the Eve 3:89
    Rudin 3:89
    A Sportsman's Notebook 3:89

turka (alla) 9:117
Turkey, Russian invasion of 3:*56*
Turner, J. M. W.
    style of painting 6:54
    Tintern Abbey 9:*18*
Tussaud, Madame, waxworks 5:109
Tuttavilla, Count Muzio 1:83
20th century
    artistic revolution 9:32-3
    changes in 9:30
    landmarks 9:30-31
    mass communication 9:33-4
    revolutions in 9:4
27 Blvd Poissonière, Paris 6:65
'twelve-note technique' 10:50
'Tyrannic Love' 4:26

U

Ullman Bernard, and Herz 6:108-9
underwear, introduction of 6:45
Unger, Caroline, and Liszt 6:91
unison 9:117
United States
    ends World War II 9:36
    and European affairs 9:34
    involvement in World War I 9:35
university life, 19th-century 8:84
University of Berlin 8:*83*
    foundation of 8:84
    Mendelssohn at 8:36
    offered chair of music 8:38
up-beat 9:117
up bow 9:117
uraemia 1:14
Urfé, Madame la Marquise d' 1:106-107
Utrecht, Peace of (1714)
    Handel's music for 4:62

V

vaccines, progress in 2:109
valse 9:117
Vallière, Louise de la 1:94, 96
valve 9:117
Vanderbilt, Cornelius 3:105
    yacht 3:*110*
Vanderbilt, Consuelo 3:*104,* 109
    on Austria 7:105
Vanderbilt, Mrs William K. 3:109-110
    art gallery 3:*105*
Varennes, disaster at 5:105, *105*
VARIATION 2:54; 9:117
    see also Index of Music
Vásáry, Tamás 6:77, 77
vaudeville 9:117; 10:22, 24
VAUGHAN WILLIAMS, Ralph *see Index of*
    Composers
Vaux-le-Vicomte, Château of, France 1:92
    fête at 3:97
Vauxhall Gardens, London 4:*98*, 99
Velluti, Giovanni Battista 10:13
veloce 9:117
Venice, Republic of, Italy 4:49ff, *49*, 60-61
    Albinoni in 4:8
    Austrian loss of 7:73
    concerts in 4:*36-7*
    decline as a music centre 10:28
    development of opera buffa 10:21

Doge of 4:50-51
Evelyn on opera performance in 10:44
exent of power and influence 4:49-53
fall of 4:56
fleet 4:49, 50-51, *50-51*, 52
Frederick the Great, King of Prussia in 4:*36*, 36-7
Handel in 4:61
　opera performed in 4:69
importance of music in 4:49
and the League of Cambrai 4:53
Mendelssohn in 8:46
opera houses
　first public 10:9, 10
　number of 10:10
and tourism 7:76
verbunkos 7:35; 9:117
VERDI, Guiseppe *see Index of Composers*
verismo 9:117; 10:34, 40, 49
Vernet, Horace, Mendelssohn and 8:47
Vernio, Count, and the Camerata 10:8-9
Versailles, France 1:91ff
　influence on European taste 5:38
　Mozart at 1:98
　water-works 4:*105*
Vestris, Auguste 3:100
Vestris, Gaetano 3:*98*, 100
Vesuvius, eruption of (AD 79) 1:*82*, 83
Vetsera, Marie 7:*105*
　death of 7:104
Viardot, Pauline 6:67
　Chopin and 6:68
vibrato 9:117; 10:85
Vichy, Tchaikovsky in 3:52
Victoire, Princess 1:*21*
　work dedicated to 1:20, *21*
Victoria, Queen of England 8:*70*, 71ff
　amusements 8:76
　and Bach revival 8:55
　and Baden-Baden 7:83
　Chopin and 6:68
　and collecting 8:74
　and family life 8:71-3
　　birth of first child 8:72
　　distaste for babies 8:72, *73*
　　sketches of children 8:*72*
　and fashion 8:78
　and The Great Exhibition 8:24, *24-5*
　　and exhibits 8:26
　homes 8:73-5
　ignoring the awkward 8:76
　and 'industrial classes' 8:75
　influence of Prince Albert on 8:77-8
　Leaves from a Journal of our Life in the Highlands 8:75
　love of music 8:76-7
　　and Mendelssohn 8:33, 39, 49, 76, 76-7
　　and Sullivan 10:47
　marriage 8:71, *71*
　mourning for Prince Albert 8:78, *78*
　on Paxton 8:23
　and photography 8:74
　and things 'Scottish' 8:74
　and travel 8:74, *74*, 78
Victoria and Albert Museum, London, funds for 8:29
vielle 9:117
Vienna, Austria 4:*40*; 6:*51*; 7:*11*
　anti-Semitism in 7:92
　audiences in 2:50-51

　and *Arabella* 10:50
　and *The Merry Widow* 10:55
　tastes of 10:29
Beethoven in 2:9-10, 27ff, 50
　conditions for leaving 2:29-30
　in fall of 2:50
　lodgings in 2:9, *30*, 47
　centenary of in 2:34
Brahms in 7:*11*, 12
　routine in 7:12
café society 6:*10*
as centre of music 10:30
Chopin in 6:63
　performances in 6:64
　works written in 6:64
coffee introduced to 5:68
court composer 10:26
death rate in 6:57
diseases in 6:57
in the 1800s 6:12, *57*, 57-8
early 19th-century painting in 6:*53*, 53-4
at the end of the 19th century 7:109
first duty of citizens of 6:53
first operetta 10:54
French take 2:50, *51, 98*
　bombardment of 5:*93*
funeral for Mahler 7:95
Haydn in 5:88, 91, 92-3
　concert in Old University 5:*92-3*
　lodgings 5:89
　mature years in 5:93
　purchases house in 5:93
hospitality of the upper classes 8:109
Liszt in 6:88, 91
　early concerts 6:88-9
Mahler in
　farewell performance 7:94
　first season 7:92
　last year in 7:94
　training in 7:88
　trials and tribulations in 7:92-3
in Mahler's time 7:104ff
medieval art group in 2:84
middle classes in 7:105, 106
modernization of 7:106, *106*
Mozart in 1:10, 11-13, 41
　concert tours to (1762) 1:18
　disaster in 1:21-2
　enemies in 1:43-5
　freelancing in 1:29-30
　friends in 1:43, 45
　lodgings in 1:*12*, 29
　The Marriage of Figaro in 10:22
　pupils in 1:43
as opera capital of the world 7:92
　types of opera in 10:26, 27, 29, 30
opera houses *see* individual names
Pachelbel in 4:8-9
Paganini in 6:13
the plague in 5:76
position of music in 2:46
punishment for prostitutes in 1:*107*
revolution in 2:100; 6:52, *58*; 7:69
the Secession in 7:108-109
Schubert in
　early years 6:9-11
　inspiration of music 6:18
　lodgings 6:11
and Schubert's songs 6:20
in Schubert's time 6:51ff
the Schumanns in 8:93

　student uprising in 6:*57*; 7:*26*
　the theatre in 6:54-6, *55*
　university scandal 7:108-109
Vivaldi in 4:40
Vienna Conservatory, Mahler at 7:88
Vienna Opera *see* Imperial Vienna Opera
Vienna Philharmonic Orchestra 7:53
　Brahms and 7:12
　director of 7:48
Vigana, Salvatore 3:100
vihuela 9:117
Villa d'Este, Liszt at 6:93, 95
'Village Musicians' 1:51
villancico 9:117
villanella/vinnelle 9:117
Villeneuve, Admiral 2:88
vingt-quatre violons du Roy, Les 4:20
viola, Telemann and 4:17-18
viola da gamba 5:*30*
　parts for in Bach's 'Brandenburg' Concertos 5:29
violin 9:41
　in Baroque era 9:9
　　makers during 9:9
　family 9:116
　Corelli and 4:12
　development of 2:62; 4:20
　　in Italy 4:47
　potential for in Baroque music 4:7
　techniques 2:62
　type played by Paginini 2:62
　see also bows: chinrest; virtuosos
viols 9:81, 117
Viotti, Giovanni 2:62
virginals 9:96, 117
virtuosos 6:104ff; 9:117
　finale furioso 6:*109*
　flamboyance of 6:108
　piano 6:61, 74
　rivalry between 6:108
　touring 6:105
　violin 2:62
VIVALDI, Antonio *see Index of Composers*
vivo 9:117
vocalise 9:117
voce 9:117
Vogl, Johann Michael 6:*17*
　and Schubert 6:11, 12, 13, 20
　　and *Erlkönig* 6:20
　and Schumann 6:24
voice 9:117
volante 9:117
volkslied 9:117
Volksoper, Vienna 10:63
Volta 4:110
volti 9:118
Voltaire, François 5:58-9, *59*, 64
　attacks on the establishment 10:24
　influence on opéra comique 10:23
voluntary 9:118
vorspiel 9:118
voyages of discovery, European in 18th-century 1:110ff
Vsevolozhsky
　and *The Nutcracker* 3:44, 45
　and *The Sleeping Beauty* 3:42
　and Tchaikovsky 3:44
vuota 9:118

W

Wagenseil, Georg Christoph 1:18
WAGNER, Richard *see Index of Composers*
Wagner tuba 10:85
Währing Cemetery, Vienna, Austria 2:15
wait 9:118
Waldmüller, Ferdinand Georg
    style of painting 6:*53*, 54
    portrait of Beethoven 2:*17*
Waldstein, Baroness 1:12
Waldstein, Count Ferdinand 1:108
    and Beethoven 2:9, 20, 27, 46
Wales, Mendelssohn in 8:37, 45, *45*
Wallis, Samuel 1:112-13
Walpole, Horace, on Piranesi's engravings
    1:86
Walpole, Sir Robert 4:96, *97*
    satire on 4:72
Walsegg-Stuppach, Count, commission for
    Mozart 1:15
Walter, Bruno 1:71
    on Mahler's Symphony No. 3 7:97-8
Walther, Gottfried, *Musicalisches Lexicon*
    5:27
WALTON, Sir William *see Index of
    Composers*
WALTZ 9:118
    see also Index of Music
Wanderlust 7:77-9
'War of the Buffoons' 4:11
War Memorial Opera House, San Francisco
    10:59
Warburton, Ernest, on Mozart and J. C.
    Bach 1:65
Wartburg fortress, Eisenach, Germany
    5:*23*, 24
Warsaw, Poland 6:63
Warsaw Conservatoire, director of 6:63
Warsaw Lyceum, N. Chopin at 6:62
Washington DC, Tchaikovsky in 3:*20-21*
Waterloo, Battle of (1815) 2:90
Watt, James 4:110
Watteroth, Professor, cantata for 6:11
Watts, Helen 4:83
Weber, Aloysia 1:11, *12*, 27
    Mozart and 1:40-41
Weber, Baron Carl von, commission for
    Mahler 7:88-9
WEBER, Carl Maria von *see Index of
    Composers*
Weber, Constanze 1:11, *13*, 29, *41*
    illness 1:14
    Mozart and 1:42, 56-7
        marriage to 1:12
    Mozart's description of 1:41
Weber family 1:29
Webern 1:52
Wechsberg, Joseph, on Bad Ischl,
    Germany 7:83
Wedgwood, Josiah 1:88, *88*; 4:110
Wegeler, Beethoven's letters to 2:10, 11
Weigl, Joseph, and development of
    Singspiel 10:30
Weihnachtsoratorium 9:118
Wieland, Christoph, and first 'German'
    opera 10:29
WEILL, Kurt *see Index of Composers*

Weimar, Germany 5:*8-9*
    J. S. Bach in 5:*9*, *9*, 26-7, 39
        court organist in 5:26
        music composed in 5:40-41
        post in 5:26
    Brahms in 7:23
        at court of 7:8-9
    concert master 7:28
    cultural prestige of 8:109
    Goethe at
        influence on theatre in 8:107
    Liszt in 6:93
        at court of 7:23
    musical director in 6:93
    19th-century court life in 8:109
    theatre in 8:107
    and tourism 7:80
Weinstock, Herbert, on Tchaikovsky and
    his mother 3:25
Weissenfels, Court of, J. S. Bach and 5:9
Wellcome, Henry 2:109
Wellington, Duke of 2:*88*
    and The Great Exhibition 8:23
Wesley, John 4:100, *100*
Wesley, Samuel, and Bach's works 8:55
'Westerners' 3:82-3, 86
Westminster Abbey, London 4:*12-13*
    Composer-in-Ordinary 4:14
    Handel memorial in 4:66
    organist 4:*13*
Westphalia, Peace of (1648) 5:22
Westrup, J. A., on Schubert's 'Trout'
    Quintet 6:24
White Swan restaurant, Vienna 2:28
'Widow of Windsor' 8:75, 78
    see also Victoria, Queen of England
Wieck, Clara 6:38; 8:*90*
    Chopin and 6:66
    concert tour 8:89
    marriage 8:91
        see also Schumann, Clara
    and Schumann 8:90ff
        Schumann's nickname for 8:89
        and piano lessons 8:89
Wieck, Friedrich
    pupils 7:29
    and Schumann 8:89
    and relationship between Clara and
        Schumann 8:91
Wilde, Oscar 3:*29*
    use of work by R. Strauss 10:50
    and *The Yellow Book* 3:28
Wilhelm I, Kaiser of Germany
    and Baden-Baden 7:83
    frugality of 8:109
    see also William I, King of Prussia
Wilhelm Ernst, Duke of Saxe-Weimar, and
    J. S. Bach 5:9-10, 26
Wilkin, Anna Magdelena *see* Bach, Anna
    Magdelena
William I, King of Prussia
    and Bismarck 7:*69*
    as German Emperor 7:74, *74*
    see also Wilhelm I, Kaiser of Germany
William, Prince of Orange 4:25, *29*, 30
Willmann, Magdalena, and Beethoven 2:18
wind band 9:118
wind ensembles 1:58
wind instruments, in Mozart's day 1:72
Winckelmann, Johann Joachim 1:84, *84*
    influence of 1:86-8

History of Ancient Art 1:87
Windsor Castle, England 8:73
witchcraft trials 4:103
    end of 9:13
Wixell, Ingvar 10:77
Wodzinska, Maria 6:66
WOLF, Hugo *see Index of Composers*
Wolff, Christian 5:25
Wolff, Dr 1:34
Wordsworth, William, and Romantic era
    9:19
Lyrical Ballads 9:19
World War I, beginnings of 9:27, *29*
World War II 9:35-6
Woronince, Liszt in 6:93
women
    Mozart's attitude to 1:45, *45*
    status in 18th century 1:45
Wren, Christopher 4:29
Wunderlich, Fritz 10:76
Württemburg, Germany
    emigration from 7:58
    organist at court of 4:9
    population control in 7:61

X Y Z

xylophone 9:59, 118
'Year of Revolutions' (1848) 9:24
    effect on Brahms 7:27
Zachow, F. W., and Handel 4:60
zanni 10:20, *20-21*
Zaremba, Nikolay 3:8
    and Tchaikovsky 3:27
    and Symphony No. 1 3:27
zarzuela 9:118; 10:53, 55, *55*
Zeitung für Theater, Musik und Posie,
    criticism of Beethoven's Violin
    Concerto 2:60
Zelazowa Wola Estate, Warsaw 6:62, *62*
ZELEMKA, Jan *see Index of Composers*
Zelter, Carl Friedrich 8:*35*
    and Bach revival 8:55
    Chopin and 6:63
    death of 8:38
    education 8:80
    and Mendelssohn 8:34
        congratulates on opera 8:35-6
        introduces to Goethe 8:34
    Schubert and 6:*16*, 18
Zeno, Apostolo 10:12
'Zilia' 8:89
Zseliz, Austria, Schubert at 6:12
Zentral-friedhof, Vienna 2:15
Ziegenhagen, Franz, commission for
    Mozart 1:38
Zimmermann, Gottfried 5:12
Zinzendorf, Count, on *Così fan Tutti* 1:45
zither 7:34; 9:118
Zitterbarth, Bartholmäus, Masonic
    certificate 1:*34*
Zollverein 7:70
Zucchi, Virginia 3:102
Zumsteeg, Johann Rudolph, Schubert and
    6:*16*, 18
Zvantsyer, Konstantin, and *Francesca da
    Rimini* 3:52
Zwicau Lyceum, Schumann at 8:88
Zywny, Wojciech, and Chopin 6:63
    farewell music for 6:63

Index of Composers

A

ALBINONI, Tomaso Giovanni
(1671-1751) 4:7, 8, *8; 9:10*
dedications:
to Maximilian Emanuel II, Elector of
Bavaria 4:8
in Florence 4:8
in Munich 4:8
in Venice 4:8
works:
catalogue of 4:16
use of in films 7:101
Adagio for Strings and Organ in G minor
4:16
Cantatas
number written *4:8*

Tomaso Albinoni

Concertos
dedications of 4:8
number written *4:8*
12 Concerti à Cinque op. 7 4:22
12 Concerti à Cinque op. 9 4:22
Operas
number written 4:8, *8*
popularity outside Italy 4:8
Griselda 4:8
Pimpinone 4:22
Zenobia 4:8
Sinfonias
number written *4:8*
Sonatas 4:8
ALBRECHTSBERGER, Johann
(1736-1809) 1:46
ALLEGRI, Gregorio (1582-1652)
Miserere 1:23
ARAIA, Francesco (1709-70)
post at Russian Court 10:41
Operas
La Forza dell'Amore 10:41
ARNE, Thomas (1710-78) 4:77
ARNOLD, Malcolm (1921)
and novel sound effects 3:55
and occasional music 4:87
Overtures
Grand Grand Overture 3:55, *55*
AUBER, Daniel (1782-1871) 8:110
and Scribe 10:33
Operas
number written 10:33
plots 10:33
La Muette de Portici
librettist 10:33
special effects 10:33

B

BACH, Carl Philipp Emanuel (1714-88)
5:*13,* 16, *16,* 17-18
and Beethoven 2:67
colleagues in Berlin 5:18
difficulty playing stringed instruments
5:17
early training 5:17
effects on musical development 2:36
Essay on the true art of playing
keyboard 5:18
and his father's (J. S. Bach) works 8:55
at Frankfurt-on-Oder University 5:17
and Frederick the Great 5:18, 58
on J. S. Bach trying organs 5:40
and keyboard instruments 5:17
posts:
in Berlin 5:12; 8:55
in Hamburg 5:18
pupils 5:18
style of music 5:17
textbook of instrumental music 5:18
and *Ursprung der musicalisch-*
Bachschen Familie 5:14-15
works:
output of 5:18
style in Berlin 5:18
Organ Music 5:17
Sonatas
effect of emotional content 2:36
BACH, Johann Christian (1735-82) 5:8, 15,
19, *19*
commission from Mannheim 5:19
engagement from Queen Charlotte of
England 5:19
finances 5:19
interest in instrumental work 5:19
and Italian opera 5:19
BACH, Johann Christoph (1642-1703) 1:46
and J. S. Bach's musical education 5:24
friendship with Mozart 1:20, 65
in Italy 5:19
liaisons 5:19
in London 5:*18,* 19; 8:55
marriage 5:19
and Mozart 5:19
in Naples 5:19
and Pachelbel 4:9
studies with Padre Martini 5:19
success of 5:19
works:
and Church cantatas 4:80
religious choral *see* Church music
for the stage 5:19
and symphony structure 1:64-5
Church music
Dixit Dominus 5:19
Requiem 5:19
Magnificat 5:27
Concertos 5:19
Operas 5:19
Amadis de Gaul 5:19

Artaserse 5:19
Catone in Utica 5:19
BACH, Johann Christoph Friedrich
(1732-95) 5:15, 16, *17,* 18-19
first post 5:18
influence of Mozart 5:19
in London 5:19
organizes opera performances 5:19
travels *see* individual cities, towns
and vocal music 5:18-19
works:
style of 5:19
Cantatas 5:19
Oratorios 5:19
BACH, Johann Sebastian (1685-1750)
5:*13,* 15, *24; 9:10*
and *Alt-Bachisches Archiv* 5:14
appointment at court of Weimar 5:9-10
in Berlin 5:12, 29
choir scholarships 5:8, 25
Chopin and 6:62
and the Church 5:22ff
see also religion
and composing:
contrapuntal outlook 4:20
development of orchestral writing
2:36
for the harpsichord 5:10
last secular work 5:12
for Easter in Eisenach 5:15
and keyboard music 5:12
maturing of style 5:26
and medieval music theory 5:27
and new-style cantatas 5:27
religious background to music 5:38-9
and religious music 5:*12*
refinements to music 5:27
sources of texts for cantatas 5:27
synthesis of styles 5:38
themes for Saxe-Weimar 5:26
use of French and Italian elements
5:25
use of instruments 9:9
Concerts: for Frederick the Great, King
of Prussia, 5:12
in Cöthen 5:29
in London 5:19
contributions to Church music 5:42
in Cöthen 5:29
and counterpoint 5:33
at court of Weissenfels 5:12
death of 5:12
survival of music after 5:39
death of first wife 5:10
dedications:
of 'Brandenburg' concertos 29
to Frederick the Great, King of Prussia
5:12
to the Margrave of Baden 5:29
of 'Musical Offering' 5:12
director of Collegium Musicum 5:12
disputes with Church authorities 5:9, 11
and distinction in secular/Church music
5:25
in Dresden 5:10
and Duke of Saxe-Weimar 5:26
disagreement with 5:10
early life 5:8
religious/musical background 5:23-4
early musical education 5:8, 24
eclipse of by sons 5:16

Archiv für Kunst und Geschichte

Johann Sebastian Bach

education in Lüneberg 5:8-9
effect of posts on music 5:38-9
18th-century criticism of 4:15
and Elector of Saxony 5:12, 27
fails to take post in Hamburg 5:10-11
family life 5:9, *11,* 16-19, 26
  in Cöthen 5:10
  family tree 5:*14*
first Church post 5:25
first employment 5:9
in Halle 5:9-10
library 5:26
  enlargement of 5:27
and Frederick the Great, King of Prussia 5:63
influence of his brother 5:8
influence of Buxtehude 5:25
influence of French/Italian styles 5:26
influence of music:
  on Modern era 5:16
  on Romantic era 5:16, 39
influence of Vivaldi 5:26
and instrumental technique 4:20
as Kantor of the Thomasschule 5:*10*
  responsibilities as 5:11
as *Konzertmeister* 5:10
leave of absence from Arnstadt 5:9, *9*
in Leipzig 5:11-12, *12,* 27
  disputes with Church council 5:27
  examination for job in 5:27
  first major work in 5:27
  gains post in 4:10
  position on return to 5:12
in Lüneberg 5:25
marriage: first 5:9, 25
  second 5:11, 26
Mendelssohn and 8:37
in Mühlhausen 5:9, 25, 39
  conflict with employers 5:25-6
  first composition in 5:25
  resigns post in 5:26
notebooks 5:26
offer from Halle 5:9-10
operations for failing eyesight 5:12

pupils 5:9
  last 5:12
rejection of principles by successors 8:55
religious commitment 5:26
  effect of on music 5:24
  foundations of 5:24
revival of work of 8:55
Schumann and 8:101
scoring:
  of Concerto no. 2 5:30
  of Concerto no. 3 5:32
  of Concerto no. 5 5:35
  of Suite no. 2 5:47
travels, to hear concerts 5:9, *9*
trying organs 5:40
  types played 5:39-40
under house arrest 5:10
Ursprung der musicalisch-Bachischen Familie 5:14-15
and Vivaldi's opus 3 4:37
in Weimar 5:9, *9,* 26-7, 39
  court organist in 5:26
  music composed in 5:40-41
  post in 5:26
work in Arnstadt 5:9
works:
  catalogue of 1:67
  Clavier-Büchlein 5:*11*
  Clavier-übung 5:12
  length of 2:37
  major ecclesiastical 5:12
  modulations in fugues 1:52
  'Musical Offering' BWV 1079 5:12, 45
  publishing 8:55
  solos for violin and for cello 5:10
  sonatas 1:58
  use of the flute in 1:61-2
  written in Cöthen 5:10
  written in Mühlhausen 5:9, 25
  written in Weimar 5:9
The Well-Tempered Clavier 2:44; 5:10, 12; 8:55
  Books 1 and 2 5:45
Arias
  Aria with 30 Variations *see* Variations
  Sheep May Safely Graze 5:26
Cantatas
  for the birthday of Duke of Weissenfels 5:9
  first 5:9
  number written at Leipzig 5:*12,* 27
  texts for 5:26, 27
  title page of secular set 5:*26*
  for Weimar 5:9, 26
  no. 82 'Ich habe Genug' 5:53
  God is my King 5:25
  Komm, du süsse Todesstunde 5:26
  Peasant Cantata 5:12
Concertos
  six concertos 'Brandenburg' 5:10, 29-30
    parts for viola da gamba 5:29, *30*
  no. 2 in F major BWV1047 5:30-32
  no. 3 in G major BWV1048 5:32-4
  no. 5 in D major BWV1050 5:35-6
    first page of 5:*34*
  Violin:
    in A minor BWV1041 5:37
    in D minor BWV1043 5:37

Fugues
  modulations in 1:52
  48 Preludes and Fugues 5:33
  The Art of the Fugue BWV1080 5:33, 53
  Fantasia and Fugue in G minor BWV542 5:41-3
  Passacaglia and Fugue in C minor BWV582 5:44
  Prelude and Fugue in E minor BWV548 5:43-4
  Toccata and Fugue in D minor BWV565 5:41
Masses
  in B minor 5:27, 42
    begins writing 5:12
  Missa Solemnis 5:42
Motets
  Actus Tragicus 5:25
Oratorios
  Christmas Oratorio NWV248 5:12, 27, 53
Organ Music 5:9, 38ff
Passions
  St John Passion 5:*12, 25,* 27
    manuscript 5:*25*
    performed by Singakademie 8:55
  St Mark Passion, first performance 5:12
  St Matthew Passion 5:*12,* 27, 37; 8:*36*
    Mendelssohn and 5:39; 8:*36,* 37, 55
Sonatas
  for Violin and Harpsichord 5:10
Suites
  dances used in 5:46
  instrumentation for 5:47
  piano transcription of 5:47

VOLUME 1
Mozart

VOLUME 2
Beethoven

VOLUME 3
Tchaikovsky

VOLUME 4
Albinoni, Corelli, Handel, Pachelbel, Purcell, Rameau, Telemann, Vivaldi

VOLUME 5
Bach, Haydn

VOLUME 6
Chopin, Liszt, Schubert

VOLUME 7
Brahms, Mahler

VOLUME 8
Berlioz, Mendelssohn, Schumann

VOLUME 9
A Guide to Classical Music

VOLUME 10
A Beginner's Guide to the Opera

no. 2 in B minor BWV1067 5:46, 47-50
no. 3 in D BWV1068 5:50-53
Variations
    Aria with 30 Variations BWV988
        Goldberg 2:54; 5:12, 45
        contrapuntal device in 5:33
BACH, Wilhelm Friedemann (1710-84)
    5:*13, 15*
    and choral Church music 5:17
    in Dresden 5:17
    early training 5:16
    failure of 5:16-17
    in Halle 5:17
    in London 5:19
    posts:
        in Dresden 5:12
        first 5:16
    travels *see* individual cities, towns
    works:
        to suit his place of work 5:17
        for teaching 5:17
    Dances
        12 Polonaises 5:17
    Fugues 5:17
    Sonatas 5:17
BALAKIREV, Mily (1837-1910) 3:36
    and 'The Mighty Handful' 10:43
    and Tchaikovksy 3:8
        letters to 3:70
        and *Romeo and Juliet* 3:70, *70*
BARTÓK, Béla (1881-1945) 2:*37*; 9:22
    influence of Beethoven 2:*37, 39*
    influence of folk music 9:33
        and gypsy music 7:35
    Operas
        Duke Bluebeard's Castle 10:51
    String quartets
        understanding 2:39
        Schuppanzigh 2:28
        Beethoven and 2:28
BEETHOVEN, Ludwig van (1770-1827)
    2:*10, 25, 43*; 7:*52*; 9:*16*
    aged thirty-four 2:66
    and C. P. E. Bach 5:127
    and J. S. Bach's music 5:12
    behaviour 2:22
    birthplace 2:*8*
    Brahms and 7:47
    and Carlsbad 7:83
    character 2:12
        Beethoven on 2:22
    and Classical style 1:77
    intimate side of 2:58
    'canonization' 2:*36*
    caricatures 2:*39*
        by Lyser 2:*14*
    Chopin and 6:62
    commissions 2:26
    and composing 2:11, *71*
        breaking 'rules' of music 2:36-7
        expanding scale of works 2:37
        'logic' of concert music 2:37-8
        on Piano Concerto No. 5 2:51
        on Symphony No. 5 2:51, 66-7
        use of five-octave compass 2:45
        use of melodies in large-scale works
            2:37
        use of *Ode to Joy* 2:77
        use of phrases 2:37, 43
        use of Scherzo 2:39
        use of themes 2:37

Ludwig van Beethoven

    and variations 2:54
    'composing secrets' 2:37
    concerts:
        in Berlin 2:10
        for Domanovecz 2:28
        at Grätz 2:25-6
        in Prague 2:10
        reliance on 2:62
        for Van Sweiten 2:28
        in Vienna 2:10, 66
    contract of 1809 2:28-9, *29*
    at Court of Bonn 2:26, 59
    creed 2:69
    criticisms of work 2:37-8
    deafness:
        effect on emotions 2:17
        onset of 2:10-12
    death mask 2:*15*
    descriptions of 2:9, 14
        in maturity 2:12
    early years 2:8-9
    effect on audiences 2:34
    enduring legacy 2:34ff
    Ertmann and 8:38, 48
    fame:
        rise to 2:34, 44, 46
        spread of 2:13
    family 2:9, 22
        effect of his brother's death 2:13
        background 2:26-7
        guardianship of nephew 2:13-14, 22
    finances 2:19
        from 1809 contract 2:30
        salary from Archduke Rudolph 2:50
        salary in Bonn 2:26, 27
        salary from Lichnowsky 2:27
    first published work 2:9
    freelance 2:10
    friends/friendships 2:9, 20-21, *20-21*, 27
        biography by 2:20, *20*
        Bonn circle 2:20
        financial problems 2:30-31
        on his lifestyle 2:17-18
        nicknames 2:28
        quarrel with Hummel 2:20

    towards end of his life 2:20-21
    and fugues of J. S. Bach 2:44
    funeral of 2:*14-15*
    and Haydn 5:92
    in Heiligenstadt 2:*17*
    'heirs' to 7:23
    on himself 2:15
    humour 2:20
    illnesses 2:14, 102
        see also deafness
    and improvisation 2:43
    influence of C. P. E. Bach 2:67
    influence of Haydn 2:9, 27, 67-8
        studies composition with 2:9
    influence of Mozart 2:67-8
        meets 2:9, 27
    influence on other composers 2:38-9
    innovations 2:36-7
    jokes played on 2:20
    lessons from his father 2:9
    letters:
        to Ameda 2:10
        about Guilietta Guicciardi 2:46
        to 'The Immortal Beloved' 2:13, 19, 20
        to Lichnowsky 2:25
        to Wegeler 2:10, 11
    lifestyle 2:17-18
    Liszt presented to 6:88
    and marriage 2:18, 19-20
    in maturity 2:11-12
    Mendelssohn and 8:35
    in his mid-thirties 2:*58*
    monument to 6:91
    and music as a moral force 9:20
    and musical puns 2:37
    musical training 2:9
    and musical content 2:38
    mystique surrounding 2:34, 38
    natural successor to 7:12, 47
    and novel sound-effects 3:55
    and oratorios 4:80
    patrons 1:36
    and the piano 6:74
        contests 2:10
        style of playing 2:38, 43, 46
        as virtuoso 2:10
    popularity 2:39
    publishers 2:*31*, 46
        letter to 2:50
    pupils 2:18, 20, *26*, 27, 46; 6:*88*
    relationships 2:13, 17ff
    and 'rescue' opera 10:35
    and Romantic harmony 1:52
    Romantic vision of 2:*38-9*; 9:*20*
    by Schimon 2:*13*
    Schubert and 6:18, 33
    Schumann and 8:101
    scoring:
        for Piano Concerto No. 4 2:51
        for Piano Concerto No. 5 2:51
        structure of concertos 1:73
    the Secessionists and 7:*108*, 109
    statue to 2:*36*
    by Steiler 2:*9*
    and structure of orchestra 2:35
    studies the violin 2:9, 59
    takes the 'cure' 2:*18*, 19
    temperament 2:17, 20, 58
    use of the orchestra 4:20
    by Waldmüller 2:*17*
    will 2:11

and women 2:13, 18
works:
  effect of musical journals on 8:101
  expressions of emotions in 9:20
Arias
  'Ah Perfido' 2:66
Concertos
  attitude to names of 2:34
  contribution to 2:42
  convention in early 2:51
  Piano:
    3rd 2:66
    No. 4 in G op. 58 2:57, 58
      'breaking rules' in 2:37
    No. 5 in E flat op. 73 'Emperor'
      1:34, 50-56
      compared with Violin Concerto
        (Beethoven) 2:58
      criticism of 2:50
      first performance 2:50-51
      last one 2:51
      title page 2:52
  Triple:
    in C major op. 56 2:65
  Violin:
    in D op. 2:61, 58-64
      'breaking rules' in 2:37
      criticism of 2:60
      first performance 2:59-60
      inscription on 2:58
      piano arrangement 2:60
      publication and popularity
        2:60-61
      speed of writing 2:60
      title page 2:60
Duets
  Duet for Two Obbligato Eyeglasses
    2:20
Fantasias
  for chorus and orchestra 2:99, 100
Masses
  in C 2:66
  Missa Solemnis 2:9, 30
  dedication of 2:30
Operas
  Fidelio 1:57; 10:35
    Mahler conducts 7:94
Overtures
  op. 84 'Egmont' 2:65
  Leonore no. 3 3:18
Piano works
  Nine Variations for piano in C minor
    2:9
Quartets
  String:
    at work on last 2:14
    'meaning' of last 2:38
  No. 1 op. 18:
    inspiration for 2:46
    op. 59 'Razumovsky' 2:28, 49; 3:62
    influence on Simpson 2:39
Romances
  for violin and orchestra:
    No. 1 op. 40 2:65
    No. 2 op. 60 2:65
Sonatas
  names of 2:44, 46
  role in development of music 2:44-5
  technique for 2:45
  Piano 2:42ff
    first 2:43

influence on 2:67
last:
  criticism of 2:38
  'meaning' of 2:38
  number 2:42
in A major op. 101 2:21
in C sharp minor, op. 27 no. 2
  'Moonlight' 2:46-8, 3:62
  autograph score 2:45
  Beethoven's instructions for
    playing 2:48
in F minor op. 57 'Appassionata'
  2:26, 48-9
  manuscript 2:48
Grande Sonata Pathétique in
  C minor op. 13 2:34, 43-6
no. 22 op. 54 2:49
no. 29 op. 106 'Hammerklavier'
  2:49
  technique for 2:45
op. 27 set:
  Beethoven's name for 2:48
op. 53 'Waldstein' 2:9
piano development and 2:45
32nd op. 111 'Arietta' 2:43
technique for 2:45
Violin:
  op. 27 'Kreutzer' 2:57
Symphonies
  changes in symphony structure 2:39
  cyclic principles in 2:39
  influence on 2:67
  names of 3:62
  replaces minuet with scherzo 2:39
  symphonic unities 2:37
  'Battle' 3:55
  No. 1 in C:
    dedication 2:28
    use of orchestra in 4:20
  No. 2 2:11
    criticism of 2:38
  No. 3 'Eroica' 2:13, 34; 3:62
    'breaking rules' in 2:37
    criticism 2:38
    dedication of 2:20, 89
    ideas behind 9:20
    importance of 2:48
    length of 2:13, 37
  No. 4 2:67
    Mendelssohn revival of 8:38
  No. 5 in C minor op. 67 2:13, 66-71
    compared with Violin Concerto
      (Beethoven) 2:58
    criticism 2:66
    dedication of 2:20
    first performance 2:66, 70
    ideas behind 9:20
    inspiration for first phase of 2:43,
      66, 69
    later interpretation 2:71
    model for other composers 2:39
    sketch of 2:68
  No. 6 'Pastoral' 2:13, 67, 3:62
    dedication of 2:20
    first performance 2:66
    influence of 2:39
    inspiration for 9:20
    as programme music 8:17
    use in cartoons 7:101
  No. 7:
    criticism of 2:38

No. 9 'Choral' 2:14, 3:62
  criticism of 2:38
  first performance 2:14
  Mendelssohn revival of 8:38
  poem for 2:77
Trios
  Piano:
    'Archduke' 2:30; 3:62
    op. 1 2:27
      dedication of 2:27
      title page 2:27
  String:
    op. 9 2:28
Variations
  Diabelli 2:54
  'Goldberg' 3:62
BELLINI, Vincenzo (1801-35) 6:110;
  10:38-9 and *bel canto* 10:40
  meets Glinka 10:42
  works:
    for specific performers 10:39
    quality of 10:40
  Operas
    essence of 10:39
    Norma:
      inspiration for 10:39
      plot 10:39
      setting for 10:38
    The Puritans:
      plot 10:39
BERG, Alban (1885-1935) 1:52
  and the 'Second Viennese School' 10:50
  and 'twelve-note technique' 10:50
  Operas
    Lulu 10:50, 50
    Wozzeck 10:50
    structure of 10:50
BERLIOZ, Hector (1803-69) 6:79; 7:26;
  8:7, 13; 9:16
  aged sixteen 8:8
  as author 8:12
    *Treatise on Modern Instrumentation
      and Orchestration* 8:12
  and Baden-Baden 7:83
  on Beethoven's Symphony No. 5 2:69,
    71

Composer	Volume
Albinoni	4
Bach	5
Beethoven	2
Berlioz	8
Brahms	7
Chopin	6
Corelli	4
Handel	4
Haydn	5
Liszt	6
Mahler	7
Mendelssohn	8
Mozart	1
Pachelbel	4
Purcell	4
Rameau	4
Schubert	6
Schumann	8
Tchaikovsky	3
Telemann	4
Vivaldi	4

Hector Berlioz

birth of his son 8:11
caricature of 8:*10*
Chopin and 6:67
in chorus of Théâtre des Nouveautés
    8:10
commission from the French
    government 8:11
and composing:
    begins 8:9
    decides to stop 8:13
    effects of swings in mood on 8:8
    programme music 6:100; 8:14, 16, 17
    time left for 8:12
    use of repeated motifs 6:98
concerts:
    conducts his own works 8:12
    for Harriet Smithson 8:14
and conducting:
    at Drury Lane 8:12
    his own works 8:12
    prominence of conductor 7:50
    tour of Russia 8:13
    treatise on 7:50
description of 8:*9*
description of Paganini 6:106-107
'discovers' *Hamlet* 8:14
discovers music 8:8-9
earliest authenticated portrait 8:*14*
early life 8:8-9
effect of death of Ferrand on 8:13
his father 8:*8*
feelings about music 8:8
finances:
    allowance stopped 8:9
    debt over *Benvenuto Cellini* 8:11
    earnings for 1832-42 8:12
    gift from Paganini 8:12
    at medical school 8:9
    for performance of Mass 8:9
    struggle against bankruptcy 8:8
gives music lessons 8:9
and Gluck's music 8:9
and Goethe's works 8:10
health 8:13
    effect of deaths of wives on 8:13

increasing use of laudanum 8:13
influence on Russian composers 8:13
and Italy 8:10
    love of countryside 8:11, *11*
    meets Mendelssohn in 8:10-11
letters:
    to Ferrand 8:10, 11
    on Harriet Smithson 8:10
    to Harriet Smithson 8:10, 14
    on his taking poison 8:11
Liszt and 6:90
'love affairs' 8:8-9
    Camille Moke 8:10
    Estelle 8:*8*, 8-9, 10, 13
    Harriet Smithson 8:10, *10,* 11, 14
    Marie Recio 8:12
marriage 8:11-12
    collapse of first 8:12
    death of second wife 8:13
Memoirs:
    begins writing 8:12
    corrections to 8:*11*
    finishes 8:13
and Mendelssohn 8:38, 47
in Moscow 8:13
most formative years 8:10
musical education:
    early 8:8
    at the Paris Conservatoire 8:9
    pupil of Lesueur 8:9
and musical criticism 8:12
    resigns from *Journal des Débats*
        8:13
and musical standards of the time 8:12
a musical vocation 8:9-10
need of a post 8:12
in Nice 8:10
in Paris 8:11
    studying medicine 8:9
and religion:
    Roman Catholicism 8:8
    taunts Mendelssohn 8:10-11
reputation in France 8:12
in Rome:
    emotional crisis in 8:10
and Romanticism 9:21
in Russia 8:13
Schumann and 8:101
and Shakespeare 8:10
struggle against French musical
    establishment 8:12-13
studies medicine 8:9
swings in mood 8:8
    effect on music 8:8
takes poison 8:11
his 'Thirty Years War' 8:11-12
thoughts of murder 8:10
travels, in Europe 8:12
Weimar School and 7:25
wins Prix de Rome 8:10
withdrawal from the world 8:13
works for the Opéra-Comique 10:34
works:
    inspiration for later 8:*11*
    public opposition to 8:8
    and publishing 8:9
    rejected by Paris Opéra 8:12
    sources of inspiration 8:9
    start of critical acclaim 8:10
    submitted for Prix de Rome 8:10
    written in Nice 8:10

    written as a student 8:9
    Death of Sardanapalus 8:10
    Eight Scenes from Faust 8:10
    Episode in the Life of an Artist see
        Symphonies: Symphony
        Fantastique
    Harold in Italy op. 16 8:11, 21
    La Damnation de Faust op. 24 8:21
    Lélio 'A Return to Life' 8:14
    Nuits d'Eté op. 7 8:21
    Romeo and Juliet 8:12
Church Music
    Te Deum 5:42
Masses
    commission from French
        Government 8:11
    written as a student 8:9
    Grande Messe des Morts 5:42
Operas
    written as a student 8:9
    Beatrice and Benedict 7:83; 8:13
    Benvenuto Cellini 8:11
    Trojans at Carthage 8:*12,* 13; 10:34
        rejection of 8:*12, 13*
        'ridiculous travesty' of 8:*12,* 13
Oratorios
    L'Enfance du Christ 4:80
Overtures
    King Lear 8:10, *63*
        influence of Beethoven in 2:39
Symphonies
    Symphonie Fantastique 6:23; 8:11,
        14-21
        first performance of 8:10, 14
        influence of Beethoven in 2:39
        inspiration for 8:10, 14
        Liszt and 6:96
        programme for 8:14, 16, 17
        scene aux champs 2:39
        success of 8:14
    Symphonie Funèbre et Triomphale
        4:87
    conducts 8-12
BIZET, Georges (1838-75) 7:110
    fate of operettas 10:53
    works for the Opéra-Comique 10:34
    Operas
        Carmen 3:52; 10:81
            inspiration for 10:40
            public reaction to 10:34
        Djamileh 10:81
        Fair Maid of Perth 10:34
        L'arlesienne 10:81
        Les Pêchers de Perles 10:34, 81
    Suites
        'L'Arlésienne' 5:49
BLOW, John (1649-1708) 4:110, 5:49
BOCCHERINI, Luigi (1743-1805) 1:46
BOIELDIEU, Adrien (1775-1834) 8:110
BONONCINI, Giovanni Battista
    (1670-1747) 4:70, 110
    rivalry with Handel 4:71
    and Royal Academy of Music 4:70-71
BORODIN, Alexander (1834-87) 3:8
    and The Mighty Handful 10:42
    works:
        Polovstian Dances 10:42
    Operas
        Prince Igor 10:42
    Symphonic poems
        In the Steppes of Central Asia 6:100

BOYCE, William (1711-79) 4:110
BRAHMS, Johannes (1833-97) 7:*8, 9, 12, 15, 17, 23, 27, 38, 46; 9:17*
  as accompanist 7:12
  aged 58 7:*13*
  aged 20 7:*7, 23*
  and anti-Wagner faction 7:27
  artistic success 7:13
  and *Bachgesellschaft* 7:68
  in Baden-Baden 7:82
  becoming better known 7:12
  beginning of career 7:8-9
  and Bismarck 7:68
  in Budapest 7:38, *40*
  in Breman 7:10
  caricatures 7:*14, 23*
  character 7:14
    effect of early experiences on 7:7, *18*
  childhood passions 7:7
  and children 7:14-15
  and classical music 7:38
  and composing:
    of concertos 7:38
    drafts part of symphony 7:47
    during holidays 7:32
    during New Music controversy 7:29
    and form of Classical 'concerto' 7:30
    golden period 7:12-13
    guide for overtures 8:60
    influence of Schumann on writing 7:47
  and lieder 6:28-30

Johannes Brahms

  and occasional music 4:87
  routine for 7:12
  shortens symphony movements 7:48
  studies composition 7:38
  thinking in keyboard terms 7:47
  time between the piano concertos 7:38
  time to complete Symphony no. 1 7:46
  writing first symphony 7:46-7
  concerts:
    in Budapest 7:38

    in Detmold 7:10
    in Hanover 7:38
    first solo 7:38
    in Leipzig 7:38
    playing Piano Concerto No. 1 7:38
    routine of tours 7:12
    of Violin Concerto 7:31-2
    with Joachim/C. Schumann 7:10
    with Reményi 7:27, 30
  and conducting 7:48, *50-51*
  and creation of German Empire 7:68
  creative holidays 7:32
  criticism of Hanslick 7:29
  criticism by Wagner 7:25-6
  death of 7:21
  and death of his mother 7:12
  death of his sister 7:14
  description 7:14
  in Detmold 7:11
  in Düsseldorf 7:9, 10
  early life 7:7
  effect of Clara Schumann on 7:14
  finances:
    playing for money 7:7-8
    from published music 7:13
    on return home 7:9
    in Vienna 7:12
  first piano lessons 7:7
  founds women's choir 7:11
  friends/friendships:
    with Elizabeth von Herzogenberg 7:13
    with Joachim 7:8, 13, 30
    memorial from 7:15
    with the Schumanns 7:9-10, 46-7
  fund for Clara Schumann 7:20
  and the 'futurists' 7:29
  in Hamburg 7:10
    founds women's choir 7:11
    house of his own in 7:11
  health:
    reaction to illness 7:15
    after Clara Schumann's death 7:14
  helps Dvořák 7:13
  and hero-worship 7:28
  holidays 7:12
  honorary degree in music from Breslau 4:87; 7:13, 26-7
  influence of Beethoven 2:39; 7:40
  influence of folk/gypsy music 7:27, 30, 35
    in Piano Concerto no. 2 7:38
  influence of Italy on 7:38, *38*
  influence of Schumann on 7:9, 17, 40
  influence of tragic events on 7:12, 14, 47
  influences on concertos 7:40
  and Johann Strauss 7:*11, 27*
  and Karlsbad 7:14, 83
  last decades 7:12-14
  in Leipzig 7:10
    plays Piano Concerto No. 1 7:11
  letters:
    to Agathe von Siebold 7:11
    to Clara Schumann 7:10, 20-21, 26
    to Elisabeth von Herzogenberg 7:13
    to Joachim 7:30
    to Schumann 7:18
  in Lichtenthal 7:12
  and his limitations 7:47
  and Liszt 7:8
    and his piano playing 7:24

  'love affairs':
    with Agathe von Siebold 7:11, 21
    with Bertha Porubsky 7:11
    with Clara Schumann 7:10, 17ff, 20-21
  and Julie Schumann 7:21
  love of the countryside 7:*8*
    and Austrian landscape 7:*30-31*
  and Mahler's interpretive genius 7:90
  and marriage 7:11, 21
  most important events in life 7:68
  and Mozart's Clarinet Concerto K. 622 1:58
  and 'New Music' 7:27, 29
    attitude towards 7:24
    and battle against 7:23ff
    and manifesto against 7:29
  offends von Bülow 7:13
  piano-playing skill 7:7, 38, *41*
    style of playing 2:38
  piano recitals 7:10
  and politics 7:27
  on Pörtschach 7:30, *30, 32*
  posts:
    conducting 7:48
    in Detmold 7:10-11
    as Director of Vienna Philharmonic Society 7:12, 48
    hope of in Düsseldorf 7:10
  publisher 7:13
    promises symphony to 7:48
  publishes Schumann manuscript 7:21
  pupils, in Detmold 7:10
  and religion 7:15
  and Reményi 7:27, *35*
    concert tours with 7:8, 30
  in Sassnitz 7:32
  and the Schumann children 7:19-20

VOLUME 1
  Mozart

VOLUME 2
  Beethoven

VOLUME 3
  Tchaikovsky

VOLUME 4
  **Albinoni, Corelli, Handel,
  Pachelbel, Purcell, Rameau,
  Telemann, Vivaldi**

VOLUME 5
  Bach, Haydn

VOLUME 6
  Chopin, Liszt, Schubert

VOLUME 7
  Brahms, Mahler

VOLUME 8
  Berlioz, Mendelssohn, Schumann

VOLUME 9
  A Guide to Classical Music

VOLUME 10
  A Beginner's Guide to the Opera

and Schumann:
  criticism by 8:101
  mental illness 7:10
  music promoted by 8:87
  visits to in asylum 7:18-19; 8:93
sex life 7:11-12
Tchaikovsky and 3:13
travel:
  love of *15*
and variations 2:54
and Wagner 7:12
  criticism of 7:26
  and *Die Meistersinger* 7:12, 25
  as rival to 7:26
in Weimar 7:23
works:
  public acceptance of style 7:12
  Clara Schumann and 7:9, 12
  for Clara Schumann 7:21
  critical response to 7:12
  inspirations for 7:30
  Joachim and 7:12
  last orchestral 7:13
  in later life 7:13-14
  most important orchestral 7:12-13
  for Prussian victory 7:74
  repertoire when composing piano
      concertos 7:40
  shorter piano pieces 7:13
  sincerity in 7:15
  submitted to Schumann 7:17
  'veiled symphonies' 7:46
  for women's choir 7:11
  Alto Rhapsody op. 53 7:15, 53
  Piano Pieces op. 118 7:45
  Scherzo in E flat minor 7:8
  serenades 7:12
  song written for Bertha Porubsky 7:11
  on writing his first symphony 7:47
  and Year of Revolution, (1848) 7:27
Chamber music
  Joachim and 7:12
  popularity of 7:12
Concertos
  Piano:
    No. 1 op. 15 7:10-11, 38, 45
    first performance 7:11
    influences on 7:40
    origin of ideas 7:47
    No. 2 in B flat op. 83 7:13, 38-44
    conception of 7:38
    first performance 7:38
    influences on 7:38
    inspiration for 7:30
    pianist's contribution to 7:38
    number of movements 3:72
  Violin:
    in D op. 77 7:13, 30-37
    first performance 7:31
    influences on 7:38
    Joachim's amendments to 7:*32*
    popularity of 7:31-2
    Double Concerto for Violin and
        Cello 7:13
Lieder
  greatest? 6:29
  number written 6:28
  sources of texts 6:28, 29
  Stockhausen and 7:12
  Cradle Song 7:11
  Four Serious Songs 7:13-14, 15

Triumphlied 7:74
  piano transcription 7:*26*
Vier ernste Gesange 6:29
Masses
  German Requiem 7:15, 47-8
    inspiration for 7:12, 15, 30, 47-8
Overtures 8:63
  Academic Festival Overture 4:87; 7:13
Quartets
  Piano:
    First Quartet 3:22
Quintets
  Clarinet Quintet 7:13
Sonatas
  'flavour' of 7:10
  in C major 7:9
Symphonies
  von Bülow's reaction to 7:24
  No. 1 in C minor op. 68 7:46-52
    critical reaction to 7:48
    dramatic mood of 7:46
    finally completes 7:12
    horn solo for 7:12, 47, *48-9*
    inspiration for 7:30
    première of 7:12, 48
    similarity to No. 9 (Beethoven)
        2:39
  No. 2 7:32
  No. 4 in E minor op. 98 7:13, 53
    conducts 7:13
Variations
  St Anthony 2:54; 7:12, 48
    première of 7:48
  on a theme of Handel 2:54; 7:12
  Variations on a theme by Haydn
      op. 56a 7:53
BRITTEN, Benjamin (1913-76) 10:47
  first opera success 10:48
  influence on Tippett 10:48
  and novel sound-effects 3:55
  on permanent national opera 10:48
  and Purcell 10:48
Operas
  Noye's Fludde 3:55
  Peter Grimes 10:47, *47*, 48
    first performance 10:48
    plot 10:48
  Billy Budd 10:48
  A Midsummer Night's Dream 10:48
  The Turn of the Screw 10:48
BRUCH, Max (1838-1920) 7:110
  and Brahms's symphonies 7:49
  honorary doctorate from Cambridge
      3:59
BRUCKNER, Anton (1824-96) 2:*36*; 7:110
  influence of Beethoven 2:*36*, 39
  influence of Wagner 1:52
BULL, John (1602-76) 2:54, *54*
  Variations
    The King's Hunt 2:54, *54*
BUXTEHUDE, Dietrich (1637-1707) 5:110
BYRD, William (1543-1623)
  Battel 8:17

C

CARISSIMI, Giacomo (1605-74) 4:80, 110
CAVALLI, Pietro
  humour in works 10:*19*
  influence on *opera buffa* 10:*19*

output of operas 10:9
use of comic elements 10:19
Operas
  Ecole Amante 10:18
  Xerxes 10:18
CHABRIER, Emmanuel (1841-94)
  fate of operettas 10:54
CHARPENTIER, Marc-Antoine
    (c. 1634-1704) 4:22
  incidental music 4:22
  influence of cantata form on 4:80
  Leçons de Tenèbres 4:22
  Pastorale 4:22
  Church music
    Magnificat 4:22
    Te Deum 4:22
  Oratorios
    Judith 4:22
CHOPIN, Fryderyk (1810-49) 6:*64, 67,
    69, 78*; 9:*17*
  aged nineteen 6:*61*
  in Carlsbad 6:66
  in Chaillot 6:69
  and composing:
    development of mature style 6:63, 70
    early attempts 6:63
    early improvisation 6:62-3
    first lessons 6:63
    and orchestration 6:63, 64
  concerts 6:82

Fryderyk Chopin

charity 6:69
in Edinburgh 6:68, *68*
first public 6:63, *63*
in London 6:68, 69
in Paris 6:65, 67, 81, 84
in Rouen 6:67
at the Salle Pleyel 6:67, 68
on 26 April 1841 6:68
in Vienna 6:63-4
salon 6:81
'concert works' 6:70

Archiv für Kunst und Geschichte

dedications:
  to Denfina Potocka 6:65
  to Liszt 6:71
  of op. 10 Etudes 6:71
  of Piano Concerto no. 2 6:65
  of Waltz op. 64 no. 1 6:65
drawing-room 6:81
in Dresden 6:64, 66, *66*
early fame 6:63
early talents 6:62
early years 6:62
early musical training 6:62
in Edinburgh 6:68, *68*
effects of 1848 Revolution on 6:84
entertaining in Paris 6:67
family 6:62
finances:
  income from concerts 6:68, 82
  in Paris 6:65, 82
  from teaching 6:82
funeral of 6:69
health 6:67-8
  failure of 6:68-9
  in Majorca 6:67
as impersonator 6:67
indecisiveness 6:61-2
influence of J. S. Bach 5:39
influence of folk-music on 6-63
influence of Hummel 6:62
influence of Liszt 6:90
in Leipzig 6:66
leaves Poland 6:64
letters:
  from Edinburgh 6:68
  to friends 6:61
  on Liszt playing the Etudes 6:71
  about Paris 6:*78*, 83
lifestyle in Paris 6:82
love life:
  and Delfina Potocka 6:65
  and George Sand 6:66-8, 81
  and Konstancia Gladkowska
    6:64
  and Maria Wodzinska 6:66
in Majorca 6:67
Mendelssohn and 8:38, 48
musical associates in Paris 6:65
and national identity 6:61
at Nohants 6:67
and opera 6:63
  on *Robert le diable* 6:78
and Paris salons 6:81-2
as performer/composer 6:70-71
  as concert virtuoso 6:82
on personalities in Paris 6:78
and pianists in Paris 6:80
as piano teacher 6:65
on playing of Scottish ladies
    6:68-9
and Polish revolt 6:65
professional début 6:63
public performances 6:65
  first 6:63, *63*
  number of 6:61
  on playing in public 6:65-6
  as a student 6:63
and publication of works 6:63
pupils 6:68
  attracting 6:82
  help from in last years 6:61
  in Paris 6:65

reputation:
  as pianist 6:61
  in Poland 6:64
and Romantic movement 6:65; 9:21
and the Rothschilds 6:65
'Salon pieces' 6:70
by Scheffer 6:*70*
and Schumann 6:66
  criticism from 8:101
  promotes Chopin's music 8:87
and singing 6:71
soirées 6:81
in Stuttgart 6:65
style of piano playing 6:71
temperament 6:82
on Thalberg 6:108
works:
  influences on 6:71
  played at professional début 6:63
  playing technique of études 6:71
  range of 6:70
  for solo piano 6:70ff
  written on Majorca 6:67
  written in Paris 6:65
  written in Vienna 6:64
  Andante spianato 6:65
  Fantasy-Impromptu in C sharp minor
    6:76
  Impromptu in F sharp 6:67
  improvisation on Polish song 6:63
  Krakowiak op. 14 6:63
  Rondo in C minor, op. 1 6:63
Ballades
  no. 1 in G minor op. 23 6:65, 72-3
Concertos
  no. 1 6:64
  no. 2 in F minor 6:64, 67, 77
    inspiration for slow movement 6:64
    Paris première 6:65
Etudes 6:77
  influences on 6:71
  playing techniques 6:71
  in C minor op. 10 no. 2 6:75-6
  in E major op. 10 no. 3 6:73
  op. 10 no. 12 'Revolutionary' 6:65
    Dreyshock and 6:109
  in G flat major op. 26 no. 9 6:65, 73
Mazurkas
  composed in Vienna 6:64
  emotion in 6:71
  first 6:63
  op. 67 no. 2 6:69
  op. 68 no. 4 6:69
Nocturnes
  style elements in 6:71
  in E flat major op. 9 no. 2 6:93
  no. 5 in F sharp minor op. 15 no. 2
    6:76
Preludes
  completion of 6:67
Scherzos
  Scherzo no. 1 in B minor 6:64, 74
  Scherzo in C sharp minor 6:67
Sonatas
  first mature 6:67
  Piano:
    no. 2 in B flat minor op. 35 6:67, 77
    in B minor G178 6:103
Variations
  on *Là ci darem* 6:63, 65
  op. 2 6:63

Composer	Volume
Albinoni	4
Bach	5
Beethoven	2
Berlioz	8
Brahms	7
Chopin	6
Corelli	4
Handel	4
Haydn	5
Liszt	6
Mahler	7
Mendelssohn	8
Mozart	1
Pachelbel	4
Purcell	4
Rameau	4
Schubert	6
Schumann	8
Tchaikovsky	3
Telemann	4
Vivaldi	4

Waltzes
  composed in Vienna 6:64
  Grande Valse Brillante no. 1 in E flat
    major op. 18 6:64, 74
  no. 6 in D flat major op. 64 no. 1 74-5
  no. 7 in C sharp minor op. 64 no. 2
    6:74-5
  op. 64 no. 1 'Minute', dedication of
    6:65
CLEMENTI, Muzio (1752-1832) 1:12; 6:110
  and J. S. Bach's music 8:55
  and Beethoven's Violin Concerto 2:60,
    61
  and Mozart 1:12, 30
  Sonatas
    Violin 2:60
COPLAND, Aaron (b. 1900)
  and film music 7:101
  The Heiress 7:101
CORELLI, Arcangelo (1653-1713) 4:7,
    12, *12*
  appointment with Cardinal Pamphili
    4:12
  and Arcadian Academy 4:12
  dedications:
    of first 12 trio sonatas 4:12
    to Queen Christina of Sweden 4:12
  and development of tonal language 4:47
    family 4:12
  patronage of 4:12
  and Purcell's music 4:14
  in Rome 4:12
  sonatas 1:58
  studies the violin 4:12
    virtuosity with 4:12, 47
  works:
    scope of 4:12
  Concertos 4:47
    influence on form of 5:29-30
    Concerti Grossi 4:12
    12 Concerti Grossi op. 6 4:22
    No. 8 4:15, 19-20
    Pastorale manuscript 4:*20*
  Sonatas
    sonate a tre op. 1-4 4:47, 5:33
    dedications of first 12 sonatas 4:12

Arcangelo Corelli

Orchestral 4:47
Violin 4:47
   12 for violin and continuo op. 5
   4:22
COUPERIN, François (1668-1733) 1:97;
   4:110
   Schumann and 8:101
CZERNY, Carl (1791-1857) 2:21, 40; 6:*88*
   and Beethoven 2:17; 6:*88*
      Piano Concerto No. 5 2:50
      Sonata in F minor op. 57 2:*47*
      Symphony No. 5 2:66
      writing Violin Concerto 2:60
   and Liszt's early training 6:88, 89
   works:
      Concertstücke 6:108

D

DARGOMIZHKY, Alexander (1813-69)
   and role of Russian vocals 10:42
   Operas
      Rusalka 10:41
      The Stone Guest 10:42
DEBUSSY, Claude (1862-1918) 3:*35*
   and chamber music 1:59
   influence on Puccini 10:50
   influence of Wagner on 10:49
      breaks with Wagnerian tradition
         10:49
   Mme von Meck and 3:10, *35*
   and whole-tone scale 1:52
   works:
      breaks with operatic tradition 10:49
      naming 3:62
   Operas
      Pelléas et Mélisande 10:49
      structure of 10:49
   Symphonic poems
      Prélude à l'après-midi d'un Faune
         6:100
DELIBES, Clément
   and music for dance/drama 3:44
   and the Opéra-Comique 10:34

Ballets
   Coppélia 3:44, 102
      costume design for 3:*101*
   Sylvia 3:40, 120
      title page 3:*44*
Concert suites
   Sylvia 3:40
DONIZETTI, Gaetano (1797-1848) 6:110
   and *bel canto* 10:40
   influence on opéra comique 10:53
   as successor to Rossini 10:22
   works:
      number of operas written 10:40
      for opera buffa 10:40
      for specific performers 10:39
   Operas
      essence of 10:39
      style of 10:40
      The Daughter of the Regiment 10:40
      Don Pasquale 10:40, 81
      Love Potion 10:40
      Lucia di Lammamoor 10:40, 81
      plot 10:39
DOWLAND, John (1563-1626) 4:22
DVOŘÁK, Antonín (1841-1904) 9:22
   attitude to operetta 10:54
   Brahms and 7:13
   and composing:
      guide for overtures 8:60
   influence of Beethoven 2:39
   influence of personality on works 9:22
   and naming works 3:61
   Tchaikovsky and 3:13
   Symphonic poems
      Slavonic Dances 6:100
   Symphonies
      No. 9 'New World':
         original numbering 3:62

E

ELGAR, Edward (1857-1934)
   influence of folk music on 9:33
   Concertos
      Violin 2:64
   Oratorios
      The Dream of Gerontius 4:80

F

FALLA, Manuel de (1876-1946)
   and Diaghilev 3:44
FAURÉ, Gabriel (1845-1924)
   and chamber music 1:59
   Tchaikovsky and 3:13
FIELD, John (1782-1837) 6:110
   and Bach's music 8:55
   tour of Europe 8:55
   Nocturnes 6:71
FROBERGER, Johann Jacob (1616-67)
   and use of dances in suites 5:49
FUX, Johann (1660-1741) 5:110

G

GABRIELI, Giovanni (1557-1612) 5:38
   influence on Baroque music 4:47
   and instrumental music 4:29

Sonatas
   for wind instruments 4:20
GASSMANN, Florian Leopold (1729-74)
   1:46
GAY, John (1685-1732) 4:62, 69
   Operas
      The Beggar's Opera 4:*70-71, 72, 98-9;*
         10-*45*
      German adaptation of 10:29
      librettist 10:29
      success of 10:46
GIARDINI, Felice de (1716-96) 5:110
GLINKA, Mikhail (1804-57) 9:*27;* 10:42
   and composing:
      influence of *bel canto* 10:42
      influence of folk music 10:42
      influence of The Mighty Handful
         10:42
   in Italy 10:42
   musical background 10:42
   musical training 10:42
   and Nationalism 9:22
      founds Nationalist school
         10:42
   Tchaikovsky and 3:51
   works:
      on *Ivan Susanin* 10:42
   Operas
      Ivan Susanin 10:42
      setting for 10:*42*
      A Life for the Tsar 3:38; 9:*27*
      Ruslan and Lyudmila 10:42
   Overtures
      Spanish Overtures 3:51
GLUCK, Christoph Willibald (1714-87)
   1:11, 46; 2:*34;* 4:22; 10:*25*
   death of 1:15
   and music for dance/drama 3:44
   and opera reform 10:*25,* 26
   and *opera seria* 1:41
   and the operatic overture 2:35-6
   and Piccini 1:28
   and simplicity of composition 10:*25*
   works:
      in the French Style 10:26
      use of castrati in 10:26
   Operas
      Berlioz and 8:9
      styles of 4:22
      Alceste 4:22
      Iphigenie en Tauride 5:19
      Orfeo ed Euridice 4:22; 10:26
      librettist 10:26
GOUNOD, Charles (1818-93)
   fate of operettas 10:53
   Tchaikovsky and 3:13
GRÉTRY, André (1741-1813)
   and opéra comique 10:26, *26*
   greatest success 10:26
   Operas
      Richard Coeur de Lion 10:26
GRIEG, Edvard (1843-1907) 3:36
   honorary doctorate from Cambridge
      University 3:59
   on Mozart's last symphony 1:64
   Tchaikovsky and 3:13
   Concertos
      Piano 3:66
   Suites
      Holberg Suite 5:49
      'Peer Gynt' 5:49

Royal College of Music

H

HANDEL, George Frideric 4:14, *14, 59,*
  60ff, 65, 69; 9:*11*
  admirers of 9:9
  aged 22 4:*61*
  in Aix-la-Chapelle 4:64
  career in London 4:63-4
  and Chapel Royal 4:64
  commission from George II, King of
    England 4:64
  composing:
    adopts Italian style 10:28
    at the popular level 9:9
    routine in London 4:62
    use of instruments 9:9
    use of the flute 1:61-2
  concerts:
    in Foundling Hospital 4:77, *77*
    of oratorios 4:65
    for Queen Anne 4:61
  and conducting 4:61-2
  contract with Heidegger 4:64
  and copyright of works 4:*62*
  copyist/secretary to 4:63
  on Corelli 4:12
  dedications:
    to Earl of Burlington 4:62
    of *Teseo* 4:62
  description of 4:60
  in Dresden 4:63
  in Dublin 4:65
    Messiah in 4:76-7
  and Earl of Caernarvon 4:70
  early life 4:60
  early music studies 4:60
  failure of 'English' works 4:65
  first post 4:60

George Frideric Handel

Archiv für Kunst und Geschichte

  friends/friendships:
    advice from 4:72-3
    and Heidegger 4:69
    and Telemann 4:60

  at Halle University 4:60
  in Hamburg 4:60
  in Hanover 4:61, 62
    conditions for taking the post 4:61
  and honorary doctorate from Oxford
    University 4:64
  illnesses 4:64, 66
  important contacts in Italy 4:61
  influence of cantata form on 4:80
  influence of Cardinal Ottoboni on
    4:12, 38
  influence on form of opera 4:68
  influence of Italian music on 10:46
  instrument combination 4:20
  interest in oratorios 4:65
    organizes season of 4:65-6
  and Italian operatic style 4:61
  and King's Theatre 4:73
  letters:
    to Charles Frederick 4:84
    to Duke of Montague 4:84
    to Jennens 4:65, 77
  in London 4:62, 65-6
    first visit to 4:61-2
  and London as operatic centre 10:46
  monument to 4:66
  music for Peace of Utrecht (1713) 4:62
  music for Treaty of Aix-la-Chapelle
    (1748) 4:66
  and occasional music 4:87
  and *opera seria* style 10:46
  in Oxford 4:64
  pupils 4:*72-3*
  and recruitment of singers 4:70, 72
  as resident composer 4:63
  rivalry with Bononcini 4:71
  in Rome 4:61
  and Royal Academy of Music 4:63, 70-71
  salary:
    in London 4:64
    from Royal family 4:64
    at King's Theatre 4:72
  and Scarlatti 4:*69*
  Schumann and 8:101
  and success of *Messiah* 4:65
  tastes of his 'public' 4:65
  travels:
    last journey to Europe 4:66
    see also individual countries, cities,
      towns ·
  'truancy' 4:62-3
  in Tunbridge Wells 4:66
  in Venice 4:61
    opera performed in 4:69
  works:
    for Ruspoli 4:61
  Hercules 4:66
  Il trionfo del tempo e del disinganno
    4:12
  Semele 4:66
  Anthems
    Zadok the Priest 4:64, 87
  Arias
    use of Italian in 10:28
    'I know that my redeemer liveth' 4:77
    'Let the Bright Seraphim' 4:87
    Silent Worship 4:72
  Church music
    Dixit Dominus 3:61
    Jubilate 4:62
    Te Deum 4:62

VOLUME 1
  Mozart

VOLUME 2
  Beethoven

VOLUME 3
  Tchaikovsky

VOLUME 4
  Albinoni, Corelli, Handel,
  Pachelbel, Purcell, Rameau,
  Telemann, Vivaldi

VOLUME 5
  Bach, Haydn

VOLUME 6
  Chopin, Liszt, Schubert

VOLUME 7
  Brahms, Mahler

VOLUME 8
  Berlioz, Mendelssohn, Schumann

VOLUME 9
  A Guide to Classical Music

VOLUME 10
  A Beginner's Guide to the Opera

  Concertos
    Concerti Grossi op. 6 4:91
  Organ 4:65
    Concerti op. 4 4:91
    Twelve Grand Concertos for Strings
      op. 6 4:65
  Odes
    L'Allegro, il Penseroso ed il Moderato,
      libretto for 4:91
  Operas 4:67ff
    change in style of 4:72
    declining popularity of 4:73
    18th-century reception of 4:15
    for London 4:62
      first 4:61, *64*
      for King's Theatre 4:72
    Italian-style 4:62
    last two 4:75
      failure of 4:65
    restructuring 4:73
    for Royal Academy of Music 4:71
    written in Italy 4:69
  Admeto 4:71
  Agrippina 4:69
    reception in Venice 4:61
  Alcina 4:64, 73, *73*
  Alessandro 4:71
  Almira 4:60
  Ariodante 4:64
  Daphne 4:60
  Deidamia 4:75
  Ezio 4:72
  Florindo 4:60
  Giulio Cesare in Egitto 4:71
    librettist 4:71
  Il pastor fido 4:62, 69
  Imeneo 4:75

Lothario 4:72
Orlando 4:73
Ottone, Cuzzoni and 4:71
Partenope 4:72
Poro 4:72
Radamisto 4:71
  libretto for 4:71
Rinaldo 4:61, *64,* 72
  first performance of 4:69
  librettist 4:69
  method of conducting 4:61-2
  Sallé and 4:73
  scenario for 4:*64*
Rodelinda 4:71, 72
  librettist 4:71
Roderigo 4:69
Serse 4:83
Siroe 4:72
  title page 4:*72*
Sosarme 4:72
Tamerlano 4:71
  librettist 4:71
Teseo 4:62, 69-70
  libretto for 4:70
Tolomeo 4:70
Handel/Bononcini:
Operas
  Muzio Scevola 4:71
Oratorios
  differences in performances 4:78
  in Dublin 4:65
  first 4:61
  in London 4:65-6
    first in 4:*80*
  occasional 4:66
  reception of 4:66
  Athlaia 4:64
  Belshazzar 4:66
    librettist 4:75
  Deborah 4:73
  Esther 4:63, 72, *80*
  Israel in Egypt 3:19; 4:65
  Jeptha 4:66, 80, 83
  Judas Maccabaeus 4:66
  Messiah 1:20; 4:21; 65, 73, 75-82
    cast at first performance 4:76-7
    librettist 4:75-6
    original score 4:*76*
    popularity in Dublin 4:65
    popularity in London 4:66, 77
  La Resurrezione 4:61
  Samson 4:65, 76
    inspiration for 4:65
  Saul 4:65, 83
    librettist 4:75
  Solomon 4:66
    title page 4:*21*
    Sinfonia from Act III 4:21
  Susanna 4:66
  Theodora 4:66
Serenades
  Acis and Galatea 4:63
Sonatas 1:58
  trio 5:33
Suites
  Music for the Royal Fireworks 4:21, 66, 84-6; 9:9
  Suites de Pièces pour le Claverin, title page 4:*62*
Water Music 4:21, 63, 84, 88-91

HAYDN, Joseph (1732-1809) 1:45; 2:*10;* 5:*87, 95;* 9:*10*
appointments:
  first court 5:89
  first permanent 5:89
  from Porpora 5:89
and Beethoven 2:9, 17, 46; 5:92
  composition lessons with 2:27
and chamber music 1:58
Chopin and 6:62
and Classical style 1:77

Archiv für Kunst und Geschichte

Joseph Haydn

commissions from Paris music society 5:99
and composing:
  character of music 6:7
  development of formula for 5:95
  experiments with instrumental combinations 5:95
  development of orchestral writing 2:36
  'monothematic' movements 1:77
  and special effects 5:95
  and symphonic development 2:67
  and the symphony 1:64; 5:99
  turning point in musical development 5:90
  use of orchestration 6:*23*
  and variation form 2:54
concerts:
  in London 5:91-2
  in Vienna 5:*92-3, 93*
death of 5:93
death of patron 5:91
dedication from Mozart 1:72
and development of the orchestra 5:99
made Doctor of Music at Oxford University 5:92
on *Don Giovanni* 1:44
early life 5:88
Entwurf-Katalog 5:93
finances:
  fees for copyright 5:91
  fees from Salomon 5:91
  pension from Prince Esterhazy 5:91
  salary as *Kapellmeister* 5:89

on Franck 5:88
and Freemasons 1:35, 43; 5:91
friendships:
  with Polzelli 5:89, 90-91
  with von Genzinger 5:89, 92-3
  with Mozart 1:12-13, 15, *42, 43;* 5:91
at Eszterhaza:
  isolation of 5:90
  as *Kapellmeister* 5:89, 90, 93
  opera performances at 5:90
in London 5:91-2
  on life in London 5:92
  symphonies for 5:99
marriage 5:89, 93
on Mozart 1:13, 30
and musical gatherings 5:*89*
musical sources 1:49-50
name book given to Liszt 6:88
and Napoleonic Wars 5:93
new contract with Prince Esterhazy 5:90
and novel sound-effects 3:55
and orchestra development 4:20
and Porpora 4:4
publishes music 5:90
puts affairs in order 5:93
as rival attraction to Playel 5:92
and Salomon 5:99
Schubert and 6:18
singing ability 5:88, *88*
Sturm und Drang period 5:99
in Vienna 5:88, 91, 92-3
  concert in Old University 5:*92-3*
  honours from Vienna 5:99
  lodgings 5:89
  mature years in 5:93
  purchases house in 5:93
at Vivaldi's funeral 4:40
and women 5:89
works:
  catalogue of 1:67
  length of 2:37
  written at Eszterhaza 5:90, 91
  naming 5:99
Church music
  Salve Regina in E major 5:89
Concertos
  Cello, in D 5:101
Masses
  for Princess Hermenegild 5:93, *93*
  style for 5:42
Operas
  fee from Salomon for 5:91
  occasions written for 5:90
  written for Eszterhaza 5:90
  L'incontro inproviso 5:91
Oratorios
  The Creation 5:*92-3,* 101
    librettist 5:93
    private performance of 5:93
  The Seasons 5:93
    librettist 5:93
Quartets
  early 5:89
  op. 54 5:55, 64, 91
  String 1:58
    first 5:89
    surprises in 1:77
    op. 76 no. 1-6 5:101
Symphonies
  early 5:89
  fee from Salomon for 5:91

first 5:89
nicknames for 3:62
number written 2:67; 5:99
   for London 5:95
numbering of 5:99
of 'Sturm und Drang' period 5:99
'Toy' 3:55
No. 2 in E flat 'Philosopher' 3:62
No. 6 Le Matin 5:99
No. 7 Le Midi 5:99
No. 8 Le Soir 5:99
No. 31 'Hornsignal' 5:99
No. 45 in F sharp minor 'Farewell'
   3:62; 5:99
No. 49 'La Passione' 5:99
No. 55 'Schoolmaster' 5:*99*
'London':
   No. 94 in G 'Surprise' 5:95-6, 99
      reviews of 5:95
      variations 2:54
   No. 96 'Miracle' 5:99
   No. 101 'The Clock' 5:96-100
   No. 103 the 'Drum Roll' 5:99
'Paris':
   No. 82 in C 'Bear' 3:62, 5:99
   No. 83 in G minor 'Hen' 3:62, 5:99
   No. 85 'The Queen' 5:99
HAYDN, Michael (1737-1806) 1:40; 5:110
HENZE, Hans Werner (b.1926)
  and contemporary German opera 10:52
  Operas
   The Bassarids 10:52
   We Come to a River 10:52
   The Young Lord 10:52
HOLST, Gustav (1874-1934)
  influence of folk music on 9:33
HONNEGER, Arthur (1892-1955)
  and novel sound-effects 3:55
HUMMEL, Johann (1778-1837) 2:40
  and Beethoven 2:20
   at his funeral 2:15
  Chopin and 6:62

J

JANÁČEK, Leos (1854-1928)
  success of works 10:51-2
  Operas
   The House of the Dead 10:51
   Jenufa 10:51
   Katia Kabanova 10:51
   The Macropulus Case 10:51

K

KODÁLY, Zoltán (1882-1967)
  and Church music 5:42
  and gypsy music 7:35
KUHNAU, Joseph (1660-1722)
  Bible Pieces, as programme music 8:17
  and Telemann 4:10

L

LEHÁR, Franz (1870-1948)
  attitude to operetta 10:54-5
  collaboration with Tauber 10:55
  re-use of material 10:53

Composer	Volume
Albinoni	4
Bach	5
Beethoven	2
Berlioz	8
Brahms	7
Chopin	6
Corelli	4
Handel	4
Haydn	5
Liszt	6
Mahler	7
Mendelssohn	8
Mozart	1
Pachelbel	4
Purcell	4
Rameau	4
Schubert	6
Schumann	8
Tchaikovsky	3
Telemann	4
Vivaldi	4

  Operettas
   Frederica 10:81
   Das Land des Lachelns 10:81
   The Merry Widow 10:54, 81
     worldwide appeal of 10:55
LEONCAVELLO, Ruggero (1857-1919)
  and light opera 10:33
  verismo operas 10:34
  Operas
   I Pagliacci 10:40, 82
LESUEUR, Jean-François (1760-1837) 8:110
  Berlioz as pupil of 8:9
LISZT, Franz (1811-86) 2:*36*, 62; 6:*61, 71,*
  87, 89, 96, 105; 9:*17*
  aged sixteen 6:*88*
  at Bayreuth 6:*94-5,* 95
  and Beethoven 2:*36*
   and importance of 7:24-5
   and monument to 6:91
   presented to 6:88
  and Berlioz 8:8
  books about 6:91-2, 95
  and Brahms 7:8-9, 23
   plays Scherzo in E flat minor 7:8-9
   plays sonata 7:9
  breaking pianos 6:74
  caricature 7:*24*
  cataleptic fits 6:90
  change in career 6:93
  Chopin and 6:65, 71, *71,* 78
   and études 6:65
  and composition 6:90, 93
  and composing:
   attitudes to work 6:96
   development of the 'symphonic
     poem' 9:20
   and display element of music 6:98
   ideas on concertos 6:98
    opening of First 6:96
   influence of Sayn-Wittgenstein 6:93
   inspiration for symphonic poems
     6:100
   musical maturity 6:93
   and 'thematic transformation' 6:98
   use of repeated motifs 6:98
  concert tours 6-89

  concerts 6:*107*
   audience behaviour at 6:91
   Beethoven at 6:88
   in Budapest 6:89
   clique of followers at 7:28
   in Hungary 6:*92*
   in Paris 6:89, 91
   showdown with Thalberg 6:108
   in Vienna 6:88-9, 91
  and conducting 6:96
  'death' of 6:90
  dedications:
   to Litolff 6:98
   of Piano Concerto no. 1 6:98
  effect of Paris revolt on 6:90
  effect of piano playing on audience
   6:104, *104-105*
  influence on later pianists 6:109
  family life 6:90
   children 6:90, 91, 93
  finances:
   fortune from concerts 6:91
   stipend for studies 6:88
  first public appearance 6:88
  followers 7:28
  in France 6:89
  on his 'homeland' 6:90
  in Hungary 6:91, *92*
  and Hungarian gypsies 6:88, 91
   music of 7:35
  and Hungarian national conservatory
   6:*92*
  influence of J. S. Bach 5:39
  influence of Berlioz on 6:90, 96
  influence of Chopin on 6:90
  influence of Litolff on 6:98
  influence of Paganini on 6:90, 96
  in Ireland 6:89
  in Italy 6:90
  letters:
   to Hiller 6:65

Franz Liszt

BBC Hulton Picture Library

   from Marie d'Agoult 6:91
   on Thalberg 6:108
  lifestyle and musical convention
   7:27

love affairs 6:91
  and Carolyne de Saint-Cricq 6:90
  and Carolyne Sayn-Wittgenstein 6:92-3
  emotional crisis over 6:90
  and Marie d'Agoult 6:90, 91-2
  and Olga Janina 6:95
  first 6:89-90
'marriage' 6:93
and 'New Music' 7:23, 25
in old age 6:95
'old school' reaction to 7:24
and Paris Conservatoire 6:89
on Paris salon society 6:89
performances of *Galop Chromatique* 6:92
performs for Prince Esterhazy 6:88
piano playing:
  for friends 7:26
  playing technique 6:71
  virtuosity 6:88, 89-90, 96
present from Erard 6:89
and 'programme music' 8:17
promotion of modern music 7:27-8
pupils 6:90
  favourite 6:90
reaction to piano playing 6:91
regime in later life 6:95
on 'rejuvenating' music 6:100
and religion 6:89, 93-5
  effect on music 6:94
  takes minor orders 6:93
in Rome 6:93
royal command performance 6:89
on Schumann 7:24
  and his operas 7:27-8
sex appeal 6:91
showdown with Thalberg 6:108
'showmanship' 6:109; 7:24
strain of early career 6:89
successes:
  with concerts 6:91
  success in Paris 6:89
  social 6:91
in Switzerland 6:90
teaching 6:90, 93
  advice to Rubinstein 6:109
  Weimar masterclasses 6:109
'three-cornered existence' 6:95
travel:
  devotees with 7:28
  tours in Europe 6:91
and virtuoso playing 2:72; 6:71
vocation 6:90
on von Bülow 7:29
and Wagner 6:93, 95
in Weimar 6:93
  hostility in 7:27
  post in 6:93; 7:23
in Woronince 6:93
works:
  reception of sacred music 6:94, *95*
  Années de pèlerinage 6:90, *90-91*
  Hungarian Rhapsodies G359 6:103
  inspiration for 6:*88-9*
  Rigoletto Paraphrase G434 6:103
  Symphonische Dichtung 6:100
Concertos 6:96
  Piano:
    prototypes for 6:96
    no. 1 in E flat major 6:98-100
      première of 6:96

    no. 2 in A major 6:101-102
      première 6:96
      orchestral score 6:*98*
  Sonatas
    Piano:
      in B minor 7:9
  Symphonic poems
    effect on music development 6:100
    Ce qu'on entend sur la montagne 6:100
    Die Ideale 6:100
    Hunneschlacht 6:100
LULLY, Jean-Baptiste (1632-87) 1:97; 4:110; 5:46, *46*; 10:16, *16*, 18
  and Académie Royale de Musique 10:18
  in *Ballet de la Nuit* 10:16
  changes outlook on composition 10:18
  commissions for ballets 10:18
  death of 10:18
  and French/Italian taste 10:18
  and music for dance/drama 3:44
  and opera-ballets 3:98
  partnership with Molière 10:18
  posts:
    Master of the King's Music 10:18
    with Mlle de Montpensier 10:16
  talents 10:16, 18
  treatment of rivals 10:18
  use of the orchestra 4:20
  Operas
    name for 10:18
    Cadmus et Hermione 10:18
  Overtures 5:46, *46*

M

MACDOWELL, Edward (1861-1908) 7:110
MACHANT, Guillaume de (c. 1300-77) 5:42
MAHLER, Gustav (1860-1911) 7:*29, 87, 93*; 9:*17*
  aged six 7:*88*
  becomes increasingly reclusive 7:93
  and Brahms 7:90
  caricatures of 7:*92*, 97
  changes religion 7:92
  commission from Baron von Weber 7:88-9
  and conducting 7:*94*
  criticism of innovative methods 7:90, 92, 97
  crucial period for 7:88
  and composing:
    'arrival' 7:94
    a creative period 7:93-4
    ideas on the compass of 7:97
    orchestral colouring 7:97
    reputation 7:91
    slowness of 7:91
    types of passages in 7:97
    and experiences of everyday life 7:97
    use of folk tunes 7:97
    use of the orchestra 7:97
    use of the orchestra in Lieder 6:29
    use of percussion 7:*92*, 97
    use of vocal movements 7:97
    'world' of symphonies 7:97
  concerts, conducts last 7:95

Gustav Mahler

Österreichische Nationalbibliothek

  and conducting:
    criticism of 7:89, 90
    time left for composing 7:97
  and cow-bells 7:97
  death of 7:95
  début 7:88
  declining years 7:94-5
  dedications:
    of Symphony no. 10 7:95
    to his wife 7:95
  early life 7:88
  education 7:88
  effect of *Familiengesetz* on 7:88
  effects of family deaths on 7:89-90
  emotional upheavals 7:91-2
  family 7:88
    birth of second child 7:94
    care of his sister 7:93
    first child 7:93, *93*
  finances, support from his family 7:88
  friends/friendships:
    introduced by his wife 7:93
    and Mengelberg 7:90
    and Richard Strauss 7:91
    and von Bülow 7:90
  health:
    analysis with Freud 7:95, *95*
    depression 7:88
    effect of criticism on 7:92-3
    effects of family tragedies on 7:94
    failing 7:95
    heart disease diagnosed 7:94
  influence of Wagner 1:52
  in Kassel 7:88
  and Klimt 7:109
  literary background 7:97
    love of poetry 7:97
  love life:
    and Alma Schindler 7:93
    and Anna von Mildenburg 7:91
    and Baroness von Weber 7:89
    and Joanna Richter 7:88
    and Natalie Bauer-Lechner 7:90, *90*
  and love of nature 7:97-8
  marriage 7:93
    reconciliation with wife 7:95
    regime imposed on 7:93

and 'New Music' controversy 7:*29*
in New York 7:94-5
and novel sound-effects 3:55
and 150th anniversary of Mozart's birth
   7:94
popularity of music 7:98
posts:
   first with an opera company 7:88
   with Royal Budapest Opera 7:89, 90
   with Hamburg Opera 7:90
   with Imperial Vienna Opera 7:91,
      92-3, 94
   in Laibach 7:88
   in Leipzig 7:88-9, *89*
   with Metropolitan Opera 7:94
   at Stadttheater, Olmütz 7:88
in Prague 7:88
regime in Vienna 7:93
and Secession 7:109
start of career 7:88-90
summer retreat 7:92, 93
and Tchaikovsky 7:90-91
   and première of *Onegin* 7:91
training at the Vienna Conservatory 7:88
triumph of first Viennese season 7:92-3
and uncut Wagner operas 7:92
and the understanding of man 7:97
use of music in films 7:*99*, 101
world view of a composer 7:97
works:
   completes work of Weber 7:88-9
   early criticism of 7:89
   first mature 7:88
   first song 7:88
Lieder
   sources of texts 6:29
   Kindertötenlieder 6:29; 7:93-4
   Der Klagende Lied 7:88
   Des Knaben Wunderhorn 6:29, *29*
   Lieden eines fahrenden Gesellen 7:88
   Rückert-Lieder 7:93, 103
Operas
   Die drei Pintos 7:88-9
Symphonies 7:97ff
   and development of 7:98
   'musical madness' 7:93
   structure of 7:97
   Das Lied von der Erde, 7:95
      ideas behind 7:97
   No. 1 in D major 'The Titan' 7:103
      finishes 7:89-90
      title page 7:*90*
      Viennese reception of 7:92
   No. 2 7:91, 103
   No. 3 in D minor 'A Summer
      Morning's Dream' 7:102-103
      Walter on 7:97-8
   No. 4 7:92
      premières 7:93
      revises 7:93
   No. 5 in C sharp minor 7:98-9
      writes two movements of 7:93
   No. 6 7:93
      novel sound-effects in 3:55; 7:*92*
   No. 7 in E minor 'Song of the Night'
      7:97, 100-101
   No. 9 in D 7:95, 103
   No. 10 7:95
      manuscript for 7:*95*
MASCAGNI, Pietro (1863-1945)
   influence of Wagner 10:50

verismo opera 10:34
Operas
   Cavalleria Rusticana 10:40, 49, 82
      Zeffirelli and 10:52
MASSENET, Jules (1842-1912)
   fate of operettas 10:53
   and the Opéra-Comique 10:34
   première of works 10:34
   Tchaikovsky and 3:13
Operas
   Thaïs, use of *Elégie* in films 7:101
MENDELSSOHN, Felix (1809-47) 8:*49,*
   52; 9:*16*
academic studies
   awarded university place 8:36
   at Berlin University 8:36, 37, 83
   and Terence's *Andria* 8:36, 83
   and university entrance 8:83
advice from his father 8:41
aged twelve 8:*34*
aged twenty 8:*33*
as artist 8:35
   Birmingham 8:*38*
   view of Lucerne 8:*36*
and Bach revival 5:12, 39; 8:55
   St Matthew Passion 8:*36,* 37, 55
and Beethoven 8:35
   plays Piano Concerto 8:77
   and symphonies 8:38
   and Violin Concerto 2:60
in Berlin:
   as musical director 8:39
and Birmingham Music Festival 8:*38,* 39
and British folk music 8:37
broadens his outlook 8:41
and Cerubini 8:36
and Chopin 6:63, 65, 66; 8:38, 48

Felix Mendelssohn

The Illustrated London News

commissions in London 8:43
and composing:
   beginnings 8:34
   routine in Rome 8:47
on conditions in Florence 8:47
on conditions in Switzerland
   8:48

VOLUME 1
   Mozart

VOLUME 2
   Beethoven

VOLUME 3
   Tchaikovsky

VOLUME 4
   Albinoni, Corelli, Handel,
   Pachelbel, Purcell, Rameau,
   Telemann, Vivaldi

VOLUME 5
   Bach, Haydn

VOLUME 6
   Chopin, Liszt, Schubert

VOLUME 7
   Brahms, Mahler

VOLUME 8
   Berlioz, Mendelssohn, Schumann

VOLUME 9
   A Guide to Classical Music

VOLUME 10
   A Beginner's Guide to the Opera

and conducting:
   appointment in Leipzig 8:38, *39,* 48
   and Düsseldorf Music Festival 8:38
   St Matthew Passion 8:36, 37, 55
   in London 8:43
criticism of Berlioz 8:8
death of 8:33, 39
   obituary 8:*49*
   Queen Victoria and 8:*49*
dedications:
   of Scottish Symphony 8:76
   to Queen Victoria 8:76
and Dorothea von Ertmann 8:38
drawing of the Thomasschule 5:*10*
in Düsseldorf 8:38
early genius 8:33
in Edinburgh 8:*44, 44*
educational expectations 8:81-2
effect of Fanny's death on 8:39
in England 8:37, 38, 39, 76-7
   climax of visits 8:39, 48-9
   crossing to 8:42
family 8:33, 39
   friends of 8:34
favourite Paris theatre 6:81
finances:
   salary in Leipzig 8:38
in Florence 8:47
founds Leipzig Conservatory 8:39
friends 8:33
   Berlioz 8:10-11, 38, 47
   in London 8:42
   Moscheles 8:37,. 42
   in Rome 8:47
and Goethe 8:33, 34-5, *35*
   influence of Goethe on 8:61
   last visit to 8:38

influence of Schumann songs on 8:61
influence of Weber on 8:61-2
    as model for orchestration 8:62
and Handel revival 8:38
and Immerman 8:38
injuries 8:37
and Italy 8:38, 46-7
    ignorance of classical music in 8:47
    on irreverence of Italians 8:47
later achievements 8:38
in Leipzig:
    and cultural activity 8:109
    and Gewanhaus 8:38, *39*, 101
    repertoire in 8:38
letters:
    on daily routine 8:34
    to David about Violin Concerto
        8:52
    on Edinburgh 8:44
    on Goethe 8:34
    hand-drawn note 8:*42*
    on Italian beggars 8:*46*
    on London 8:37, 41, 42
    on Parisian music style 8:48
    on pianists in Paris 6:80-81
    to his sister 8:37
and Leipzig Conservatory 7:23, 25
and Liszt 8:38, 48
literary influences 8:61
    of Shakespeare 8:61
in London 8:37, *37*
    attachment to 8:37, 39, 41
    behaviour in 8:42-3
    début in 8:37
    greatest success in 8:44
    introduced to society 8:42
    lodgings 8:42
    number of visits to 8:41
    performances in 8:43
love of literature 8:34
marriage 8:38-9
and Meyerbeer 8:38, 48
misses Fanny's wedding 8:37, 45
in Munich 8:48
music studies 8:34
    principal tutor 8:34, *35*
musical influences on 8:61-2
in Naples 8:47-8
and 'New Music' 7:23
and Paganini 8:38, 48
in Paris 8:48, *49*
'phrensied' behaviour 8:42-3
and Piano Concerto in A minor
    (Schumann) 8:98
as performer:
        early 8:33
        playing before Goethe 8:*35*
        review of piano playing 8:37
posts:
        Director of Singakademie 8:38
        music director in Berlin 8:39
        offered chair of music at Berlin 8:37
relationship with his sister 8:37-8
        reliance on 8:37
and religion 8:10, 11
in Rome 8:46
    in apartment in 8:46-7
and Schubert's last symphony 8:38
short-lived happiness 8:38-9
and Sir George Smart 8:37
and Sir Thomas Attwood 8:45

and Sir Walter Scott 8:44-5
starts a newspaper 8:34
in Switzerland 8:48, *48*
    and countryside 8:*48*
    with family 8:35
and Symphony No. 1 in B flat major
    (Schumann) 8:94
and Taglioni 6:81
on Thalberg 6:108
and travel 8:38
    Grand Tour 8:41ff
    with Klingemann 8:37, 44ff
    passion for 8:35
    in Scotland 8:37, 44-5
in Venice 8:46
and Victoria and Albert 8:33, 39, 48-9,
    76, 76-7
    improvisations for 8:49, 77
    introduction to Prince Albert 8:49
    journal entry on 8:49
    popularity with 8:76-7
    Victoria sings song by 8:49
and *Walpurgisnacht* (Goethe) 8:47
on yodelling 8:35
works:
    for Birmingham Music Festival
        8:*38*, 39
    first fully mature 8:36
    first important 8:76
    inspiration for 8:41
    for liberation of the natives of Ceylon
        8:43
    operettas 8:62
    for parents' wedding anniversary
        8:39
    rejected by Paris Conservatoire 8:48
    showed to Fanny first 8:37
Concertos
    Piano:
        No. 1 in G minor 8:51
    Violin 8:52-4
        encouragement from David 8:52
Octets
    in E flat op. 20 8:67
    String:
        completes 8:36
        inspiration for 8:36
Operas
    The Uncle from Boston 8:35-6
Oratorios
    Elijah op. 70 8:39, 67
        first performance 8:*38*, 77
    St Paul 4:80
Overtures 8:60ff
    as symphonic poems 8:60
    Calm Sea and Prosperous Voyage
        op. 27 8:*41*, 67
    The Hebrides op. 26 'Fingal's Cave'
        8:62-3, 76
        inspiration for 8:37, 41, 45
    A Midsummer Night's Dream op. 21
        8:36, 66-7, 76
        influence of Weber on 8:62
        inspiration for 8:36
    Ruy Blas op. 95 8:63-5
    The Tale of the Fair Melusina op. 32
        8:65-6
Symphonies
    in C minor, conducts in London 8:43
    no. 3 in A minor 'Scottish' 8:44, 51
        inspiration for 8:37, 41

Composer	Volume
Albinoni	4
Bach	5
Beethoven	2
Berlioz	8
Brahms	7
Chopin	6
Corelli	4
Handel	4
Haydn	5
Liszt	6
Mahler	7
Mendelssohn	8
Mozart	1
Pachelbel	4
Purcell	4
Rameau	4
Schubert	6
Schumann	8
Tchaikovsky	3
Telemann	4
Vivaldi	4

    no. 4 in A major op. 90 'Italian' 8:56-9
        description of 8:47
        inspiration for 8:38, 41, 47
    no. 5 in D 'Reformation' 8:51
        begins to write 8:38
        rejection of 8:48
    Twelve String Symphonies op. posth.
        8:67
MENOTTI, Gian Carlo (b. 1911)
    success of works 10:52
    Operas
        Amahl and the Night Visitors 10:52
        The Consul 10:52
MESSIAEN, Olivier (b. 1908)
    and Church music 5:42
    and novel sound-effects 3:55
    Symphonies
        'Turangalîla' 3:55
MEYERBEER, Giacomo (1791-1864) 8:110;
    10:*32*
    and castrati voice 10:13
    Chopin and 6:67
    and Scribe 10:33
    Mendelssohn and 8:38, 48
    success in Paris 6:78
    Operas
        Il Crociato in Egitto 10:13
        Les Huguenots 6:81; 10:33
            librettist 10:33
            setting for 10:*33*
        Robert le Diable 6:78; 10:*32-3*, 33
            librettist 10:33
MONTEVERDI, Claudio (1567-1643) 10:*9*
    impact of early opera 10:9
    use of comic elements 10:19
    Church music
        Vespro della Beata Vergine 4:22
    Operas
        first 10:9
        influence of 4:47
        masterpiece 10:9
        La Favola d'Orfeo 4:20, 22, 47; 10:9
            first performance 10:9
            title page 10:*8*
        L'Incoronozione di Poppaea 4:22, 47;
            10:9

Li Ritorno d'Ulisse 4:22, 47; 10:9
Songs
Madrigals of Love and War 4:22
MOZART, Wolfgang Amadeus 1:*9, 14, 19, 23, 28, 33, 44;* 9:*11*
aged eleven 1:*72*
and Aloysia Weber 1:11
in Augsburg 1:11
and Baron Grimm 1:11
and Beethoven 2:9, 27, 67-8
bleeding 2:103
in Bologna 1:23
chamber works 1:15
character 1:18, 40-41
  of music 6:7
child prodigy 1:18ff
children 1:12, *13,* 64
  death of first 1:12
Chopin and 6:62
on Clementi 1:12
collaboration with Da Ponte 1:13, 14
and Colloredo 1:9-10
  dismissed by 1:26
  letters to 1:28
  rows with 1:41
commissions:
  for Archduke Ferdinand 1:23
  for carnival in Milan 1:23
  for Count Firmian 1:23
  for Duc de Guines 1:27, *60,* 61
  for Franz Ziegenhagen 1:38
  from Joseph II of Austria 10:30
  from Walsegg-Stuppach 1:15
competition with Clementi 1:12
concerts:
  amounts received for 1:30
  benefit-type 1:36
  freelance 1:30
  in England 1:20, *20-21*
  in Mannheim 1:26
  in Munich 1:18
  in Paris 1:20, 27
  subscription 1:*41,* 72
  in Vienna 1:18-19, 43; 5:91
and Constanze Weber 1:12, 30
dances 1:15
dancing, love of 1:51
death of 5:92
dedications:
  to Anton Stadler 1:36
  to Count-Archbishop of Salzburg 1:21
  to Haydn 1:30, 72; 5:91
  to Princess of Nassau-Weilburg 1:20
  to Princess Victoire 1:20, *21*
  to Puchberg 1:45
description, aged ten 1:21
and development of *opera buffa* 10:22
development of orchestral writing 2:36
and directing the orchestra 7:50
and Duc de Guines 1:27
early life 1:8
early musical ability 1:8, 9
education 1:9
effect of mother's death on 1:28, 41
enemies 1:43-5
in England:
  popularity in 46
  visit to cancelled 1:13
exhibition tours 1:9
  earliest 1:18

finances 1:13, 14, *14,* 30-31, *31*
  annuity from the Emperor 1:14
  debts at death 1:30
  effects of illnesses on 1:44
  lends to friends 1:36
first published compositions 1:20
in Florence 1:23
as freelance musician 1:25ff
  teaching 1:26, 29-30
friends 1:43
  circle diminishes 1:45
  deaths among 1:44
  Haydn 1:12-13; 5:91
  solo parts for 1:56
funeral 1:15
humanitarianism 1:39ff
illnesses 1:14-15, 20, 21, 31, 34, 44
improvisation 1:19
influence of J. C. Bach 1:20, 65; 5:12, 19
influence of *Commedia dell'Arte* 10:22
influence of Haydn 1:58
influence on Tchaikovsky 10:43
in Italy 1:9, 19, 22-3
as *Kammermusicus* 1:*26,* 30
  salary 1:30
as *Konzertmeister* 1:22, 26
by Lange 1:14, *25*
length of works 2:37
letter to Abbé Bullinger 1:*11*
letters to Puchberg 1:14
librettist 1:13
lifestyle 1:20-21
in London 1:20
looking for a position 1:26-7
love, views on 1:42
in Mannheim 1:11, 26
marriage 1:12, 30, *41,* 42
  contract 1:*13*
  views on 1:42
Masonic oration on death of 1:33
in Milan 1:23
in Munich 1:11, 18, *18,* 26
  concert tours 1:18
  opera for carnival in 1:*10*
  preview tour to 1:18
  success in 1:29
musical sources 1:49-50
and novel sound-effects 3:55
and occasional music 4:87
150th anniversary of birth of 7:94
operatic works 1:13-15
  and limitations on 1:26
  see also Operas
and orchestral development 4:20
orchestration for *Messiah* 1:20
and Order of the Golden Spur 1:23
in Paris 1:11, 19-20, 27, *27,* 60-61
  disillusioned with society in 1:41
and the piano:
  composing specifically for 6:74
  on his piano concertos 1:77
in Prague 1:13, 30, 43-4, *44*
pupils in Vienna 1:29-30, 43
in Rome 1:23
in Salzburg 1:29
  dismissal from 1:29
  as organist 1:11
  resignation from 1:11
  return to 1:22
  salary in 1:29
  working conditions 1:11

Schubert and 6:18, 33
  'compliment' to 6:*33*
scoring:
  of Clarinet Concerto K.622 1:57
  of Flute and Harp Concerto in C major K.299 1:61
  of Piano Concerto No. 21 in C K.467 1:74
  of Piano Concerto No. 22 1:78-9
  of Serenade in G major K.525 1:57
  of Symphony No. 40 in G minor 'Tragic' 1:66
  of Symphony No. 41 in C major 'Jupiter' 1:69
sight reading 1:19-20
social life 1:40
temperament 1:21
and Thomas Linley 1:23
treatment of opera characters 10:22

Gesellschaft der Musikfreude in Wein

Wolfgang Amadeus Mozart

use of music in films 7:101
and variation of form 2:54
at Versailles 1:98
and the Weber family 1:27
works:
  effect of music journals on 8:101
  sacred 1:19
  see also Cantatas; Oratorios; Masses
Arias
  for Nancy Storace 1:45
  Tchaikovsky and 3:23
Cantatas
  A Little Masonic Cantata 1:38
  Hymn to the Sun 1:36
  K.6129 1:38
  Masonic 1:33, 36, 38
  Masonic Joy 1:36, 37
    title page 1:*36*
Chamber music 1:15
  number of pieces 1:58
Concertos
  influence of J. C. Bach 5:19
  number of movements 1:72-3
  number written 3:72
  numbers remaining 1:72
  use of themes 3:72

Jeunehomme 1:10
Clarinet:
  K.622 1:56-60
    dedication 1:36
Clavier 1:43
Flute:
  in G major K.313 1:63
Flute and Harp 1:27
  K.299 1:56, 60-63
Piano 1:9
  contrast between K.467 and K.466
    1:74
  first remaining 1:72
  K.175 1:79
  C minor K.491 1:79
  D minor K.466 1:74
  E flat K.499 1:72
  No. 9 K.271 1:9, 79
  No. 20 K.466 1:79
  No. 21 1:72, 74-8
  No. 22 1:72, 78-9
  No. 27 K.595 1:79
Violin 1:9
  No. 5 in A K.219 1:55
Dances 1:15, 48ff
  number written 1:51
  themes for 1:51
  gavotte 1:61, 63
  Three German Dances K.605 1:51
    'Sleigh Ride' 3:55
Duets
  Piano 1:12
    in D 1:12
    'Haydn' 1:40
  String 1:40
    for violin and viola 1:40
Masses 1:9
  style of 5:42
  C minor 1:12
  Requiem in D minor K.626 1:15, 63
    Lacrymosa from 1:*15*
    played for Chopin's funeral 6:69
Operas
  for Count Firmain 1:23
  humour in 10:53
  for national theatre 1:41
  number written 10:22
  popularity of 10:30
  success with 1:23, 30
  written in Italy 1:22
  Ascanio in Alba 1:23
  Bastien und Bastienne 1:22, *29, 34*
    solos for Stadler in 1:56
  Cosí fan Tutte 1:14; 10:82
    gala conducted by Mahler 7:94
    origin of characters 10:22
    theme of 1:45
  Die Entführung aus dem Serail
    1:12, 41-2; 5:19; 10:30, 82
    title page 10:*30*
    translation of 10:30
  Die Zauberflöte 1:15, 35, 45; 10:27, 82
    Act II, scene 19 1:*15*
    central theme 1:40
    designs for 2:*22, 80-81, 83*
    Masonic influences 1:33, 37
    novel sound-effects in 3:55
    success of 1:31
  Don Giovanni 1:13-14, 15, 44; 10:82
    Casanova and 1:108
    origin of characters 10:22

  overture for 1:14, 44
  payment for 1:30
  success of 1:14
  Idomeneo 1:*10,* 11, 29; 10:82
    plot 1:41
    title page 1:*10*
  La Clemenza di Tito 1:15; 10:82
  La finta semplice 1:22
  Lucio Silla 1:23, *23;* 10:82
  Mitridate, Rè di Ponto 1:23
  Le Nozzi di Figaro 1:13, 71, 78; 10:19,
    22, 82
    comparisons with Symphony
      No. 41 1:69
    librettist 1:43; 10:22
    opposition to 1:43
    origin of characters 10:22
    success of 1:13
Quartets
  dedicated to Haydn 5:91
  Piano:
    K.478 1:65
  String:
    dedicated to Haydn 1:30, *42,* 72
    No. 19 in C K.465 'Dissonance' 1:55
    structure 1:58
Serenades 1:48ff
  for outdoor performance 4:87
  G major K.525 'Eine kleine
      Nachtmusik, 1:*48,* 48-51
    catalogue note 1:*50*
    manuscript 1:*48*
  No. 7 K.250 'Haffner' 1:55; 4:87
  F major K.522 'A Musical Joke' 1:51-5
    title 1:*53*
Sonatas
  first published keyboard 1:20
  Harpsichord and Violin:
    Opus 1 1:20
      title page 1:*21*
  Piano 1:12
  Violin:
    first published score 1:20
Songs
  Masonic 1:36, *36*
  Fellow Craft's Journey 1:36
  For the Closing of the Lodge 1:36
  For the Opening of the Lodge 1:36
Symphonies
  canon 1:64-5
  influence of J. C. Bach on 5:19
  C major K.338 1:71
  C major K.551 1:74
  G minor K.183 1:65
  K.16, structure of 1:65
  K.19, structure of 1:65
  Haffner 1:65
  Linz 1:65
  No. 29 in A major K.201 1:65
  No. 31, K.297 'Paris' 1:11, *27, 28,* 105
  No. 38 in D major 'Prague' 1:13, 64
  No. 39 in E flat major 1:64
  No. 40 in G minor K.550 'Tragic' 1:64,
    65-8, 74
    comparison with No. 5 (Beethoven)
      2:70
  No. 41 in C major 'Jupiter' 1:64, 68-71
Trios
  Piano:
    K.496 in E, Chopin and 6:68
    K.498 1:56

MUSSORGSKY, Modest Petrovich
    (1839-81) 3:8,36
  avoidance of musical trends 10:42
  influence of personality on music
    9:22
  and the Mighty Handful (Balakirev,
    Borodin, Cui, Mussorgsky and
    Rimsky-Korsakov) 10:42

Modest Mussorgsky

  and Nationalism 9:22
  Operas
    Boris Gudunov 10:*41,* 42, 43
      popularity outside Russia 10:*43*
  Symphonic poems
    St John's Night on a Bare Mountain
      6:100

N

NOVERRE, Jean-Georges (1727-1810) 3:99
  Letters on Dancing and Ballets 3:99-100
  Ballets
    Les Fêtes Chinoises 3:99

O

OFFENBACH, Jacques (1819-1880) 8:110
  and operetta 10:33, 53-4
  opens new theatre 10:53
  re-use of materials 10:53
  speed of orchestrating 10:33, 53-4
  works:
    subjects 10:53
    Les Contes d'Hoffmann 10:53
      setting for 10, *34*
  Operettas
    overtures to 8:63
    La Belle Helene 10:53
    La Vie Parisienne 9:26
    The Grand Duchess 10:53
    Orpheus in the Underworld 9:26;
      10:53
    The Tales of Hoffman 3:44, 45

ORFF, Carl (1895-1982)
 official acceptance of 10:51

P

PACHELBEL, Johann (1653-1706)
 and the Bach family 4:9
 and development of the overture 5:46
 effect on music of post held 5:38
 examination of musical progress 4:9
 family 4:9
 marriages 4:9
 in Nuremburg 4:9
 post as organist 4:8
 in Stuttgart 4:9
 studies 4:8
 in Vienna 4:8-9
 works:
  for harpsichord 4:22
  Cannon and Gigue 4:19
  Chaconne in F minor 1:72; 4:22
 Suites
  in G for Strings and Continuo 4:22
PACINI, Giovanni (1796-1867) 8:110
PAGANINI, Niccolò (1782-1840) 2:62;
  6:13, *71*, 104, *104*, 105-7, 110
 Chopin and 6:71, *71*
 descriptions of 6:106-107
 gift to Berlioz 8:12
 and Karlsbad 7:83
 Liszt and 6:90
 Mendelssohn and 8:38, 48
 technique 6:71, 106
 tours 6:105, 106
 use of publicity 6:107
 and variations 2:54
 and virtuoso playing 3:72
 see also Sonatas; Variations
PALESTRINA, Giovanni Pierluigi da
  (c.1525-94)
 'imitative' composition 5:33
 Masses 5:42
  basis of composition 5:33
PERGOLESI, Giovanni Battista (1710-36)
 number of operas written 10:12

 Church music
  Stabat Mater 4:15
 Operas
  influence on Baroque music 4:47
  Il Prigioner Superbo 10:20
PERI, Jacopo (1561-1633)
 and the Camerata 10:9
 influence on Baroque music 4:47
 Operas
  Euridice 10:9
   first performance 10:9
   librettist 10:9
  Dafne 10:9
   librettist 10:9
POULENC, Francis (1899-1963)
 and Church music 5:42
 Operas
  Le Dialogue des Carmelites 10:52
PROKOFIEV, Serge (1891-1953)
 and Diaghilev 3:44
 and film music 7:101
 works:
  opposition to 10:43
  types of 10:43
  Alexander Nevsky 7:101
 Ballets
  Cinderella 3:44
  Romeo and Juliet 3:44
 Operas
  The Fiery Angel 10:43
  The Love of Three Oranges 10:43,
   50-51
  War and Peace 10:43
PUCCINI, Giacomo (1858-1924) 7:110
 influence of contemporaries 10:50
 style of later works 10:50
 verismo style 10:34, 50
 Operas
  La Bohème 10:40, 50, 82
  La Fanciulla del West 10:83
  Madam Butterfly 10:40, 50, 82
  Manon Lescaut 10:83
  La Rondine 10:83
  Il Tabarro 10:83
  Tosca 10:50, 82
  Turandot 10:50, 82
   finished by Alfano 10:50
PURCELL, Henry (1659-95) 4:7, *13*,
  13-14, 87; 10:44
 appointments for the King 4:14
 Britten and 10:48
 dedications:
  to Charles II, King of England 4:14
  of *Sonnata's of III Parts* 4:14
 description of 4:14
 effect of work on health 4:14
 and funeral of Queen Mary of England
  4:14, 30, 87
 incidental music 4:14
 and musical effects 4:14
 and occasional music 4:87
 patronage 4:30
 posts and music at Westminster Abbey
  4:*13*, 14
 and suites 5:49
 works:
  chamber music 4:14
  for Charles II 4:87
  contribution to Church music 4:14
  first published 4:13
  numbers of 4:14

Composer	Volume
Albinoni	4
Bach	5
Beethoven	2
Berlioz	8
Brahms	7
Chopin	6
Corelli	4
Handel	4
Haydn	5
Liszt	6
Mahler	7
Mendelssohn	8
Mozart	1
Pachelbel	4
Purcell	4
Rameau	4
Schubert	6
Schumann	8
Tchaikovsky	3
Telemann	4
Vivaldi	4

The National Portrait Gallery, London

Johann Pachelbel

 for private performance 10:45
 scope of 4:14
 Anthems
  for Westminster Abbey 4:14
 Music dramas
  The Indian Queen 4:16
 Odes 4:14
  Ode on St Cecilia's Day 4:22, 87
  For the Queen's Birthday 4:87
 Operas
  Dido and Aeneas 4:14, 22; 10:*44*, 45
 Overtures
  The Indian Queen 4:16
 Pastiches
  The Fairy Queen 4:22
 Sonatas
  Sonnata's of III Parts 4:14
 Songs 4:14
  first published 4:13
  for Westminster Abbey 4:14
 Suites
  for harpsichord 4:14

R

RAMEAU, Jean-Philippe (1683-1764)
  4:7, *10-11*, 11; 9:*11*; 10:*18*
 'character pieces' 4:11
 criticism of style 4:11
 description of 4:11
 dismissal from Clermont 4:11
 on harmony 10:26
 influence of cantata form on 4:80
 in Lyons 4-11
 La Poule 4:11, *18:19*
 marriage 4:11
 in Milan 4:11
 and music for dance/drama 3:44
 as organist 10:18
 in Paris 4:11
  work produced in 4:11
 Rousseau's attack on 10:25-6
 studies 4:11
 and tragédies-lyriques 10:18

Jean-Philippe Rameau

works:
 for the harpsichord 10:18
 Pièces de Claverin, Livre I 4:22
 third collection of keyboard works
  4:11
Ballets
 Les Indes Galantes 4:22
Operas
 first 4:11
  criticism of 4:11
 Castor et Pollux 4:22; 10:18
 Dardanus 10:18
 Hippolyte et Aricie 4:11; 10:18
  librettist 4:11
Piano works
 Pièces de Claverin, Livre I 4:22
Suites
 Nouvelles Suites de Pièces de Claverin
  4:18
 frontispiece *4:18*
RAVEL, Maurice (1875-1937)
 Diaghilev and 3:44
 inspiration from folk heritage 9:23
 works:
  inspiration for *Bolero* 9:23
 Operas
  L'Enfant et les Sortilèges 10:50-51
  'Revolutionary' 10:31-2
   style of 10:31
   use of 10:31
  The Chance of Liberty 10:31
  The Triumph of the Republic 10:31
 Suites
  Le Tombeau de Couperin 5:49
REICHA, Antoine (1770-1836) 2:40
RIMSKY-KORSAKOV, Nicholay
 Andreyevich (1844-1908) 3:8, 36
 finishes Borodin's *Prince Igor* 10:42
 influence of Berlioz 8:13
 influence of personality on work 9:22
 and The Mighty Handful 10:42
 and Tchaikovsky's Symphony No. 6 3:61
 Operas
  themes of 10:42
  Golden Cockerel 10:42, 51

RODERIGO, Joaquin (b. 1902)
 influence of folk music on work 9:33
ROSSINI, Gioacchino (1792-1868) 2:40
 and *bel canto* 10:40
 Chopin and 6:78
 combines Italian/French elements 10:33
 influence on opéra comique 10:53
 popularity in England 10:46
 retirement 10:38
 souvenir fan 10:*22*
 style of opera 6:72, 10:38
 successors to 10:22
 and the Théâtre Italien 10:33
 use of the orchestra 6:23
 Church music
  Stabat Mater 5:42
 Operas
  inspiration for 10:38
  Barber of Seville 6:*72;* 10:19, 22, 38, 83
   Chopin and 6:63
   costume design 6:65
   at the Théâtre Italien 10:32
  La Cenerentola 10:83
  L'Italiana in Algeri 10:83
  Otello
   inspiration for 10:38
   Malibran in 8:42, *43*
  William Tell 10:33
 Overtures
  William Tell, use in films 7:101
ROUSSEAU, Jean-Jacques (1712-78) 1:46,
 117
 attacks: on the establishment 10:24
  on Rameau 10:25-6
 on children's clothes 6:50
 influence on opera 10:22, 23, 24
 and 'nature' 1:115
 and opera buffa 10:24-5
 see also Index of Music, OPERAS
RUBINSTEIN, Nikolay (1835-81) 3:27, 36,
 66
 and Mme von Meck 3:32
 and Tchaikovsky 3:8, 11, 31
  and '1812' Overture 3:49
  and Piano Concerto No. 1 3:56, 66, 67

S

SAINT-SAËNS, Camille (1835-1921)
 honorary doctorate from Cambridge
  University 3:59
 and the Opéra-Comique 10:34
 Tchaikovsky and 3:29
 use of music in films 7:101
 works:
  The Swan 7:101
 Symphonic poems
  Danse Macabre 6:100
SALIERI, Antonio (1750-1825) 1:13, 30, *45,*
 46; 6:*9*
 and Haydn's *The Creation* 5:93
 influence on Joseph II of Austria 10:30
 influence on *Singspiel* 10:30
 jealous of Mozart 1:43
 and Schubert 6:*9,* 10-11
 Liszt and 6:88
SATIE, Eric (1866-1925)
 and Diaghilev 3:44
 'Dessicated Embryos' 3:62
 naming pieces 3:62

Ballets
 Agon 3:44
 Apollo 3:44
 Danses Concertantes 3:44
 The Firebird 3:44
 Jeu de Cartes 3:44
 Orpheus 3:44
SCARLATTI, Alessandro (1660-1725) 10:*12*
 and Naples as opera centre 10:20
SCARLATTI, Domenico (1685-1757) 4:22,
 47, *69*, 110
 and Arcadian Academy 4:12
 on Corelli 4:12
 Schumann and 8:101
 Church music
  Stabat Mater 4:22
 Sonatas
  number written for harpsichord 4:22
SCHOENBERG, Arnold (1874-1951)
 and atonality 1:52; 7:109
 bafflement at works 9:32
 Gurrelieder 3:55
 Mahler and 7:93
 and novel sound-effects 3:55
 and 'Second Viennese School' 10:50
 and 'serial' music 9:32
 and 'twelve-note technique' 10:50
 Operas
  Moses und Aron 10:52
SCHUBERT, Franz Peter (1797-1828)
 6:*7, 11, 17;* 9:*17*
 achievements as songwriter 6:15
 aged sixteen 6:*33*
 burial of 6:13, 56
 character 6:8, 9
 'character' of music 6:7
 commissions for operettas 6:24
 and composing 6:11-12, *38*
  acceptance of early style 6:12
  and counterpoint 6:10, 13
  demands on pianist/singer 6:20
  'discovering' himself 6:33
  forms used for songs 6:28
  mechanics of 6:21
  method for early songs 6:18
  offers from publishers 6:13
  and symphonic writing 6:33
  form of Symphony no. 8 6:36
  speed of writing symphonies 6:33
  use of folk-songs 6:15-16
  using link between songs 6:21
  use of repeated motifs 6:98
  use of unrelated keys 1:52
 concerts:
  success of *Erlkönig* at 6:20
  of 26 March 1828 6:13
 death of 6:49
 dedications to Goethe 6:20
 description of 6:9
 diaries 6:9, 11
  on love of nature 6:17
  on marriage 6:11
  on Mozart concert 6:9
 early brilliance 6:18-19
 early life 6:9-10
 effect of drink on 6:8-9
 epitaph 6:13
 family life 6:9
  music in 6:53
  number in 6:57
  in family string quartet 6:53

and fashion 6:48-9
fashion during Schubert's life 6:43ff
finances:
    from drawing-room appearances 6:12
    from Count Esterhazy 6:24
    from privately published songs 6:20
    at school 6:10
friends/friendships 6:17
    choosing poems for songs 6:20
    effect of *Winterreise* on 6:13
    finding lodgings with 6:11
    loyalty of 6:7
    nickname for 6:9
    portraits by 6:9
    and publishing his works 6:12, 20
    travels with Vogl 6:12, 20
in Hungary 6:13
illness 6:12-13
and improvisation 6:12
increasing popularity 6:12
influence of Beethoven 2:15, 38; 6:18, 33
influence of Haydn 6:18
influence of minor composers on 6:18
influence of Mozart 2:38; 6:9, 18, 33
influence of Vogl on career 6:11
by Klimt 6:*12-13*
leaves home 6:11
letters:
    to Kupelwieser 6:12-13
    mentions of songs 6:21
literary influences 6:17
lodgings 6:24
love affairs:
    Mme Jenny 6:11
    'Pepi' 6:12
    Therese Grob 6:*10*, 11
and marriage 6:11

Franz Schubert

monument to 6:*13*
and Müller's poems 6:21
musical influences 6:18
and musical soirées 6:53
offer of scholarship 6:11
poetic inspiration 6:17, 53
political/economic changes during life
    of 6:43

posts:
    with Count Esterhazy 6:12
    difficulty obtaining 6:11
    lost through uncooperation 6:12
    Music Director, Laibach 6:11
public recognition 6:19-20
and publishing works 6:12, 20-21
    difficulties 6:20
    'Trout' Quintet 6:24
pupils:
    Esterhazy children 6:12
reputation in Vienna 6:20
and Romanticism 9:20
school report 6:10
school uniform 6:10, 50
as schoolmaster 6:11
Schumann and 8:101
sells copyright to songs 6:20
singing talents 6:9-10
in Steyr 6:24
studies:
    of Handel 6:13
    with Salieri 6:*9*, 10-11
style of piano playing 2:38
travels:
    tour in Upper Austria 6:12, 24
    see also individual cities, towns
and the Viennese authorities 6:12
on *Winterreise* cycle 6:21
working hours 6:8
'Year of indecision' 6:33
at Zseliz 6:12
works:
    catalogue of 1:67
    earliest compositions 6:9-10
    effect of musical journals on 8:101
    greatness revealed in 6:15
    how circulated 6:53
    masses 6:11
    octets 6:13
    and oratorios 4:80
    rediscovery of 8:61
    for Steyr music society 6:24
    unfinished 6:8
    and variations 2:54
    written when schoolmaster 6:11
    Impromptus D899, D935, D946
        6:39
    Rosamunde incidental music 6:39
Cantatas
    first commission 6:11
    for Salieri's birthday 6:11
Lieder 6:15ff
    'apprentice' 6:18
    catalogue of 6:18
    early 6:18
    first published 6:12, 20
    first surviving 6:18
    first to be well known 6:15
    the great song-cycles 6:20-21
    model for style of 6:*16*
    number written 6:15
        of early 6:11
    published by friends 6:20
    sources of texts 6:16-17, 18-19
    use of 6:19
    Der Abend 6:18
    An die Musik 6:11-12, 20
    Daphne am Bach, reshaping of 6:21
    Erlafsee 6:20
    Erlkönig 6:12, *18-19*, 19, 20, 33

VOLUME 1
Mozart

VOLUME 2
Beethoven

VOLUME 3
Tchaikovsky

VOLUME 4
Albinoni, Corelli, Handel,
Pachelbel, Purcell, Rameau,
Telemann, Vivaldi

VOLUME 5
Bach, Haydn

VOLUME 6
Chopin, Liszt, Schubert

VOLUME 7
Brahms, Mahler

VOLUME 8
Berlioz, Mendelssohn, Schumann

VOLUME 9
A Guide to Classical Music

VOLUME 10
A Beginner's Guide to the Opera

Die Forelle 6:11-12, 15, 20
Gretchen am Spinnrade 6:11, 18,
    18, 33
Hagar Klage 6:18
Heidenröslein 6:19
    title page 6:*20*
Dere Leiermann 6:21
Der Lindenbaum 6:21
Der Müller und der Bach 6:21
Die Schöne Müllerin cycle 6:20-21, 31
    inspiration for 6:17, 20-21
Der Tod und das Mädchen 6:12, 20
Der Wageiser 6:28
Winterreise cycle 6:13, 20-21, *21*, 39
    mood when writing 6:21
    texts for 6:17
Wohin? 6:21
Operas
    early attempts 6:11
    first commission 6:12
    Fierabras 6:21
Quartets
    String 6:11
        Deutsch number 6:24
    Quintets
        Piano:
            in A major op. 114 'Trout' 6:12,
                24-30
                first performance 6:24
                loss of original manuscript
                    6:24, 26
        String 6:13
            in C major D956 6:31
    Sonatas
        Piano:
            in A 6:24
            in F minor, own name for 6:98

Songs 4:15
see also Lieder
Symphonies 6:11
no. 1 6:33
in C major 6:13
revision of 6:13
no. 4 6:33
influence of Beethoven on 6:12
no. 5 in B flat major D485 6:33-5
influence of Mozart on 6:12
no. 8 in B minor 'Unfinished' 6:12, 36-8
manuscript for third movement 6:37
no. 9 in C major 'The Great' 6:39
Trios
Piano:
in E flat 6:13
SCHUMANN, Robert (1810-56) 7:*13*; 8:*87, 88, 94*
and Allgemeine musikalische Zeitung 8:101
and Bach revival 8:55
in Berlin 8:93
and Brahms 8:87
C major sonata 7:9
diary entry on 7:9
as inspiration for 7:30
musical criticism of 8:101
piano pieces 7:46
reception of 7:17
visits from in asylum 8:93
career:
as concert pianist 8:89-90
conflicts with Clara's 8:91-2
and Chopin 6:66; 8:87
and Clara Wieck 8:90ff, *91*
confronts Clara's father 8:91
encouragement from 8:94
legal battle over 8:91
and composing:
effect of legal battle on 8:91
effect of personality on 8:87
Lieder 6:28
method 8:98
most productive period 8:93
for solo piano 8:90, 91
sources of inspiration 3:62
studies counterpoint 8:92
while in asylum 8:93
while studying with Wieck 8:89
concerts:
of Symphony No. 1 8:94
with Clara 8:91-4
and contemporary music 8:101
and court life 8:109
criticism:
of Chopin 8:101
of *Tannhäuser* 7:25
damage to right hand 8:89-90
death of 8:93
description 8:88
diaries:
'characters' in 8:88
entry on madness 8:90
in Dresden 8:92
on cultural activity in 8:109
and gaining position in 8:93
in Düsseldorf:
with Clara 8:93

lowering of artistic standards 8:93
quarrels with authorities 8:93
early years 8:88-9
education 8:88
effects of family deaths on 8:88, 90
engagement 8:90
family 7:*19*
births of children 8:92
deaths in 7:*21*
father and mother 8:*88*
fears about Düsseldorf 8:*92*
final years 8:93
finances:
on 21st birthday 8:89
friends:
Davidsbündler 8:90
'names' for 8:89
visits from in asylum 8:93
health:
effect of Russian tour on 8:92
holiday for 8:93
progressive collapse of 8:92-3
illnesses 8:90
collapse of nervous system 8:93
committed to asylum 8:93
declared insane 7:10, 18
failing hearing 8:92
mental breakdown 8:92
inherited? 8:88
vertigo 8:92
imaginary brotherhood 8:90
as independent conductor 8:89-90

Robert Schumann

influence of J. S. Bach 5:39
influence of Beethoven 2:38-9
influence on contemporary music 8:101
influence of Schubert's songs on 8:89
influence of Schunke on 8:90
as journalist 8:90
and Karlsbad 7:83
law studies 8:89
in Leipzig 8:89, 91-2
and Leipzig Conservatory 7:23
'leisure' during life of 8:102ff
and literature 8:87

life at university 8:89
on Liszt's 'showmanship' 6:109; 7:24
manners 8:88
marriage 8:91
in Moscow 8:92
as music critic 8:101
contributions to journals 8:101
Neue Bahnen 7:18
Neue Zeitschrift für Musik 7:18, 25; 8:87, 91, 92
policy 8:101
and 'New Music' 7:23; 8:101
and dispute over 7:25
and opera 8:92
on *Faust* 8:92
further endeavours 8:93
personality 8:87-8
piano lessons 8:89
posthumous portrait 8:*93*
posts:
in Düsseldorf 8:93
and music director at Leipzig 8:93
in Prague 8:93
and pseudonyms 8:87-8
and revolution in Dresden 8:*92, 93*
in the Rhineland 8:*88-9*
and Romanticism 8:87; 9:21
and Rochlitz 8:101
in Russia 8:92
and Schubert's last symphony 8:38
suicide attempt 7:10, 18; 8:93
on virtuosos 6:105
working visits, effect on health 8:93
works:
choral 8:92
cyphers in 8:87
'Kinderscenen' 3:62
main types of 8:90
style 8:93
two greatest chamber works 8:91
written at university 8:89
Fantasie in A minor for piano and orchestra 8:91, 98
Concertos
Cello:
in A minor op. 129 8:100
Piano:
in A minor op. 54 8:98-9
completes 8:92, 98
first performance 8:98
first movement 8:91
origins 8:94
in D minor:
first movement 8:98
in F 8:98
in F minor 8:98
Dances
'Davidsbündlertänze' 3:62
Lieder
influence on Mendelssohn 8:61
number composed 6:28
Dichterliebe cycle 6:28; 8:91
Frauenliebe und -leben 8:91
Liederkreis 8:91
Operas
Liszt and 7:27-8
Faust, pieces for 8:92, 93
Genoveva 8:93
Oratorios
Das Paradies und die Peri 8:92

Overtures
  in E flat minor op. 115 'Manfred'
    8:93, 100
Quartets
  Piano 8:91
Quintets
  Piano 8:91
  performance in Moscow 8:92
Symphonies
  cyclic principle in 2:39
  last
    première of 8:38
  nearly completes first 8:90
  C minor:
    sketches for 8:94
  G minor:
    sketches for 8:94
  No. 1 in B flat major op. 38 'Spring'
    3:62; 8:91, 94-7
    first performance 8:94
    orchestration of 8:94
    origins 8:94
    performance in St Petersburg 8:92
  No. 2:
    influence of Beethoven 2:39
  No. 3 in E flat major op. 97 'Rhenish'
    8:100
  No. 4:
    cyclic principle 2:39
SCHÜTZ, Heinrich (1585-1672)
  effect on music of post held 5:38
  influence of Italian style on 5:38
SIBELIUS, Jean (1865-1957) 9:22
  influence of Beethoven 2:39
SKRYABIN, Alexander (1872-1915)
  3:36
  and 'colour' of harmonies 6:23
SMETANA, Bedřich (1824-84) 9:22
  influence of Liszt 6:100
  Symphonic poems
    Hakon Jarl 6:100
    Ma Vlast 6:100
    Richard III 6:100
    Walenstein's Lager 6:100
SPOHR, Louis (1784-1859) 2:62; 3:40
  on Beethoven's last works 2:38
  on programme music 8:17
  and prominence of conductor 7:50
  Faust 8:17
STANFORD, Sir Charles (1852-1924)
  and Brahms's Symphony No. 1 7:48
STRAUSS, Johann (the Younger;
    1825-99) 3:8
  problems with libretti 10:54
  and revolution 9:26
  style of 9:26
  Operettas
    Die Fledermaus 10:54, 83
      librettist 10:54
    Indigo 10:54
    Die Zigeunerbaron 10:54, 83
      librettist 10:54
  Waltzes
    Blue Danube, use as film music
      7:101
STRAUSS, Richard (1864-1949) 1:71
  and Diaghilev 3:44
  guide for overtures 8:60
  influence of Mozart 10:50
  influence of Wagner 1:52
  and programme music 8:17

Composer	Volume
Albinoni	4
Bach	5
Beethoven	2
Berlioz	8
Brahms	7
Chopin	6
Corelli	4
Handel	4
Haydn	5
Liszt	6
Mahler	7
Mendelssohn	8
Mozart	1
Pachelbel	4
Purcell	4
Rameau	4
Schubert	6
Schumann	8
Tchaikovsky	3
Telemann	4
Vivaldi	4

  and Romanticism 9:32
  shock of style 10:50
  use of counterpoint 10:50
  works:
    Ein Heldenleben 8:17
  Operas
    major success 10:50
    overtures to 8:63
    Arabella 10:50
    Ariadne auf Naxos 10:50, 83
    Capriccio 10:83
    Elektra 10:50
      librettist 10:50
    Der Rosenkavalier 10:50, 83
    Salome 7:94, 94; 10:50-51, 83
      shock of 10:50
  Suites
    'Der Rosenkavalier' 5:49
STRAVINSKY, Igor (1882-1971)
  attitude to opera form 10:43
  and Church music 5:42
  and Diaghilev 3:44
  influence on Puccini 10:50
  influence on Schoenberg 1:52
  shock of works 9:32
  Operas
    'opera-oratorio' 10:43
    The Nightingale 10:43
    Les Noces 10:43
    Oedipus Rex 10:43
    The Rake's Progress 10:43, 52
      experiments in 10:52
  Suites
    'Firebird' 5:49
SULLIVAN, Sir Arthur (1842-1900) 9:26;
    10:56
  collaboration with Gilbert 10:47,
    55-6
  influence on British and American
    theatre 10:56
  and serious opera 10:47
  works:
    'Onward Christian Soldiers' 10:56
  Operas
    Ivanhoe 10:47
    Thespis 10:56

  Operettas
    The Gondoliers 10:56
    Iolanthe 10:56
    The Mikado 10:56
    Patience 10:56
    HMS Pinafore 10:56
    Princess Ida 10:56
    Ruddigore 10:56
    The Sorcerer 10:56
    Trial by Jury 10:56
    The Yeoman of the Guard 10:56

T

TCHAIKOVSKY, Pyotr Ill'yich (1840-93)
  3:7, 8, 9, 13, 16, 31, 49, 58-9, 66; 9:16
  aged twenty-one 3:9
  and Antonia Milyukova 3:10
  in Baltimore 3:21
  in Bayreuth 3:52
  with Bob Davidov 3:61
  and Carnegie 3:19
  childhood 3:25
    sensitivity in 3:7, 23
  composing:
    conditions for 3:31
    creative period 3:9
    creative stream after Piano Concerto
      No. 1 3:66
    ideas on a sixth symphony 3:58
    lessons in 3:8
    most productive period 3:71
    stimulus for ballets 3:44
  commissions 3:13
    from Imperial Theatre, Moscow 3:10
    from Mme von Meck 3:10, 32, 33
    from Vsevolozhsky 3:44
  concerts:
    at Lyceum Theatre 3:21
    in Moscow 3:13
    for opening of New York Music Hall
      3:17, 18
    Russian Music Society 3:56-7
    in Washington 3:22
    in St Petersburg 3:13
  conducting 3:12-13
    conducts Pathétique Symphony 3:13
    tours in Europe 3:13
  controversy over Wagner 3:21
    and criticism 3:7
  dedications:
    to Mme von Meck 3:12
    of Piano Concerto No. 1 3:67
    of Romeo and Juliet 3:71
    of Symphony No. 4 3:33
    of Symphony No. 6 3:61
    to Von Bülow 3:67
  and Désirée Artôt 3:8, 29
  divorce 3:34-5
  early training 3:7
  emotional problems 3:9, 12-13, 24-5
    and Symphony No. 6 3:58
  family 3:25
    with his brothers 3:28-9
    and twins (brothers) 3:27
  favourite painting 3:59
  finances 3:9, 34
    annuity from Mme von Meck 3:12,
      16, 33
  in Florence 3:11, 35

friendships/relationships 3:9, 27-8
   possible lovers 3:29
   romantic attachments 3:10-12
and Germany 3:16
homosexuality 3:8, 9-10, 13, 23ff, 31
honorary doctorate from Cambridge
   University 3:*23, 59*
ideal heroines and real women 3:29
illnesses:
   depression 3:29
   early 3:7
   mental 3:12, 27
   nervous 3:8, 13
incidental music 3:57
influence of Bizet 3:52
influence of Glinka 3:51
influence of 'western' music on 10:43
and Italy 3:16
and Knabe pianos 3:21
last years 3:13
letters:
   to Bob Davidov 3:58, 59
   to Grand Duke Constantin 3:58
   to Jurgenson 3:40, 59
   to/from Mme von Meck 3:11, 13, 35
   to/from Antonina Milyukova 3:11
   to Modest 3:16, 58
   to Sacha 3:28
   on Symphony No. 6 3:58
and Mme von Meck 3:29, 33
   break with 3:35
and marriage 3:10, 11, 29, 33-4
   effect on music of 3:51
meets Mahler 7:90-91
and The Mighty Handful 10:43
in Moscow 3:8-9, 27
   conducts concerts in 3:13
   flat in 3:9
   at Moscow Conservatoire 3:8
   and Moscow Exhibition of Industrial
      Arts 3:49
and his mother 3:7, 25
music:
   classes 3:8, 27
   'pain' in 3:23-4
   personal refuge in 3:29
   as a refuge 3:29
   Romanticism in 3:29
nostalgia for Russia 3:10
and novel sound-effects 3:55
pupils 3:33
in Rome 3:*50-51*, 51
'secret instrument' 3:45
at St Petersburg Conservatoire
   3:17-8, *12-13*
conducts concerts in 3:13
suicide attempts 3:12, 29, 34
and Taneyev 3:38
temperament 3:7
and theatrical music 3:38
and travels 3:9, 16
   in Europe 3-26-7, 28
at Vichy 3:52
and Wagner 3:*52* ·
   reviews *The Ring* cycle 3:52
in Washington 3:*20-21*
works:
Ballets 3:38ff
   and general level of music for
      3:13, 44-5
   sources of inspiration for 3:13, 44-5

Pyotr Tchaikovsky

The Nutcracker 3:13, 16, 22, 38,
   44-8, 102
   first London performance 3:45
   hostility to 3:58
   setting for 3:*44-5*
   title page 3:*22*
The Sleeping Beauty 3:13, 38, 42-3,
   102
   first performance 3:13, *43*
   Petipa's requirements for 3:44
   St Petersburg performances 3:44
Swan Lake 3:10, 29, 38-41, 102
   manuscript 3:*41*
   piano arrangement 3:39
   substitution of music in 3:40
canzonetta 3:8
Concert suites
   The Nutcracker 3:45
   The Sleeping Beauty 3:42
   Swan Lake 3:40-41
   Third Suite 3:18, 21
Concertos
   for opening of New York Music Hall
      3:19
   use of themes 3:72
   Piano 3:21
      and technical difficulties of 3:66
      No. 1 in B flat minor 3:10, 19, 66-9
         manuscript 3:*67*
         changes to 3:67
      No. 3:
         origin of first movement 3:58
   Violin 3:12, 51
      in D op. 35 3:73
Fantasias
   Fatum 3:8
Marches
   Coronation March op. 31 3:56-7
Operas
   and Italian opera 3:8
   number written 3:38

Eugene Onegin 3:10, 48, 52; 10:43
   finishes work on 3:12
   première 7:91
   setting for 7:*90-91*
   source of inspiration for 3:13
   Tatyana letter scene 3:*10*
Hyperbole 3:26
The Maid of Orleans 3:51
The Oprichnik 3:9
The Queen of Spades 3:13; 10:42
Undine 3:8
Vakula the Smith 3:10, 13, 66
The Voyevoda 3:8, 28
Yolanta 3:44
   hostility towards 3:58
Orchestral works 3:49ff
   Francesca da Rimini op. 10 3:52-5
      source of inspiration for 3:52
      success of 3:55
      Tchaikovsky on 3:55
   Italian Capriccio op. 3:45, 51
      source of inspiration for 3:51
   The Tempest 3:10, *32-3*
      Mme von Meck and 3:32
Overtures
   in F 3:8
   Festival Overture: the Year 1812
      3:12, 49-51
   Romeo and Juliet 3:8, 29, 70-73
      modifications to 3:70-71
      source of inspiration for 3:70
Quartets
   String 3:9
      Second 3:10, 66
      Third 3:3-10
Serenades
   String:
      in C op. 48 3:73
      Serenade for Strings 3:21
Sextets
   op. 70 'Souvenir de Florence'
      3:48
Sonatas
   Piano 3:51
Songs
   first published 3:8
   Mezza notte 3:8
Symphonies
   No. 1 3:8
      criticism of 3:8
      strain of writing 3:27
   No. 2 op. 17 'Little Russian' 3:65
   No. 3 3:10
   No. 4 in F minor op. 36 3:10, 29, 65
   No. 5 in E minor op. 64 3:13, 65
   No. 6 in B minor op. 74 'Pathétique'
      3:13, 23, 29, 58-64
      first draft 3:58
      'hidden meanings' 3:61
      manuscript 3:*61*
      title page 3:61
   'Manfred' op. 58 3:12, 29, 57
      source of inspiration for 3:12
Trios
   Piano 3:22
      in A minor op. 50 3:57
Variations
   on a Rococo Theme for Cello and
      Orchestra op. 33 3:10, 73
Waltzes
   Anastasie Valse 3:26

TELEMANN, Georg Philipp (1681-1767)
4:7, 10, *10*
C. P. E. Bach and 5:18
and development of the overture 5:46
effect on music of post held 5:38
friendship with Handel 4:60
influence of Handel 4:10
marriage 4:10
musical style 4:17
and musical theory 4:10
Musique de Table 4:22
position in Hamburg 5:18
resignation from Hamburg post 4:10
and *sonata da chiesa* 4:18, 80
in Sorau 4:10
and unusual instruments 4:17-18
works:
number written 4:10
Musique de Table 4:22
Cantatas
for Hamburg 4:10
number written 4:10
Chamber music
number written 4:10
Church music
contribution to Hamburg's 4:10
Concertos
number written 4:10
Viola:
in G 4:17-18

Georg Philipp Telemann

Masses
number written 4:10
Operas
first 4:10
number written 4:10
Oratorios
number written 4:10
Passions
number for Hamburg 4:10
St Mark 4:22
Quartets
The 'Paris' Quartets 4:22
Songs
number written 4:10

Song Book (1730) 4:*10*
Suites
number written 4:10
TIOMKIN, Dimitri (1899-1979)
and film music 7:101
High Noon 7:101
TIPPETT, Sir Michael (b. 1905) 10:*47*
influence of Britten 10:48
and occasional music 4:87
Operas
The Ice-Break 10:48
King Priam 10:*46, 48*
The Knot Garden 10:48
The Midsummer Marriage 10:48
setting for 10:*49*

V

VAUGHAN WILLIAMS, Ralph (1872-1958)
2:*37*
and Church music 5:42
influence of Beethoven 1:52; 2:*37*
influence of folk music on 9:33
Operas
Hugh the Drover 10:47, 51
Symphonies
No. 4, similarity to No. 5 (Beethoven)
2:39
VERDI, Giuseppe (1813-1901)
development of operatic form 10:40
influence on Romantic opera 10:37
popularity in England 10:46
as successor to Rossini 10:22
works:
best-loved 10:40
masterpieces 10:40
number of operas written 10:40
Arias
approach to 10:40
Masses
Requiem 5:42
Operas
structure of 10:40
Aïda 10:84
Don Carlos 10:84
Falstaff 10:40, 84
La Forza del Destino 10:84
Otello 10:40, 84
Rigoletto 10:40, 84
Simon Boccanegra 10:84
La Traviata 10:40, 84
Il Trovatore 10:40
VIVALDI, Antonio (1678-1741) 4:*42*, 49
in Amsterdam 4:40
in Austria 4:40
J. S. Bach and 5:26
banned from Ferrara 4:38
commissions from Roger 4:37-8
concerts, for Prince Frederick 4:40
dedications:
to Count Gambara 4:36
to Count Morzin 4:39, 41-2, *42*
to Charles VI of Austria 4:39
to Ferdinand of Tuscany 4:37
to Frederick IV of Denmark 4:36
of *Il cimento dell'armonica* 4:39,
41-2, *42*
of *L'estro armonica* 4:37
of *La cetra* 4:39
of *La stravaganza* 4:37

VOLUME 1
Mozart

VOLUME 2
Beethoven

VOLUME 3
Tchaikovsky

VOLUME 4
Albinoni, Corelli, Handel,
Pachelbel, Purcell, Rameau,
Telemann, Vivaldi

VOLUME 5
Bach, Haydn

VOLUME 6
Chopin, Liszt, Schubert

VOLUME 7
Brahms, Mahler

VOLUME 8
Berlioz, Mendelssohn, Schumann

VOLUME 9
A Guide to Classical Music

VOLUME 10
A Beginner's Guide to the Opera

to Vettor Delfino 4:37
of set of 12 trio sonatas 4:36
early music training 4:35
and engraved music 4:37
'entourage' 4:38
fame outside Venice 4:37ff
by Ghezzi 4:*33, 38*
illnesses 4:35
influence of Cardinal Ottoboni 4:12
and Ospidale della Pietà 4:35-7
popularity with Venetian audience 4:40
and the priesthood 4:*34*, 34-5
on his publishers 4:39
pupils 4:37
in Rome 4:38
and sale of manuscripts 4:39
travels in Europe 4:38-40
works:
for the Pietà 4:37
first published 4:37
number of operas written 10:12
payment for 4:37
programme music 4:39
and publishing 4:37
Church music
Gloria in D, RV589 4:48
Vespers for the Pietà 4:37
Concertos
commissioned by Roger 4:37-8
for the Pietà 4:37
'Dresden' 4:40
*Il aminto dell'armonia e
dell'inventione* 4:39, 41ff
La cetra 4:39
L'estro armonico 4:37, 48
Violin:
for himself 4:36-7

Antonio Vivaldi

The Four Seasons 4:39, 41-2
 Autumn (No. 3 in F) 4:44-5
 Spring (No. 1 in E) 4:42-4
 Summer (No. 2 in G minor) 4:44
 Winter (No. 4 in F minor) 4:45-8
 as programme music 8:17
La stravaganza 4:37, 48
Masses
 for the Pietà 4:37
Motets
 for the Pietà 4:37
Operas
 interest in 4:38
 promotions in Italian centres 4:40
 Aristide:
 librettist 4:*35*
 Griselda:
 librettist 4:*35*
 Orlando finto pazzo 4:38
 Ottone in Villa 4:38
Oratorios
 for the Pietà 4:37
 Moyses Deus Pharaonis 4:37
 Juditha triumphans 4:37
Pastiches
 Nerone fatto Cesare 4:38
Sonatas
 12 trio sonatas 4:36, 5:33
VIVALDI, Giovanni Battista
 4:*33, 34*
 and A. Vivaldi's early training 4:35
Operas
 La fedelta sfortunata 4:34

W

WAGNER, Richard (1813-83) 2:*36*; 3:*52*
 Art and Revolution 7:29
 and Beethoven's Symphony No. 5 2:71
 Brahms and 7:12
 criticism of on doctorate 7:26-7
 as rival to 7:26
 caricatures of 7:*25, 27*
 and chromatic harmony

Concerning Poetry and Composition
 7:27
 contribution to 19th-century culture
 10:36
 criticisms of 7:25
 and devotees 7:28
 genius of 10:36-7
 and Hanslick 8:101
 influence of J. S. Bach 5:39
 influence of Beethoven 2:*36,* 39
 influence on Nietzsche 10:36
 influence on Tchaikovsky's *Francesca
 da Rimini* 3:55
 and instrument development 3:55
 and Karlsbad 7:83
 letters:
 to Schott 7:25-6
 lifestyle and musical conventions
 7:27
 links music with drama 9:20
 Liszt and 6:93
 literary ability 10:37
 and 'New Music' 7:23, *27*
 patron 2:31; 10:37
 popularity in England 10:46
 and prominence of conductor 7:50
 revolutionary activities 7:27
 and Romantic movement 10:35, 37
 and Schopenhauer 7:26
 Tchaikovsky controversy over 3:21, *52*
 treatise on conducting 7:50
 use of symbolism/mythology 10:37
 waning of influence 10:49
 on Weber's *Der Freischütz* 10:36
 works:
 in exile 10:36
 and national consciousness 10:37
 structure of operas 10:37
 Siegfried's Death 10:37
Operas
 Mahler conducts uncut versions
 7:92
 as ultimate expression of
 Romanticism 9:20
 von Bülow and 7:29
 Die Meistersingers:
 Brahms and 7:12
 model for Beckmesser 7:25; 8:101
 setting for 7:*24*
 The Flying Dutchman 10:36
 starting point for 8:104
 Lohengrin 10:36
 C. Schumann on 7:29
 Liszt's performances of 7:29
 Parsifal 10:36-7, 84
 excerpts from 3:21
 The Ring 10:84
 Alberich 7:*25*
 begins work on 10:37
 first complete performance 10:37
 interpretations of 10:52
 sends copy to Schopenhauer 7:26
 Tchaikovsky and 3:52
 use of in animated cartoons
 7:101
 Tannhäuser 10:36
 criticism of 7:25
 Tristan und Isolde 10:37, 84
 importance of 2:48
WALTON, Sir William (1902-83)
 and film music 7:101

works:
 Henry V 7:101
 Oratorios
 Belshazzar's Feast 4:80
WEBER, Carl Maria von (1786-1826) 2:40;
 10:*36*
 commission for London 10:37
 death of 8:88; 10:36
 letters:
 on *Der Freischütz* 10:36
 on success of *Oberon* 10:36
 Mendelssohn and 8:61
 and prominence of conductor 7:50
 and Romantic movement 10:35
 Schumann and 8:101
 use of the orchestra 6:23
 Operas
 Der Freischütz 10:*35*
 Chopin and 6:63
 first performance 8:61
 librettist 10:35-6
 plot 10:36
 success of 10:36
 title page 8:*62*
 Oberon 10:36
 Scherzos
 influence on Mendelssohn 8:62
WEILL, Kurt (1900-50) emigrates 10:51
 music denounced 10:51
 use of dance rhythms 10:51
 Operas
 *The Rise and Fall of the City of
 Mahogonny* 10:51
 The Threepenny Opera 10:*51*
 librettist 10:51
 see also individual types
WOLF, Hugo (1860-1903) 7:110
 influence of Wagner 6:29
 and Lieder 6:29
 Lieder
 texts for 6:29

Z

ZELENKA, Jan (1679-1745) 5:110

Composer	Volume
Albinoni	4
Bach	5
Beethoven	2
Berlioz	8
Brahms	7
Chopin	6
Corelli	4
Handel	4
Haydn	5
Liszt	6
Mahler	7
Mendelssohn	8
Mozart	1
Pachelbel	4
Purcell	4
Rameau	4
Schubert	6
Schumann	8
Tchaikovsky	3
Telemann	4
Vivaldi	4

Index of Music

A

ANTHEMS
Handel:
  Zadok the Priest 4;64, 87
Purcell:
  for Westminster Abbey 4:14
ARIAS
Bach, J. S.:
  Aria with 30 Variations *see* **VARIATIONS**
  Sheep May Safely Graze 5:26
Beethoven:
  'Ah Perfido' 2:66
Handel:
  use of Italian in 10:28
  'I know that my redeemer liveth' 4:77
  Let the Bright Seraphim 4:87
  Silent Worship 4:72
Mozart:
  for Nancy Storace 1:45
  Tchaikovsky and 3:23
Verdi:
  approach to 10:40

B

BALLADES
Chopin:
  no. 1 in G minor op.23, 6:65, 72-3
BALLETS
  Ballet Comique de la Reine Louise 3:97
  Ballet de la Nuit 3:97
  La Fille mal Gardée 3:100
  Le Lac de Fées 3:110
  La Liberazione di Tirrenio 3:97
  Medée et Jason 3:98
  Ondine 3:102
  Pas de Quatre 3:102
  La Sylphide 3:100, 101; 6:81
    influence on *Swan Lake* 3:39
Adam:
  Giselle 3:101-102
    influence on *Swan Lake* 3:39
Delibes:
  Coppélia 3:44, 102
    costume design for 3:*101*
  Sylvia 3:40, 120
    title page 3:*44*
Noverre:
  Les Fêtes Chinoises 3:99
Perrot:
  La Esmeralda 3:*101*, 102
Prokofiev:
  Cinderella 3:44
  Romeo and Juliet 3:44
Rameau:
  Les Indes Galantes 4:22
Satie:
  Agon 3:44
  Apollo 3:44
  Danses Concertantes 3:44
  The Firebird 3:44
  Jeu de Cartes 3:44
  Orpheus 3:44
Tchaikovsky 38ff

and general level of music for 3:13, 44-5
sources of inspiration for 3:13, 44-5
The Nutcracker 3:13, 16, 22, 38, 44-8, 102
  first London performance 3:45
  hostility to 3:58
  setting for 3:*44-5*
  title page of 3:*22*
The Sleeping Beauty 3:13, 38, 42-3, 102
  first performance 3:13, *43*
  Petipa's requirements for 3:44
  St Petersburg performances 3:44
Swan Lake 3:10, 29, 38-41, 102
  manuscript 3:*41*
  piano arrangement 3:39
  substitution of music in 3:40
Vigano:
  Psamos, King of Egypt 3:99

C

CANTATAS
Albinoni:
  number written 4:*8*
Bach, J. C. F. 5:19
Bach, J. S.:
  for the birthday of Duke of Weissenfels 5:9
  first 5:9
  number written at Leipzig 5:*12*, 27
  texts for 5:26, 27
  title page of secular set 5:*26*
  for Weimar 5:9, 26
  no. 82 'Ich habe Genug' 5:53
  God is my King 5:25
  Komm, du süsse Todesstunde 5:26
  Peasant Cantata 5:12
Carissimi 4:80
Mozart:
  A Little Masonic Cantata 1:38
  Hymn to the Sun 1:36
  K. 619 1:38
  Masonic 1:33, 36, 38
  Masonic Joy 1:36, 37
    title page 1:*36*
Schubert:
  first commission 6:11
  for Salieri's birthday 6:11
Telemann:
  number written 4:10
  for Hamburg 4:10
CHAMBER MUSIC
Brahms:
  Joachim and 7:12
Mozart 1:15
  number of pieces 1:58
Purcell 4:14
Telemann:
  numbers written 4:10
CHURCH MUSIC
Bach, J. C.:
  Dixit Dominus 5:19
  Requiem 5:19
  Magnificat 5:27
Berlioz:
  Te Deum 5:42
Charpentier:
  Magnificat 4:22
  Te Deum 4:22

Composer	Volume
Albinoni	4
Bach	5
Beethoven	2
Berlioz	8
Brahms	7
Chopin	6
Corelli	4
Handel	4
Haydn	5
Liszt	6
Mahler	7
Mendelssohn	8
Mozart	1
Pachelbel	4
Purcell	4
Rameau	4
Schubert	6
Schumann	8
Tchaikovsky	3
Telemann	4
Vivaldi	4

Handel:
  Dixit Dominus 4:61
  Jubilate 4:62
  Te Deum 4:62
Haydn:
  Salve Regina in E major 5:89
Monteverdi:
  Vespro della Beata Vergine 4:22
Purcell:
  contribution to 4:14
Pergolesi:
  Stabat Mater 4:15
Rossini:
  Stabat Mater 5:42
Scarlatti:
  Stabat Mater 4:22
Telemann:
  contribution to Hamburg's 4:10
Vivaldi:
  Gloria in D, RV589 4:48
  Vespers for the Pietà 4:37
  see also **MASSES; MOTETS; PASSIONS**
CONCERT SUITES
Delibes:
  Sylvia 3:40
Tchaikovsky:
  The Nutcracker 3:45
  The Sleeping Beauty 3:42
  Swan Lake 3:40-41
  Third Suite 3:18, 21
'concert works', Chopin 6:70
CONCERTOS
Albinoni:
  dedications of 4:8
  number written 4:8
  12 Concerti a Cinque op. 7 4:22
  12 Concerti a Cinque op. 9 4:22
Bach, J. C. 5:19
Bach, J. S.:
  six concertos 'Brandenburg' 5:10, 29-30
    parts for viola da gamba 5:29, *30*
  no. 2 in F major BWV1047 5:30-32
  no. 3 in G major BWV1048 5:32-4
  no. 5 in D major BWV1050 5:35-6
    first page of 5:*34*
Violin:

in A minor BWV1041 5:37
in D minor BWV1043 5:37
Beethoven:
    attitude to names of 2:34
    contribution to 2:42
    convention in early 2:51
    Piano:
        3rd 2:66
        No. 4 in G op. 58 2:57, 58
            'breaking rules' in 2:37
        No. 5 in E flat op. 73 'Emperor' 2:34,
            50-56
            compared with Violin Concerto
                (Beethoven) 2:58
            criticism of 2:50
            first performance 2:50-51
            last one 2:51
            title page 2:*52*
    Triple:
        in C major op. 56 2:65
    Violin:
        in D op. 81 2:61, 58-64
            'breaking rules' in 2:37
            criticism of 2:60
            first performance 2:59-60
            inscription on 2:58
            piano arrangement 2:60
            publication and popularity 2:60-61
            speed of writing 2:60
            title page 2:*60*
Brahms:
    Piano: No. 1 op. 15 7:10-11, 38-45
        first performance 7:11
        influences on 7:40
        origin of ideas 7:47
    No. 2 in B flat op. 83 7:13, 38-44
        conception of 7:38
        first performance 7:38
        influences on 7:38
        inspiration for 7:38
        pianist's contribution to 7:38
        number of movements 3:72
    Violin:
        in D op. 77 7:13, 30-37
            first performance 7:31
            influences on 7:38
            Joachim's amendments to 7:*32*
            popularity of 7:31-2
    Double Concerto for Violin and Cello
        7:13
Chopin:
    no. 1 6:64
    no. 2 in F minor 6:64, 67, 77
        inspiration for slow movement
            6:64
        Paris première 6:65
Corelli 4:47
    influence on form of 5:29-30
    Concerti Grossi 4:12
    12 Concerti Grossi op. 6 4:22
    No. 8 4:15, 19-20
    Pastorale manuscript 4:*20*
Elgar:
    Violin 2:64
Frederick the Great, King of Prussia:
    Flute 9:9
Grieg:
    Piano 3:66
Handel:
    Concerti Grossi op. 6 4:91
    Organ 4:65

Concerti op. 4 4:91
Twelve Grand Concertos for Strings
    op. 6 4:65
Haydn:
    Cello, in D 5:101
Liszt 6:96
    Piano:
        prototypes for 6:96
        no. 1 in E flat major 6:98-100
            première of 6:96
        no. 2 in A major 6:101-102
            première 6:96
        orchestral score 6:*98*
Joachim:
    Hungarian Concerto 7:29
Mendelssohn:
    Piano: no. 1 in G minor 8:51
    Violin 8:52-4
        encouragement from David 8:52
Mozart:
    influence of J. C. Bach 5:19
    number of movements 1:72-3
    number written 3:72
    numbers remaining 1:72
    use of themes 3:72
    Jeunehomme 1:10
    Clarinet:
        K. 622 1:56-60
            dedication 1:36
    Clavier 1:43
    Flute:
        in G major K. 313 1:63
    Flute and Harp 1:27
        K. 299 1:56, 60-63
    Piano 1:9
        contrast between K. 467 and K. 466
            1:74

first remaining 1:72
K. 175 1:79
C minor K. 491 1:79
D minor K. 466 1:74
E flat K. 449 1:72
No. 9 K. 271 1:9, 79
No. 20 K.466 1:79
No. 21 1:72, 74-8
No. 22 1:72, 78-9
No. 27 K. 595 1:79
Violin 1:9
    No. 5 in A K. 219 1:55
Schumann:
    Cello: in A minor op. 129 8:100
    Piano:
        in A minor op. 54 8:98-9
            completes 8:92, 98
            first performance 8:98
            first movement 8:91
            origins 8:94
        in D minor:
            first movement 8:98
            in F 8:98
            in F minor 8:98
Tchaikovsky:
    for opening of New York Music Hall 3:19
    use of themes 3:72
    Piano 3:21
        and technical difficulties of 3:66
        No. 1 in B flat minor 3:10, 19, 66-9
            manuscript of 3:67
            changes to 3:67
        No. 3:
            origin of first movement 3:58
    Violin 3:
        12, 51
        in D op. 35 3:73
Telemann:
    number written 4:10
    Viola:
        in G 4:17-18
Vivaldi:
    commissioned by Roger 4:37-8
    for the Pietà 4:37
    'Dresden' 4:40
    Il aminto dell'armonia e dell'invenzione
        4:39, 41ff
    La cetra 4:39
    L'estro armonico 4:37, 48
    Violin:
        for himself 4:36-7
        The Four Seasons 4:39, 41-2
            Autumn (No. 3 in F) 4:44-5
            Spring (No. 1 in E) 4:42-4
            Summer (No. 2 in G minor) 4:44
            Winter (No. 4 in F minor) 4:45-8
            as programme music 8:17
    La stravaganza 4:37, 48

VOLUME 1
Mozart

VOLUME 2
Beethoven

VOLUME 3
Tchaikovsky

VOLUME 4
**Albinoni, Corelli, Handel,
Pachelbel, Purcell, Rameau,
Telemann, Vivaldi**

VOLUME 5
Bach, Haydn

VOLUME 6
Chopin, Liszt, Schubert

VOLUME 7
Brahms, Mahler

VOLUME 8
Berlioz, Mendelssohn, Schumann

VOLUME 9
A Guide to Classical Music

VOLUME 10
A Beginner's Guide to the Opera

D

DANCES
Bach, W. F.:
    12 Polonaises 5:17
Dowland:
    in lute music 4:22
Mozart 1:15, 48ff
    number written 1:51
    themes for 1:51

gavotte 1:61, 63
Three German Dances K. 605 1:51
'Sleigh Ride' 3:55
Schumann:
'Davidsbündlertänze' 3:62
see also **FOLK DANCES**
DUETS
Beethoven:
Duet for Two Obbligato Eyeglasses
2:20
Mozart:
Piano 1:12
in D 1:12
'Haydn' 1:40
String 1:40
for violin and viola 1:40

E

ETUDES
Chopin 6:77
influences on 6:71
playing techniques 6:71
in C minor op. 10 no. 2 6:75-6
in E major op. 10 no. 3 6:73
op. 10 no. 12 'Revolutionary' 6:65
Dreyshock and 6:109
in G flat major op. 26 no. 9 6:65, 73

F

FANTASIAS
Beethoven:
for chorus and orchestra 2:99 100
Tchaikovsky:
Fatum 3:8
FUGUES
Bach, J. S.:
modulations in 1:52
48 Preludes and Fugues 5:33
The Art of the Fugue BWV1080
5:33, 53
Fantasia and Fugue in G minor BWV542
5:41-3
Passacaglia and Fugue in C minor
BWV582 5:44
Prelude and Fugue in E minor BWV548
5:43-4
Toccata and Fugue in D minor BWV565
5:41
Bach, W. F. 5:17

L

LIED/LIEDER
Brahms:
greatest? 6:29
number written 6:28
sources of texts 6:28, 29
Stockhausen and 7:12
Cradle Song 7:11
Four Serious Songs 7:13-14, 15
Triumphlied 7:74
piano transcription 7:26
Vier ernste Gesange 6:29

Mahler:
sources of texts 6:29
Kindertötenlieder 6:29, 7:193-4
Der Klagende Lied 7:88
Des Knaben Wunderhorn 6:29, *29*
Lieden eines fahrenden Gesellen
7:88
Rückert-Lieder 7:93, 103
Schubert 6:15ff
'apprentice' 6:18
catalogue of 6:18
early 6:18
first published 6:12, 20
first surviving 6:18
first to be well known 6:15
the great song-cycles 6:20-21
model for style of 6:*16*
number written 6:15
of early 6:11
published by friends 6:20
sources of texts 6:16-17, 18-19
use of 6:19
Der Abend 6:18
An die Musik 6:11-12, 20
Daphne am Bach, reshaping of 6:21
Erlafsee 6:20
Erlkönig 6:12, *18-19*, 19, 33
rejection by publishers 6:20
Die Forelle 6:11-12, 15, 20
Gretchen am Spinnrade 6:11, 18, *18*,
33
Hagar Klage 6:18
Heidenröslein 6:19
title page 6:*20*
Der Leiermann 6:21
Der Lindenbaum 6:21
Der Müller und der Bach 6:21

Die Schöne Müllerin cycle 6:20-21, 31
inspiration for 6:17, 20-21
title page 6:*19*
Der Tod und das Mädchen 6:12, 20, *20*
Der Wageiser 6:28
Winterreise cycle 6:13, 20-21, *21, 39*
mood when writing 6:21
texts for 6:17
Wohin? 6:21
Schumann:
influence on Mendelssohn 8:61
number composed 6:28
Dichterliebe cycle 6:28; 8:91
Frauenliebe und — leben 8:91
Liederkreis 8:91
Wolf:
texts for 6:29

M

MARCHES
Frederick the Great, King of Prussia:
'Hohenfriedberg' 5:58
Tchaikovsky:
Coronation March op. 31 3:56-7
MASSES
Bach, J. S.:
in B minor 5:27, 42
begins writing 5:12
Missa Solemnis 5:42
Beethoven:
in C 2:66
Missa Solemnis 2:9, *30*
dedication of 2:30
Berlioz:
commission from French Government
8-11
written as a student 8:9
Grande Messe des Morts 5:42
Brahms:
German Requiem 7:15, 47-8
inspiration for 7:12, 15, 30, 47-8
Haydn:
for Princess Hermenegild 5:93, *93*
style of 5:42
Marchaut:
Messe de Nôtre Dame 5:42
Mozart 1:9
style of 5:42
C minor 1:12
Requiem in D minor K. 626 1:15, 63
Lacrymosa from 1:*15*
played for Chopin's funeral 6:69
Palestrina 5:42
basis of composition 5:33
Schubert 6:11
Telemann:
number written 4:10
Verdi:
Requiem 5:42
Vivaldi:
for the Pietà 4:37
MAZURKAS
Chopin:
composed in Vienna 6:64
emotion in 6:71
first 6:63
op. 67 no. 2 6:69
op. 68 no. 4 6:69

VOLUME 1
Mozart

VOLUME 2
Beethoven

VOLUME 3
Tchaikovsky

VOLUME 4
Albinoni, Corelli, Handel,
Pachelbel, Purcell, Rameau,
Telemann, Vivaldi

VOLUME 5
Bach, Haydn

VOLUME 6
Chopin, Liszt, Schubert

VOLUME 7
Brahms, Mahler

VOLUME 8
Berlioz, Mendelssohn, Schumann

VOLUME 9
A Guide to Classical Music

VOLUME 10
A Beginner's Guide to the Opera

MOTETS
Bach, J. S.:
    Actus Tragicus 5:25
Vivaldi, for the Pietà 4:37
MUSIC DRAMAS
Purcell:
    The Indian Queen 4:16

N

NOCTURNES
Chopin:
    style elements in 6:71
    in E flat major op. 9 no. 2 6:93
    no. 5 in F sharp minor op. 15 no. 2 6:76
Field 6:71

O

OCTETS
Mendelssohn:
    in E flat op. 20 8:67
    String:
        completes 8:36
        inspiration for 8:36
Schubert 6:13
ODES
Handel:
    L'Allegro, il Penseroso ed il Moderato,
    libretto for 4:91
Purcell 4:14
    Ode on St Cecilia's Day 4:22, 87
    For the Queen's Birthday 4:87
OPERAS
Almahide 4:68
    contributors to 4:71
Artaxerses, use of libretto for 10:12
Albinoni:
    number written 4:8, *8*
    popularity outside Italy 4:8
    Griselda 4:8
    Pimpinone 4:22
    Zenobia 4:8
Araia:
    La Forza dell'Amore 10:41
Auber:
    number written 10:33
    plots 10:33
    La Muette de Portici: librettist 10:33
        special effects for 10:33
Bach, J. C.:
    5:19
    Amadis de Gaul 5:19
    Artaserse 5:19
    Catone in Utica 5:19
Bach, J. C. F.:
    organizes performances 5:19
Balfe:
    The Bohemian Girl 10:46-7
Barber:
    Antony and Cleopatra 10:52
    Vanessa 10:52
Bartók:
    Duke Bluebeard's Castle 10:51
Beethoven:
    Fidelio 1:57; 10:35
        Mahler conducts 7:94

Bellini:
    essence of 10:39
    Norma:
        inspiration for 10:39
        plot 10:39
        setting for 10:*38*
    The Puritans:
        plot 10:39
Berg:
    Lulu 10:50, *50*
    Wozzeck 10:50
        structure of 10:50
Berlioz:
    written as a student 8:9
    Beatrice and Benedict 7:83; 8:13
    Benvenuto Cellini 8:11
    Trojans at Carthage 8:*12,* 13; 10:34
        rejection of 8:*12, 13*
        'ridiculous travesty' of 8:*12*, 13
Bernstein:
    Trouble in Tahiti 10:52
    West Side Story (musical) 10:52
Bizet
    Carmen 3:52; 10:81
        inspiration for 10:40
        public reaction to 10:34
    Djamilch 10:81
    Fair Maid of Perth 10:34
    L'arlesienne 10:81
    Les Pêchers de Perles 10:34, 81
Bononcini:
    Astarto 4:71
Borodin:
    Prince Igor 10:42
Britten:
    Noye's Fludde 3:55
    Peter Grimes 10:47, *47,* 48
        first performance 10:48
        plot 10:48
    Billy Budd 10:48
    A Midsummer Night's Dream 10:48
    The Turn of the Screw 10:48
Cambert:
    Pomone 10:18
Camerata:
    Dafne 10:9
    Euridice 10:9
Cavalli:
    Ecole Amante 10:18
    Xerxes 10:18
Coffey:
    The Devil to Pay 10:29
        translation of 10:29
Dallapiccola:
    Ulisse 10:52
Dargomizhky:
    Rusalka 10:41
    The Stone Guest 10:42
Debussy:
    Pelléas et Mélisande 10:49
        structure of 10:49
Donizetti:
    essence of 10:39
    style of 10:40
    The Daughter of the Regiment 10:40
    Don Pasquale 10:40, 81
    Love Potion 10:40
    Lucia di Lammamoor 10:40, 81
        plot 10:39
Gay:
    The Beggar's Opera 4:70-71, 72, *98-9;*

Composer	Volume
Albinoni	4
Bach	5
Beethoven	2
Berlioz	8
Brahms	7
Chopin	6
Corelli	4
Handel	4
Haydn	5
Liszt	6
Mahler	7
Mendelssohn	8
Mozart	1
Pachelbel	4
Purcell	4
Rameau	4
Schubert	6
Schumann	8
Tchaikovsky	3
Telemann	4
Vivaldi	4

    10:*45*
    German adaptation of 10:29
    librettist 10:29
    success of 10:46
Gershwin:
    Porgy and Bess 10:52
    librettist 10:52
Glinka:
    Ivan Susanin 10:42
        setting for 10:*42*
    A Life for the Tsar 3:38; 9:27
    Ruslan and Lyudmila 10:42
Gluck:
    Berlioz and 8:9
    styles of 4:22
    Alceste 4:22
    Iphigenie en Tauride 5:19
    Orfeo ed Euridice 4:22; 10:26
        librettist 10:26
Gounod:
    Faust 10:34, 81
    Mireille 10:34, 81
    Romeo et Juliette 10:81
Grétry:
    Richard Coeur de Lion 10:26
Halevy:
    La Juive: setting for 10:*32-3*
Handel 4:67ff
    change in style of 4:72
    declining popularity of 4:73
    18th-century reception of 4:15
    for London 4:62
        first 4:61, *64*
        for King's Theatre 4:72
    Italian-style 4:62
    last two 4:75
        failure of 4:65
    restructuring 4:73
    for Royal Academy of Music 4:71
    written in Italy 4:69
    Admeto 4:71
    Agrippina 4:69
        reception in Venice 4:61
    Alcina 4:64, 73, *73*
    Alessandro 4:71
    Almira 4:60

Ariodante 4:64
Daphne 4:60
Deidamia 4:75
Ezio 4:72
Florindo 4:60
Giulio Cesare in Egitto 4:71
   librettist 4:71
Il pastor fido 4:62, 69
Imeneo 4:75
Lothario 4:72
Orlando 4:73
Ottone, Cuzzoni and 4:71
Partenope 4:72
Poro 4:72
Radamisto 4:71
   libretto for 4:71
Rinaldo 4:61, *64,* 72
   first performance of 4:69
   librettist 4:69
   method of conducting 4:61-2
   Sallé and 4:73
   scenario for 4:*64*
Rodelinda 4:71, 72
   librettist 4:71
Roderigo 4:69
Serse 4:83
Siroe 4:72
   title page 4:*72*
Sosarme 4:72
Tamerlano 4:71
   librettist 4:71
Teseo 4:62, 69-70
   libretto for 4:70
Tolomeo 4:70
Handel/Bononcini:
   Muzio Scevola 4:71
Haydn:
   fee from Salomon for 5:91
   occasions written for 5:90
   written for Eszterhaza 5:90
   L'incontro improviso 5:*91*
Henze:
   The Bassarids 10:52
   We Come to a River 10:52
   The Young Lord 10:52
Hindemith:
   Mathis der Maler 10:52
Holst:
   Savitri 10:47
Isouard:
   Aladdin 10:32
Janácek:
   The House of the Dead 10:51
   Jenufa 10:51
   Katia Kabanova 10:51
   The Macropulus Case 10:51
Lully:
   name for 10:18
   Cadmus et Hermione 10:18
Leoncavello:
   Pagliacci 10:40, 82
Locke/Laws:
   The Siege of Rhodes, librettist 10:45
Mahler:
   Die drei Pintos 7:88-9
Manelli:
   Andromeda 10:9
Mascagni:
   Cavalleria Rusticana 10:40, 49, 82
      Zeffirelli and 10:52
Massenet:

Thaïs, use of *Elégie* in films 7:101
Mendelssohn:
   The Uncle from Boston 8:35-6
Menotti:
   Amahl and the Night Visitors 10:52
   The Consul 10:52
Meyerbeer:
   Il Crociato in Egitto 10:13
   Les Huguenots 6:81; 10:33
      librettist 10:33
      setting for 10:*33*
   Robert le Diable 6:78; 10:*32-3,* 33
      librettist 10:33
Monteverdi:
   first 10:9
   influence of 4:47
   masterpiece 10:9
   La Favola d'Orfeo 4:20, 22, 47; 10:9
      first performance 10:9
      title page 10:*9*
   L'Incoronazione di Poppaea 4:22, 47; 10:9
   Il Ritorno d'Ulisse 4:22, 47; 10:9
Mozart:
   for Count Firmain 1:23
   humour in 10:53
   for national theatre 1:41
   number written 10:22
   popularity of 10:30
   success with 1:23, 30
   written in Italy 1:22
   Ascanio in Alba 1:23
   Bastien und Bastienne 1:22, *29, 34*
      solos for Stadler in 1:56
   Così fan Tutte 1:14; 10:82
      gala conducted by Mahler 7:94
      origin of characters 10:22

theme of 1:45
Die Entführung aus dem Serail 1:12, 41-2; 10:30, 82
   title page 10:*30*
Die Zauberflöte 1:15, 35, 45; 10:27, 82
   Act II, scene 19 1:*15*
   central theme 1:40
   designs for 2:*22, 80-81,* 83
   Masonic influences 1:33, 37
   novel sound-effects in 3:55
   success of 1:31
   translation of 10:30
Don Giovanni 1:13-14, 15, 44; 10:82
   Casanova and 1:108
   origin of characters 10:22
   overture for 1:14, 44
   payment for 1:30
   success of 1:14
Idomeneo 1:*10,* 11, 29; 10:82
   plot 1:41
   title page 1:*10*
Il Seraglio 5:19
La Clemenza di Tito 1:15; 10:82
La finta semplice 1:22
Lucio Silla 1:23, *23;* 10:82
Mitridate, Rè di Ponto 1:23
Le Nozzi di Figaro 1:13, 71, 78; 10:19, 22, 82
   comparisons with Symphony No. 41 1:69
   librettist 1:43; 10:22
   opposition to 1:43
   origin of characters 10:22
   success of 1:13
Mussorgsky:
   Boris Gudunov 10:*41,* 42, *43*
   popularity outside Russia 10:*43*
Paisiello:
   The Barber of Seville 10:22, 42
Pergolesi:
   influence on Baroque music 4:47
   Il Prigioner Superbo 10:20
Peri:
   Euridice 10:9
      first performance 10:9
      librettist 10:9
   Dafne 10:9
      librettist 10:9
Pfitzner:
   Palestrina 10:52
Piccinni:
   influence on Baroque music 4:47
Porta:
   numitore 4:71
Poulenc:
   Le Dialogue des Carmelites 10:52
Prokofiev:
   The Fiery Angel 10:43
   The Love of Three Oranges 10:43, *50-51*
   War and Peace 10:43
Puccini:
   La Bohème 10:40, 50, 82
   La Fanciulla del West 10:83
   Madam Butterfly 10:40, 50, 82
   Manon Lescaut 10:83
   La Rondine 10:83
   Il Tabarro 10:83
   Tosca 10:50, 82
   Turandot 10:50, 82
      finished by Alfano 10:50

VOLUME 1
Mozart

VOLUME 2
Beethoven

VOLUME 3
Tchaikovsky

VOLUME 4
Albinoni, Corelli, Handel, Pachelbel, Purcell, Rameau, Telemann, Vivaldi

VOLUME 5
Bach, Haydn

VOLUME 6
Chopin, Liszt, Schubert

VOLUME 7
Brahms, Mahler

VOLUME 8
Berlioz, Mendelssohn, Schumann

VOLUME 9
A Guide to Classical Music

VOLUME 10
A Beginner's Guide to the Opera

Purcell:
Dido and Aeneas 4:14, 22; 10:*44*, 45
Rameau:
first 4:11
criticism of 4:11
Castor et Pollux 4:22, 10:18
Dardanus 10:18
Hippolyte et Aricie 4:11; 10:18
librettist 4:11
Ravel:
L'Enfant et les Sortilèges 10:50-51
Rimsky-Korsakov:
themes of 10:42
Golden Cockerel 10:42, 51
Rossini:
inspiration for 10:38
Barber of Seville 6:72; 10:19, 22, 38, 83
Chopin and 6:63
costume design 6:*65*
at the Théâtre Italien 10:32
La Cenerentola 10:83
L'Italiana in Algeri 10:83
Otello: inspiration for 10:38
Malibran in 8:42, *43*
William Tell 10:33
Rousseau:
Le Devin du Village 10:24-5, *25*
Schoenberg:
Moses und Aron 10:52
Schubert:
early attempts 6:11
Fierabras 6:21
first commission 6:12
Schumann:
Liszt and 7:27-8
Faust, pieces for 8:92, 93
Genoveva 8:93
Schweitzer:
Alceste 10:29
Shostokovich:
Lady Macbeth of Mtsensk 10:43
The Nose 10:43
Smyth:
The Wreckers 10:47
Spohr:
Faust 8:17
Spontini:
Fernando Cortez 10:32
Stanford:
The Travelling Companions 10:47
Strauss, R.:
major success 10:50
overtures to 8:63
Arabella 10:50
Ariadne auf Naxos 10:50, 83
Capriccio 10:83
Elektra 10:50
librettist 10:50
Der Rosenkavalier 10:50, 83
Salome 7:94, *94;* 10:*50-51*, 83
shock of 10:50
Stravinsky:
'opera-oratorio' 10:43
The Nightingale 10:43
Les Noces 10:43
Oedipus Rex 10:43
The Rake's Progress 10:43, 52
experiments in 10:52
Sullivan:
Ivanhoe 10:47
Thespis 10:56

Composer	Volume
Albinoni	4
Bach	5
Beethoven	2
Berlioz	8
Brahms	7
Chopin	6
Corelli	4
Handel	4
Haydn	5
Liszt	6
Mahler	7
Mendelssohn	8
Mozart	1
Pachelbel	4
Purcell	4
Rameau	4
Schubert	6
Schumann	8
Tchaikovsky	3
Telemann	4
Vivaldi	4

Suppé:
Das Pensionat 10:54
Taylor:
The King's Henchmen 10:52
Peter Ibbetson 10:52
Tchaikovsky:
and Italian opera 3:8
number written 3:38
Eugene Onegin 3:10, 48, 52; 10:43
finishes work on 3:12
première 7:91
setting for 7:*90-91*
source of inspiration for 3:13
Tatyana letter scene 3:*10*
Hyperbole 3:26
The Maid of Orleans 3:51
The Oprichnik 3:9
The Queen of Spades 3:13, 10:42
Undine 3:8
Vakula the Smith 3:10, 13, 66
The Voyevoda 3:8, 28
Yolanta 3:44
hostility towards 3:58
Telemann:
first 4:10
number written 4:10
Tippett:
The Ice-Break 10:48
King Priam 10:*46*, 48
The Knot Garden 10:48
The Midsummer Marriage 10:48
setting for 10:*49*
Vaughan Williams:
Hugh the Drover 10:47, 51
Verdi:
structure of 10:40
Aïda 10:84
Don Carlos 10:84
Falstaff 10:40, 84
La Forza del Destino 10:84
Otello 10:40, 84
Rigoletto 10:40, 84
Simon Boccanegra 10:84
La Traviata 10:40, 84
Il Trovatore 10:40
Vivaldi, A.:

interest in 4:38
promotions in Italian centres 4:40
Aristide: librettist 4:*35*
Griselda: librettist 4:*35*
Orlando finto pazzo 4:38
Ottone in Villa 4:38
Vivaldi, G. B.:
La fedelta stortunata 4:34
Wagner:
Mahler conducts uncut versions 7:92
as ultimate expression of Romanticism 9:20
von Bülow and 7:29
Die Meistersingers: Brahms and 7:12
model for Beckmesser 8:101, 7:25
setting for 7:*24*
The Flying Dutchman 10:36
starting point for 8:104
Lohengrin 10:36
C. Schumann on 7:29
Liszt's performances of 7:29
Parsifal 10:*36-7*, 84
excerpts from 3:21
The Ring 10:84
Alberich 7:*25*
begins work on 10:37
first complete performance 10:37
interpretations of 10:52
sends copy to Schopenhauer 7:26
Tchaikovsky and 3:52
use of in cartoons 7:101
Tannhäuser 10:36
criticism of 7:25
Tristan und Isolde 10:37, 84
importance of 2:48
Weber:
Der Freischütz 10:35
Chopin and 6:63
first performance 8:61
librettist 10:35-6
plot 10:36
success of 10:36
title page 8:*62*
Oberon 10:36
Weill:
The Rise and Fall of the City of Mahagonny 10:51
The Threepenny Opera 10:*51*
librettist 10:51

OPERETTAS
Gilbert and Sullivan:
The Gondoliers 10:56
Iolanthe 10:56
The Mikado 10:56
Patience 10:56
HMS Pinafore 10:56
Princess Ida 10:56
Ruddigore 10:56
The Sorcerer 10:56
Trial by Jury 10:56
The Yeoman of the Guard 10:56
Lehár:
Frederica 10:81
Das Land des Lachelns 10:81
The Merry Widow 10:54, 81
worldwide appeal of 10:55
Offenbach:
overtures to 8:63
La Belle Hélène 10:53
La Vie Parisienne 9:26
The Grand Duchess 10:53

Orpheus in the Underworld 9:26, 10:53
The Tales of Hoffman 3:44, 45
Solomon:
  Billee Taylor 10:55
  Polly 10:55
Strauss, J.:
  Die Fledermaus 10:54, 83
    librettist 10:54
  Indigo 10:54
  Die Zigeunerbaron 10:54, 83
    librettist 10:54
ORATORIOS 4:80
Bach, J. C. F. 5:19
Bach, J. S.:
  Christmas Oratorio BWV248 5:12, 27, 53
Berlioz:
  L'Enfance du Christ 4:80
Carissimi:
  Jephte 4:80
Charpentier:
  Judith 4:22
Elgar:
  The Dream of Gerontius 4:80
Gounod:
  The Redemption 4:80
Handel:
  differences in performances 4:78
  in Dublin 4:65
  first 4:61
  in London 4:65-6
    first in 4:*80*
  occasional 4:66
  reception of 4:66
  Athlaia 4:64
  Belshazzar 4:66
    librettist 4:75
  Deborah 4:73
  Esther 4:63, 72, *80*
  Israel in Egypt 3:19, 4:65
  Jeptha 4:66, 80, 83
  Judas Maccabaeus 4:66
  Messiah 1:20; 4:21, 65, 73, 75-82
    cast at first performance 4:76-7
    librettist 4:75-6
    original score 4:*76*
    popularity in Dublin 4:65
    popularity in London 4:66, 77
  La Resurrezione 4:61
  Samson 4:65, 76
    inspiration for 4:65
  Saul 4:65, 83
    librettist 4:75
  Solomon 4:66
    title page 4:*21*
    Sinfonia from Act III 4:21
  Susanna 4:66
  Theodora 4:66
Haydn:
  The Creation 5:*92-3*, 101
    librettist 5:93
    private performance of 5:93
  The Seasons 5:93
    librettist 5:93
Honegger:
  Joan of Arc at the Stake 3:55
Mendelssohn:
  Elijah op. 70 8:39, 67
    first performance 8:*38*, 77
  St Paul 4:80

Schumann:
  Das Paradies und die Peri 8:92
Telemann:
  number written 4:10
Walton:
  Belshazzar's Feast 4:80
Vivaldi:
  for the Pietà 4:37
  Moyses Deus Pharaonis 4:37
  Juditha triumphans 4:37
ORCHESTRAL WORKS
Gershwin:
  An American in Paris 3:55
Tchaikovsky 3:49ff
  Francesca da Rimini op. 3:10, 52-5
    source of inspiration for 3:52
    success of 3:55
    Tchaikovsky on 3:55
  Italian Capriccio op. 45 3:45, 51
    source of inspiration for 3:51
  The Tempest 3:10, *32-3*
    Mme von Meck and 3:32
ORGAN MUSIC
Castrum doloris 5:9
Bach, C. P. E. 5:17
Bach, J. S. 5:9, 38ff
see also **FUGUES**
OVERTURES
Arnold:
  Grand Grand Overture 3:55, *55*
Beethoven:
  op. 84 'Egmont' 2:65
  Leonore no. 3 3:18
Berlioz:
  King Lear 8:10, *63*
    influence of Beethoven in 2:39
Brahms 8:63
  Academic Festival Overture 4:87; 7:13
Glinka:
  Spanish Overtures 3:51
Lully 5:46, *46*
Mendelssohn 8:60ff
  Calm Sea and Prosperous Voyage op. 27 8:*41*, 67
  The Hebrides op. 26 'Fingal's Cave' 8:62-3, 76
    inspiration for 8:37, 41, 45
  A Midsummer Night's Dream op. 21 8:36, 66-7, 76
    influence of Weber on 8:62
    inspiration for 8:36
  Ruy Blas op. 95 8:63-5
  The Tale of the Fair Melusina op. 32 8:65-6
  see also **SYMPHONIC POEMS**
Purcell:
  The Indian Queen 4:16
Rossini:
  William Tell, use in films 7:101
Schumann:
  in E flat minor op. 115 'Manfred' 8:93, 100
Tchaikovsky:
  in F 3:8
  Festival Overture: the Year 1812 3:12, 49-51
  Romeo and Juliet 3:8, 29, 70-3
    modifications to 3:70-71
    source of inspiration for 3:70

P

PASSIONS
Bach, J. S.:
  St John Passion 5:*12, 25,* 27
    manuscript 5:*25*
    performed by Singakademie 8:55
  St Mark Passion, first performance 5:12
  St Matthew Passion 5:*12,* 27, 37, 8:36
    Mendelssohn and 5:39, 8:*36,* 37, 55
Telemann: number for Hamburg 4:10
  St Mark Passion 4:22
PASTICHES
Purcell:
  The Fairy Queen 4:22
Vivaldi:
  Nerone fatto Cesare 4:38
PIANO WORKS
Beethoven:
  Nine Variations for piano in C minor 2:9
Rameau:
  Pièces de Claverin, Livre I 4:22
PRELUDES
Chopin:
  completion of 6:67

Q

QUARTETS
Bartók:
  String: understanding 2:39
  Schuppanzigh Quartet 2:28
    Beethoven and 2:28

VOLUME 1
Mozart

VOLUME 2
Beethoven

VOLUME 3
Tchaikovsky

VOLUME 4
Albinoni, Corelli, Handel, Pachelbel, Purcell, Rameau, Telemann, Vivaldi

VOLUME 5
Bach, Haydn

VOLUME 6
Chopin, Liszt, Schubert

VOLUME 7
Brahms, Mahler

VOLUME 8
Berlioz, Mendelssohn, Schumann

VOLUME 9
A Guide to Classical Music

VOLUME 10
A Beginner's Guide to the Opera

Beethoven:
  String: at work on last 2:14
    'meaning' of last 2:38
  No. 1 op. 18: inspiration for 2:46
  op. 59 'Razumovsky' 2:28, 49; 3:62
    influence on Simpson 2:39
Brahms:
  Piano: First Quartet 3:22
Haydn:
  early 5:89
  op. 54 5:55, 64, 91
  String 1:58
    first 5:89
    surprises in 1:77
    op. 76 no. 1-6 5:101
Mozart:
  dedicated to Haydn 5:91
  Piano:
    K. 478 1:65
  String:
    dedicated to Haydn 1:30, *42*, 72
    No. 19 in C K. 465 'Dissonance' 1:55
    structure 1:58
Schubert:
  String 6:11
    Deutsch number 6:24
Schumann:
  Piano 8:91
Tchaikovsky:
  String 3:9
  Second 3:10, 66
  Third 3:10
Telemann:
  The 'Paris' Quartets 4:22

QUINTETS
Brahms:
  Clarinet Quintet 7:13
Schubert:
  Piano: in A major op. 114 'Trout' 6:12,
    24-30
    first performance 6:24
    loss of original manuscript 6:24, 26
  String 6:13
    in C major D956 6:31
Schumann:
  Piano 8:91
    performance in Moscow 8:92

R

ROMANCES
Beethoven:
  for violin and orchestra: No. 1 op. 40
    2:65
  No. 2 op. 60 2:65

S

SACRED MUSIC
Mozart 1:9
see also **CANTATAS; ORATORIOS;**
  MASSES
SCHERZOS
Weber:
  influence on Mendelssohn 8:62
SERENADES
Handel:

Acis and Galatea 4:63
Mozart 1:48ff
  for outdoor performance 4:87
  G major K.525 'Eine kleine Nachtmusik
    1:*48*, 48-51
    catalogue note 1:*50*
    manuscript 1:*48*
  No. 7 K. 250 'Haffner' 1:55; 4:87
  F major K. 522 'A Musical Joke' 1:51-5
    title 1:*53*
Tchaikovsky:
  String: in C op. 48 3:73
  Serenade for Strings 3:21
SEXTETS
Tchaikovsky:
  op. 70 'Souvenir de Florence' 3:48
SINFONIAS
Albinoni:
  number written 4:*8*
SONATAS
Albinoni 4:8
Bach, C. P. E.:
  effect of emotional content 2:36
Bach, J. S.:
  for Violin and Harpsichord 5:10
Bach, W. F. 5:17
Beethoven:
  names of 2:*44*, 46
  role in development of music 2:44-5
  technique for 2:45
  Piano 2:42ff
    first 2:43
    influence on 2:67
    last: criticism of 2:38
    'meaning' of 2:38
    number 2:42
    in A major op. 101 2:*21*
    in C sharp minor, op. 27 no. 2
      'Moonlight' 2:46-8; 3:62
      autograph score 2:*45*
      Beethoven's instructions for playing
        2:48
    in F minor op. 57 'Appassionata' 2:26,
      48-9
      manuscript 2:*48*
    Grande Sonata Pathétique in C minor
      op. 13 2:34, 43-6
    no. 22 op. 54 2:49
    no. 29 op. 106 'Hammerklavier' 2:49
      technique for 2:45
    op. 27 set: Beethoven's name for 2:48
    op. 53 'Waldstein' 2:9
      piano development and 2:45
    32nd op. 111 'Arietta' 2:43
      technique for 2:45
  Violin:
    op. 27 'Kreutzer' 2:57
Brahms:
  'flavour' of 7:10
  in C major 7:9
Chopin:
  first mature 6:67
  Piano:
    no. 2 in B flat minor op. 35 6:67, 77
    in B minor G178 6:103
Clement:
  Violin 2:60
Corelli:
  sonate a tre op. 1-4 4:47; 5:33
  dedications of first 12 sonatas 4:12
  Orchestral 4:47

Composer	Volume
Albinoni	4
Bach	5
Beethoven	2
Berlioz	8
Brahms	7
Chopin	6
Corelli	4
Handel	4
Haydn	5
Liszt	6
Mahler	7
Mendelssohn	8
Mozart	1
Pachelbel	4
Purcell	4
Rameau	4
Schubert	6
Schumann	8
Tchaikovsky	3
Telemann	4
Vivaldi	4

Violin 4:47
  12 for violin and continou op. 5 4:22
Frederick the Great, King of Prussia:
  Flute 5:*59*
Gabrieli:
  for wind instruments 4:20
Handel:
  trio 5:33
Liszt:
  Piano: in B minor 7:9
Mozart:
  first published keyboard 1:20
  Harpsichord and Violin: Opus 1 1:20
    title page 1:*21*
  Piano:
    1:12
  Violin:
    first published score 1:20
Paganini:
  Violin: *Sonata à mouvement perpetual*
    6:106
Purcell:
  Sonnata's of III Parts 4:14
Scarlatti:
  number written for harpsichord 4:22
Schubert:
  Piano: in A 6:24
  in F minor, own name for 6:98
Tchaikovsky:
  Piano 3:51
Vivaldi:
  12 trio sonatas 4:36, 5:33
SONGS (*see also* **LIEDER**)
Dowland:
  Bookes of Songs 4:22
  A Pilgrimes Solace 4:22
Monteverdi:
  Madrigals of Love and War 4:22
Mozart:
  Masonic 1:36, *36*
  Fellow Craft's Journey 1:36
  For the Closing of the Lodge 1:36
  For the Opening of the Lodge 1:36
Purcell 4:14
  first published 4:13
  for Westminster Abbey 4:14

Schubert 4:15
  see also **LIEDER**
Tchaikovsky:
  first published 3:8
  Mezza notte 3:8
Telemann:
  number written 4:10
  Song Book (1730) 4:*10*
SUITES
Bach, J. S.:
  dances used in 5:46
  instrumentation for 5:47
  piano transcription of 5:47
  no. 2 in B minor BWV1067 5:46, 47-50
  no. 3 in D BWV1068 5:50-53
Bizet:
  'L'Arlésienne' 5:49
Grieg:
  Holberg Suite 5:49
  'Peer Gynt' 5:49
Handel:
  Music for the Royal Fireworks 4:21, 66,
    84-6
  Suites de Pièces pour le Claverin, title
    page 4:*62*
  Water Music 4:21, 63, 84, 88-91
Purcell:
  for harpsichord 4:14
Pachelbel:
  in G for Strings and Continuo 4:22
Rameau:
  Nouvelles Suites de Pièces de Claverin
    4:18
    frontispiece 4:*18*
Ravel:
  Le Tombeau de Couperin 5:49
Strauss, R.:
  'Der Rosenkavalier' 5:49
Stravinsky:
  'Firebird' 5:49
Telemann:
  number written 4:10
SYMPHONIC POEMS
Balakirev:
  Tamara 6:100
Borodin:
  In the Steppes of Central Asia 6:100
Debussy:
  Prelude à l'après-midi d'un Faune 6:100
Dukas:
  L'apprenti-sorcier 6:100
Dvořák:
  Slavonic Dances 6:100
Liszt:
  effect on music development 6:100
  Ce qu'on entend sur la montagne
    6:100
  Die Ideale 6:100
  Hunnenschlacht 6:100
Mendelssohn:
  overtures as 8:60
Mussorgsky:
  St John's Night on a Bare Mountain
    6:100
Saints-Saëns:
  Danse Macabre 6:100
Smetana:
  Hakon Jarl 6:100
  Ma Vlast 6:100
  Richard III 6:100
  Wallenstein's Lager 6:100

VOLUME 1
Mozart

VOLUME 2
Beethoven

VOLUME 3
Tchaikovsky

VOLUME 4
Albinoni, Corelli, Handel,
Pachelbel, Purcell, Rameau,
Telemann, Vivaldi

VOLUME 5
Bach, Haydn

VOLUME 6
Chopin, Liszt, Schubert

VOLUME 7
Brahms, Mahler

VOLUME 8
Berlioz, Mendelssohn, Schumann

VOLUME 9
A Guide to Classical Music

VOLUME 10
A Beginner's Guide to the Opera

SYMPHONIES (*see also* **SYMPHONIC
  POEMS**)
Beethoven:
  changes in symphony structure 2:39
  cyclic principles in 2:39
  influence on 2:67
  names of 3:62
  replaces minuet with scherzo 2:39
  symphonic unities 2:37
  'Battle' 3:55
  No. 1 in C:
    dedication 2:28
    use of orchestra in 4:20
  No. 2 2:11
    criticism of 2:38
  No. 3 'Eroica' 2:13, 34; 3:62
    'breaking rules' in 2:37
    criticism 2:38
    dedication of 2:20, *89*
    ideas behind 9:20
    importance of 2:48
    length of 2:13, 37
  No. 4 2:67
    Mendelssohn revival of 8:38
  No. 5 in C minor op. 67 2:13, 66-71
    compared with Violin Concerto
      (Beethoven) 2:58
    criticism of 2:66
    dedication of 2:20
    first performance 2:66, *70*
    ideas behind 9:20
    inspiration for first phase of 2:43, 66,
      69
    later interpretation 2:71
    model for other composers 2:39
    sketch of 2:*68*
  No. 6 'Pastoral' 2:13, 67; 3:62

    dedication of 2:20
    first performance 2:66
    influence of 2:39
    inspiration for 9:20
    as programme music 8:17
    use in cartoons 7:101
  No. 7:
    criticism of 2:38
  No. 9 'Choral' 2:14; 3:62
    criticism of 2:38
    first performance 2:14
    Mendelssohn revival of 8:38
    poem for 2:77
    in D minor op. 125 3:62
Berlioz:
  Symphonie Fantastique 6:23; 8:11, 14-21
    first performance of 8:10, 14
    influence of Beethoven in 2:39
    inspiration for 8:10, 14
    Liszt and 6:96
    programme for 8:14, 16, 17
    scene aux champs 2:39
    success of 8:14
  Symphonie Funèbre et Triomphale 4:87
    conducts 8:12
Brahms:
  von Bülow's reaction to 7:24
  No. 1 in C minor op. 68 7:46-52
    critical reaction to 7:48
    dramatic mood of 7:46
    finally completes 7:12
    horn solo for 7:12, 47, *48-9*
    inspiration for 7:30
    première of 7:12, 48
    similarity to No. 9 (Beethoven) 2:39
  No. 2 7:32
  No. 4 in E minor op. 98 7:13, 53
    conducts 7:13
Dvořák:
  No. 9 'New World': original numbering
    3:62
Haydn:
  early 5:89
  fee from Salomon for 5:91
  first 5:89
  nicknames for 3:62
  number written 2:67, 5:99
    for London 5:95
  numbering of 5:99
  of 'Sturm und Drang' period 5:99
  'Toy' 3:55
  No. 2 in E flat 'Philosopher' 3:62
  No. 6 Le Matin 5:99
  No. 7 Le Midi 5:99
  No. 8 Le Soir 5:99
  No. 31 'Hornsignal' 5:99
  No. 45 in F sharp minor 'Farewell' 3:62;
    5:99
  No. 49 'La Passione' 5:99
  No. 55 'Schoolmaster' 5:99
  'London':
    No. 94 in G 'Surprise' 5:95-6, 99
    reviews of 5:95
    variations 2:54
    No. 96 'Miracle' 5:99
    No. 101 'The Clock' 5:96-100
    No. 103 the 'Drum Roll' 5:99
  'Paris':
    No. 82 in C 'Bear' 3:62; 5:99
    No. 83 in G minor 'Hen' 3:62; 5:99
    No. 85 'The Queen' 5:99

Mahler:
    7:97ff
    and development of 7:98
    'musical madness' 7:93
    structure of 7:97
    Das Lied von der Erde, 7:95
        ideas behind 7:97
    No. 1 in D major 'The Titan' 7:103
        finishes 7:89-90
        title page 7:*90*
        Viennese reception of 7:92
    No. 2 7:91, 103
    No. 3 in D minor 'A Summer Morning's
        Dream' 7:102-103
        Walter on 7:97-8
    No. 4 7:92
        premières 7:93
        revises 7:93
    No. 5 in C sharp minor 7:98-9
        writes two movements of 7:93
    No. 6 7:93
        novel sound-effects in 3:55; 7:*92*
    No. 7 in E minor 'Song of the Night' 7:97,
        100-101
    No. 9 in D 7:95, 103
    No. 10 7:95
        manuscript for 7:*95*
Mendelssohn:
    in C minor, conducts in London 8:43
    no. 3 in A minor 'Scottish' 8:44, 51
        inspiration for 8:37, 41
    no. 4 in A major op. 90 'Italian' 8:56-9
        description of 8:47
        inspiration for 8:38, 41, 47
    no. 5 in D 'Reformation' 8:51
        begins to write 8:38
        rejection of 8:48
    Twelve String Symphonies op.
        (posthumous) 8:67
Messiaen:
    'Turangalîla' 3:55
Mozart:
    canon 1:64-5
    influence of J. C. Bach on 5:19
    C major K. 338 1:71
    C major K. 551 1:74
    G minor K. 183 1:65
    K. 16, structure of 1:65
    K. 19, structure of 1:65
    Haffner 1:65
    Linz 1:65
    No. 29 in A major K. 201 1:65
    No. 31, K. 297 'Paris' 1:11, *27*, 28, 105
    No. 38 in D major 'Prague' 1:13, 64
    No. 39 in E flat major 1:64
    No. 40 in G minor K. 550 'Tragic' 1:64,
        65-8, 74
        comparison with No. 5 (Beethoven)
            2:70
    No. 41 in C major 'Jupiter' 1:64, 68-71
Schubert 6:11

    no. 1 6:33
    in C major 6:13
        revision of 6:13
    no. 4 6:33
        influence of Beethoven on 6:12
    no. 5 in B flat major D485 6:33-5
        influence of Mozart on 6:12
    no. 8 in B minor 'Unfinished' 6:12, 36-8
        manuscript for third movement 6:*37*
    no. 9 in C major 'The Great' 6:39
Schumann:
    cyclic principle in 2:39
    last:
        première of 8:38
    nearly completes first 8:90
    C minor:
        sketches for 8:94
    G minor:
        sketches for 8:94
    No. 1 in B flat major op. 38 'Spring' 3:62,
        8:91, 94-7
        first performance 8:94
        orchestration of 8:94
        origins 8:94
        performance in St Petersburg 8:92
    No. 2:
        influence of Beethoven 2:39
    No. 3 in E flat major op. 97 'Rhenish'
        8:100
    No. 4:
        cyclic principle 2:39
Tchaikovsky:
    No. 1 3:8
        criticism of 3:8
        strain of writing 3:27
    No. 2 op. 17 'Little Russian' 3:65
    No. 3 3:10
    No. 4 in F minor op. 36 3:10, 29, 65
    No. 5 in E minor op. 64 3:13, 65
    No. 6 in B minor op. 74 'Pathétique'
        3:13, 23, 29, 58-64
        first draft 3:58
        'hidden meanings' 3:61
        manuscript 3:*61*
        title page 3:61
    'Manfred' op. 58 3:12, 29, 57
        source of inspiration for 3:12
Vaughan Williams:
    No. 4:
        similarity to No. 5 (Beethoven) 2:39

T

TRIOS
Beethoven:
    Piano:
        'Archduke' 2:30, 3:62
        op. 1 2:27
        dedication of 2:*27*

        title page 2:*27*
    String:
        op. 9 2:28
Mozart:
    Piano: K. 496 in E. Chopin and 6:68
    K. 498 1:56
Schubert:
    Piano:
        in E flat 6:13
Tchaikovsky:
    Piano 3:22
        in A minor op. 50 3:57
TRIO SONATAS *see* **SONATAS:** trio

V

VARIATIONS
'Severn Bridge' 4:87
Bach, J. S.:
    Aria with 30 Variations BWV988
        Goldberg 2:54; 3:62; 5:12, 45
        contrapuntal device in 5:33
Beethoven:
    Diabelli 2:54
Brahms:
    St Anthony 2:54; 7:12, 48
        première of 7:48
    on a theme of Handel 2:54; 7;12
    Variation on a theme by Haydn op. 56a
        7:53
Bull:
    The King's Hunt 2:54; *54*
Chopin:
    on *Là ci darem* 6:63, 65
    op. 2 6:63
Paganini 2:54
    on *My Country Tis of Thee/God Save the
        Queen* 6:106
Tchaikovsky:
    on a Rococo Theme for Cello and
        Orchestra op. 33 3:10, 73

W

WALTZES
Chopin:
    composed in Vienna 6:64
    Grande Valse Brillante no. 1 in E flat
        major op. 18 6:64, 74
    no. 6 in D flat major op. 64 no. 1 6:74-5
    no. 7 in C sharp minor op. 64 no. 2
        6:74-5
    op. 64 no. 1 'Minute', dedication of 6:65
Strauss, J.:
    Blue Danube, use as film music 7:101
Tchaikovsky:
    Anastasie Valse 3:26